A Woman's Civil War

Cornelia McDonald, photographed in Washington D.C., circa 1890.

Cornelia Peake McDonald

A Woman's Civil War

A Diary,
with Reminiscences of the War,
from March 1862

Edited, with an Introduction by
Minrose C. Gwin

The University of Wisconsin Press

The University of Wisconsin Press
114 North Murray Street
Madison, Wisconsin 53715

3 Henrietta Street
London WC2E 8LU, England

Printed in the United States of America

Library of Congress Cataloging-in-Publication Data
McDonald, Cornelia Peake, 1822–1909.
A woman's civil war: a diary with reminiscences of the war from
March 1862 / edited with an introduction by Minrose C. Gwin.
314 pp.   cm.—(Wisconsin studies in American autobiography)
Rev. ed. of: A diary with reminiscences of the war and refugee
life in the Shenandoah Valley, 1860–1865. c1935.
Includes bibliographical references (pp. 275–296) and index.
ISBN 0-299-13260-9 (cloth)   ISBN 0-299-13264-1 (paper)
  1. McDonald, Cornelia Peake, 1822–1909—Diaries.
  2. United States—History—Civil War, 1861–1865—
Personal narratives, Confederate.
  3. United States—History—Civil War, 1861–1865—Women.
  4. Shenandoah River Valley (Va. and W. Va.)
—History—Civil War, 1861–1865.
  5. Women—Virginia—Winchester—Diaries.
  6. Winchester (Va.)—Biography.
  I. Gwin, Minrose C.
II. McDonald, Cornelia Peake, 1822–1909. Diary with reminiscences
of the war and refugee life in the Shenandoah Valley, 1860–1865.
III. Title. IV. Series.
E487.M195   1992
973.7′ 159′ 092—dc20
  [B]   91-32345

Contents

Acknowledgments

I am most deeply indebted to Nancy Sheets, who assisted with the research for this project over a period of many months. Without her tireless sleuthing in libraries around the state of Virginia, this edition would have been several more years in process. I am grateful not only for her painstaking research and firm commitment to the completion of this book, but also for her friendship, patience, and support.

I also wish to thank members of the McDonald family of Nashville, Tennessee, who made the handwritten manuscripts of Cornelia McDonald's writings available to me and offered much help and information to fill in my knowledge of their fascinating foremother.

For essential funding at a crucial point, I am particularly grateful to the Women's Research Institute, Virginia Polytechnic Institute and State University, Blacksburg, Virginia. In addition, I wish to thank the Center for Programs in the Humanities at VPI for a summer stipend which enabled me several years earlier to do the initial work on this project.

I am also grateful to William L. Andrews and Barbara Hanrahan for their commitment to the publication of Cornelia McDonald's narrative and to Suzanne L. Bunkers for her helpful suggestions on the introduction to this volume. Nicholas Murray's careful and intelligent copyediting was essential, as was Raphael Kadushin's, Carol Olsen's, and Alexa Selph's help in bringing the book to production. I am thankful, as well, for Jennifer Hawkins's assistance with proofreading.

My thanks go also to my aunt Hamer Pitner, whose knowledge of Virginia history was helpful along the way, and to Becky Cox, whose care with this manuscript, as with others, is greatly appreciated.

Finally, I thank Ruth Salvaggio for her consistent intellectual and personal support of this and other endeavors—past, present, and future.

A Woman's Civil War

Introduction

There will be narratives of female lives only when women no longer live their lives isolated in the houses and stories of men.
                    Carolyn G. Heilbrun, *Writing a Woman's Life*

On the night of March 11, 1862, the pickets were in town; part of the army had already gone, and there were hurried preparations and hasty farewells, and sorrowful faces turning away from those they loved best, and were leaving, perhaps forever. At one o'clock the long roll beat, and soon the heavy tramp of the marching columns died away in the distance. The rest of the night was spent in violent fits of weeping at the thought of being left . . ." (**21**)[1]

The Civil War journal of Cornelia Peake McDonald begins appropriately with sounds of abandonment and images of despair. As the footsteps of a male Confederacy recede in the distance, McDonald records the beginning of a personal and distinctly female battle of her own: the struggle for survival and the care of nine children in Winchester, Virginia, an area of the South which saw constant troop movement throughout the war. Her autobiography of this period, a combination of diary and reminiscence first published by family members in 1935, provides a gripping record of a white southern woman's struggle in the midst of chaos to provide nurturance and shelter—a safe place—for herself and her family.

The value of her narrative lies in its textual production of history as a domestic subject. For McDonald, history is what happens "inside the house." Her story is, in fact, about the trauma that occurs when the domestic sphere, traditionally a safe place, is disrupted and destroyed by the forces of history—when women and children are put out of their houses and have nowhere to go. At the same time, McDonald's ingenuity and tenacity in the face of that trauma reflect women's capacity to recreate for themselves and their children safe places, albeit temporary ones, in the face of danger and despair.

Reading McDonald's writings about her own experiences in the Civil War therefore leads us to consider the gendered nature of auto-biography and the ways in which women's life-writings can transform our understanding of history.

McDonald obviously believed that her narrative was important. Although she began her diary at the request of her husband, who wished to be informed of events in and around Winchester during his absence, her perseverance with the writing after his death and the nature of her subject matter make this a record of war which moves beyond the realm of family history. She kept her diary faithfully (often between the lines of printed books) from March 1862 to August 1863, but when she and her children fled Winchester, a portion was lost. Later she tried to recall the happenings of the period from March through November 1862 and rewrote the lost sections in diary form. In 1875 she added her recollections of the years before and after those recorded in the diary, particularly the period from August 1863 until the assassination of Lincoln, during which she lost her husband and found herself and her remaining children (one had died) in danger of starving. After she had reconstructed her record in a leather-bound volume of almost five hundred pages, she made eight identical copies in her own handwriting for each of her surviving children. These were entitled *A Diary with Reminiscences of the War, From March 1862,* and meticulously written in black ink in large bound scrapbooks. In 1935 her son Hunter McDonald edited and annotated her writings in combination with a family history of genealogy charts, maps, letters, and other reminiscences by family members. This large handsomely bound volume, now relegated primarily to special collections shelves of university libraries, he entitled *A Diary with Reminiscences of the War and Refugee Life in the Shenandoah Valley 1860–1865.* So it was that, like many women's texts throughout history, Cornelia McDonald's writings, through a series of circumstances, have been virtually lost to contemporary readers.

This edition retrieves McDonald's journal from its dual burial, first within the massive family history volume, and subsequently on the unfrequented shelves of library special collections. The text for this edition is derived from one of the handwritten copies made for her children.[2] This text varies somewhat from the earlier published version edited by her son, Hunter McDonald, who deleted a few sections; made changes in punctuation, spelling, and capitalization; and retitled the manuscript. Most of Hunter McDonald's notes are accurate. My notes are less concerned with detail and therefore more streamlined to suit a text which I see as having implications for women's history and women's writing generally.

Young Cornelia's early experiences may have partly prepared her for the ordeal of war at her doorstep and developed in her the ability to provide such an intense and vivid personal account of the Civil War period. Her daughter Ellen believed that her mother's memory was remarkable and recalls in her introduction to the originial volume that from age three, when her mother recalled being kissed by Lafayette, she never seemed to forget "anything that she had read or heard." Cornelia Peake was born in Alexandria, Virginia, on June 14, 1822, the youngest child in the large family of Anne Linton Lane and Humphrey Peake. Because her father, a medical doctor, had cosigned loans for friends who later defaulted on payments, the family moved several times in Cornelia's early years, first to a plantation in Prince William County, Virginia, and later to Front Royal in the Shenandoah Valley. In 1835, on a long, arduous journey, her father moved the family and their slaves to Palmyra, Missouri, where many of the slaves and some family members died of consumption. In an introduction to the family history, her daughter Ellen relates that young Cornelia slept in a small room up under the roof where she sometimes awoke with snow all over her bed— fresh-air quarters which she later believed may have saved her from severe illness and even death.

Early in life Cornelia was called upon to nurse her sick mother, who, unaccustomed to a pioneer life, was frequently ill. Young Cornelia began to read extensively during this period. While her mother slept, she would sit behind the bed curtains and read from Byron's works and other books from her father's library. Her daughter reports that, in later years, McDonald had a vivid memory of the forced migration of thousands of Pottawattomie Indians through Missouri and told her own children how she would sit up late at night making caps for their babies. McDonald thought it unfair that the Indian women walked, carrying all the burdens, while the men rode on horseback.

After her mother's death in 1837, the family moved to Hannibal, where her life became filled with social activity. When her older sister

Susan married Edward C. McDonald, his brother, Angus W. McDonald III, a lawyer twenty-three years Cornelia's senior, visited the family and began to court her. She married him on May 27, 1847, and returned to Virginia, first to Romney, where he practiced law, and then to Windlea, on a spur of the Allegheny Mountains near New Creek, Virginia, where he managed his mining interests. An enthusiastic horseback rider from her early childhood, she would ride over mountain roads to see and sketch the mountains around her. Her talent for drawing and painting, which imbues her writing with an extraordinary vividness of visual detail, was practiced within the confines of motherhood. Her son Kenneth recalls that the first thing he remembers about his mother was her sitting by the window of his room drawing the rugged landscape, and her daughter Ellen remembers her mother overseeing the children playing in the fields while she sat on an elevation and sketched the mountains and river. After the war and its many alterations to the land and the people she loved, McDonald turned to china painting, because, she told her daughter, the colors were "permanent, never fading or changing."

Cornelia McDonald and her children, photographed in Lexington, Virginia, in 1870. Standing, from left: Hunter, Donald, Kenneth, Ellen. Seated, from left: Roy, Allan, Cornelia, Harry.

The year after her marriage, she gave birth to her son Harry, the first of nine children to be born in the next fourteen years. Since her husband was often away, the family moved to Winchester, where they enjoyed a more communal social life until the Civil War erupted. After the war and her husband's death, McDonald lived as a refugee in Lexington, Virginia, until 1873, when she and most of her children moved to Louisville, Kentucky. There she set up what her daughter calls "a gay and pleasant household," completed her writings about the war, and continued her painting and charitable work until her death on March 11, 1909.

Why retrieve Cornelia McDonald's story from its dusty library shelf? This is an important text for the disciplines of literature, history, and women's studies on multiple levels, the most obvious being that these writings, in their arresting immediacy, profoundly link the historical and the personal as women's cultural narrative. As her story reveals, McDonald was acutely sensitive, artistic, and deeply religious. Her life before the war was far from luxurious, and she suffered physical as well as emotional deprivation during the

Cornelia McDonald and her children photographed in Louisville, Kentucky, in 1883.

war years. In the midst of war, she writes about her grief at the death of her baby daughter, her anxiety about the plight of a slave woman being sold away from her own children, her shock at being shown the corpse of her husband when she had not been notified of his death, her stumbling over piles of amputated limbs outside a makeshift hospital, her hysterical laughter at the retrieval of a stolen Christmas turkey, her despair, her fear, her deepening sense of impending doom. She tells exactly what it was like to be a middle-class white southern woman during the Civil War, what it meant to defend a household against numerous attempts (eventually successful) to take it over, what it was like to have to beg the shoemaker to make seven pairs of shoes for barefoot children in November, how it felt to be left behind to cope and wait.

For those interested in women's creativity and women's histories, then, McDonald's autobiographical writings constitute a long-ignored female text complex enough to generate crucial questions about women's reading and writing of their own personal and cultural histories, questions which lead us to consider the gender-related implications of what Janet Varner Gunn has called "the cultural dimension of the autobiographical act."[3] In the midst of a culture of war, McDonald's writings show the effects of that culture on white women and children, slaves and former slaves, southern landscape, and southern life. Her pain at being unable to care for her children, the fear for her own personal safety, the degradation of having to beg for food—this pain flows into sharply focused images and experiences: the frozen bleeding feet of children, her trampled lilacs and jessamine, the butchered trees, the ravaged vegetable garden, men's footsteps at the door.

Like its immediacy, the textual untidiness of this narrative leaves us with a sense of the discontinuities of southern history and the disruptions of women's lives during and after the Civil War years. I use the term *untidy* to describe not only the hybrid form of the narrative but also its original physical form. This is not altogether a diary but rather a diary, a memoir, and then another memoir constructed out of lost portions of the diary, specifically lost books on whose pages McDonald squeezed her writing literally between the printed lines. In its very construction, then, this text circles and recircles itself as it incorporates the spatial dailiness of the diary form[4] along with the diary form *as remembered* and subsequently as reshaped through memory. The diary which the exhausted McDonald reluctantly wrote almost daily because her husband wanted a record of daily events at home naturalizes the cultural trauma of the war years, while the diary she rewrites from memory must inevitably recreate that trauma and at the same time reify her own position as a subject of the history she writes. This double chronology of the real and reshaped diary reflects, within a spatial metaphor of dailiness, not only the "mobile setting of time as depth," but how a woman writer may read herself within that mobile setting.[5]

There is an important distinction, then, between the form of McDonald's autobiographical narrative of the war and that of many other women's Civil War narratives; for McDonald copies segments of past writing, reconstructs lost portions of that past writing, and in addition writes several sections based entirely on memory of events, rather than the secondary memory of lost diary entries. Other white southern women of the period either revised and added to their entire journals after the war (Mary Chesnut), or simply wrote memoirs (Louise Wigfall Wright), or copied their diaries with little revision (Kate Stone). McDonald's personal narrative is, instead, a complex interweaving of past, present, and present transposed upon past—an example *par excellence* of Josephine Donovan's observation that women's writing may reflect the "interruptibility" of women's lives and projects.[6]

More important, McDonald writes about a complex set of cultural events in what has been considered male history—a history of public events removed from the domestic sphere of nineteenth-century southern white women, but which McDonald rethinks as female experience. Years ago historians such as Joan Kelly and, on the southern scene, Anne Firor Scott began to take notice of the central problem of women's omission from historical study. The assumptions underlying such omission were, as Scott states, "that woman's natural place is in the home and that history takes place on the battlefield or in the Congress, the statehouse, the pulpit, the marketplace, or the laboratory. Women, therefore, by definition do not make history . . ."[7] More recently, Joan Scott has argued that the absence of women in history—their confinement to studies of the domestic sphere—illustrates a politics by which the discipline of history operates to repress women as historical subjects.[8] In particular, southern history, we have been told by several southern historians, is a collective, not a private experience. In *The Burden of Southern History*, for example, C. Vann Woodward says that "Much experience of importance is private and individual in nature and would in the main seem best left to the psychologist for study. The historian is more properly concerned with the public and external forces that go to make up the collective experience and give shape to the group character of a people."[9]

Under this standard, the model autobiography, as Sidonie Smith points out, is defined by "the relationship of the autobiographer to the arena of public life and discourse."[10] In contrast, women's diaries, journals, letters, and memoirs, as Suzanne L. Bunkers has shown, "came to be labeled 'private' writings, that designation not only signalling their classification as texts but also relegating them to what was judged 'woman's sphere'—the private rather than the public realm."[11] Mary Chesnut's journals have been seen as exceptions to this binary model and extolled *not* for the insights they offer into her private experience as a woman; Anne Goodwyn Jones and others have pointed out that Chesnut erases herself to produce her journal. Chesnut's writing is instead valued primarily for its depictions of the collective *public* experience of the war. Hers is, on the whole, a social history—and anyone who knows the textual history of her journals must agree with Jones that Chesnut "creates her persona by cutting out her personal voice" and "chooses to try to get into the traditional text, the dominant male culture."[12] McDonald's narrative is a far more radical text in the sense that she writes about what happens when that traditionally male domain of history— war—forces its way into personal, domestic life: when it comes *into* the house.

McDonald's personal domestic narrative of war therefore not only begins to answer Jean E. Friedman's questions—"What of women whose existence is wholly private? Is their experience any less valid historically?"[13]—but also shows how the public and private spheres may become in women's writing something else altogether, a place neither public nor private but both at the same time.[14] It has been suggested that to know women's lives we must examine the interactions between women's sphere(s) and the remainder of history.[15] In a broader sense Hélène Cixous, the French feminist theorist, has argued that women's writing "unthinks" history.[16] What happens in McDonald's narrative, however, is something quite beyond interaction with male history and distinguishable from the "unthinking" of it. From her position as the mother of first nine and then, after the death of her youngest, eight children within a specific *place*, a medium-sized, two-story house in the path of constant troop movements and battles or skirmishes, McDonald rethinks and hence rewrites the historical event of war by depicting it as a domestic activity fought daily within the female sphere—in the *house*. In this way she personalizes the public, feminizes the masculine.

In reading McDonald's autobiography, then, we may find that we are grappling with a provocative plurality within one woman's personal narrative of the Civil War. Moreover, we find this text posing theoretical questions about how we read other autobiographical texts in which women have articulated themselves personally and specifically as cultural subjects by bringing history into the domestic sphere. For example, a reading of McDonald's narrative may lead us to take Gerda Lerner's question, "What would history be like if it were seen through the eyes of women and ordered by values they define?"[17] and rephrase it as follows: What is a woman's "self-conception" like when it is developed through her own private reading of the public historical text in which she finds herself participating?

I am borrowing the term *self-conception* from historian Karl J. Weintraub, whose essay "Autobiography and Historical Consciousness" inadvertently points to some of the problems we must face in thinking within androcentric models about women's writing—specifically, white southern women's personal narratives of nineteenth-century history. Weintraub, like James Olney and Albert E. Stone, has pointed out the intricate connections between autobiography and history. "Men," he writes (the use of the term *men* in referring to autobiographers is more common than not in the traditional critical and theoretical literature about autobiography), reflect a history of "self-conceptions" which inevitably must be articulated in their autobiographies. These "self-conceptions" are based upon accepted "models" into which are compressed "essential values and convictions" of the culture: they are, indeed, "part of a man's professional self-perception." These models, Weintraub argues, have dominated "self-conceptions," and hence autobiographical form, for centuries.[18] Immediately we can see the problem for nineteenth-century southern women writers. Southern white women of the antebellum South indeed had a cultural "model," but their cultural placement on the southern chivalric pedestal had little connection to the harsh realities of the working lives of white women in the antebellum South.[19] As Anne Goodwyn Jones points out, the white southern woman was institutionalized as "the soul of the South," the preserver of southern patriarchy.[20] Wilbur J. Cash called her "the South's palladium . . . this shield-bearing Athena gleaming whitely in the clouds, the standard for its rallying, the mystic symbol of its nationality in face of the foe."[21] The problem with such a cultural model is that it/she has neither agency nor, as Jones points out, voice.

To pursue the problem further, if we think (with Gunn) of autobiography as a cultural act of reading the self, or (with Olney) of the self as producing its own order and expression through metaphor, we encounter at each theoretical turn the difficulties facing the southern white woman writer who may be reading her own voiceless position as the silent Other of the nineteenth-century cultural model and at the same time may be in the act of revising that position by writing patriarchal history from a woman's perspective—by bringing history into the house. And so, as we take her writings down from their shelf, dust them off, and begin to read, Cornelia McDonald places us outside of prevailing theories of autobiography and engages us in a critical practice which, as Domna Stanton asserts about reading women's autobiographies in general, is "committed to challenging existing discursive and ideological boundaries."[22]

One of the most provocative examples of how McDonald's writings bring history into the house can be seen in her attitudes about race, which are both consistent with and resistant to the dominant white ideology of her times. When the war broke out, Angus McDonald had purchased two slaves along with the property at Hawthorn. In addition, the McDonalds rented the services of several local slaves to help with the laundry, cooking, and child care. However, in retrospect at least, Cornelia McDonald felt that slavery was unjust. In her recollections of the year 1861, she writes as follows:

> I never in my heart thought slavery was right, and having in my childhood seen some of the worst instances of its abuse, and in my youth, when surrounded by [slaves] and daily witnessing what I considered great injustice to them, I could not think how the men I most honored and admired, my husband among the

rest, could constantly justify it, and not only that, but say it was a blessing to the slave, his master, and the country; and (even now I say it with a feeling of shame), that the renewal of the slave trade would be a blessing and benefit to all, if only the consent of the world could be obtained to its being made lawful. (247)

As I have suggested elsewhere, McDonald differs from most southern white women diarists of her period by showing genuine concern for her slaves, particularly for her children's two nurses, Catherine and Lethea, and by finding common maternal ground with African-American women.[23] When Catherine runs away to follow Union soldiers, McDonald worries that her former nurse will have difficulty surviving with two young children. After much searching she finds her "making her way painfully along the road from Harpers Ferry, with her baby in her arms and little Manuel following her, the picture of famine and grief . . . and when I saw her gaunt figure approaching the house with her poor baby on her arm and the other little one clinging to her ragged skirt, I could not believe the starved, forlorn creature could be my trim-looking, neat nurse" (65). She becomes even more concerned about Lethea when the slave woman's owner decides to sell her. She is particularly fond of her because Lethea had helped her nurse her infant daughter Bess, who had died only a few weeks before. She shares with Lethea the experience of motherhood and is particularly worried that the slave woman will be sold away from her children. She records daily arguments with Lethea's owner about the matter and mourns the fact that she does not have the money to buy Lethea. More than a decade later, Lethea's sorrow haunts her. As she recreates the crisis, she writes in an entry for October 12, 1862, "I cannot endure the thought of her grief; to be torn from her husband and perhaps from her children" (82). And on October 20, after Lethea is taken, with one but not both of her children, McDonald recalls, ". . . I would not have believed that the sorrow of a poor servant and her departure would have made me so sad. I thought of that beautiful and sad lament of Jeremiah. 'Weep not for him that dieth, neither bemoan him; but weep for him that goeth away, for he shall return no more, nor see his native country' " (84).

In the diary segment of her autobiography, however, perhaps without the perspective of hindsight, McDonald criticizes African-

American women who came into the South with Union troops and freed women who dress in finery. She is sarcastic in her comments about former slaves who leave the South in government wagons "on their way to the land of Promise" (**119**). One of her drawings in the original volume, entitled "The Milroy Valentine," depicts a white woman being sent out of the room while two black women are being allowed to speak with the much-despised Maj. Gen. R. H. Milroy, whose troops held Winchester. At the urging of friends, McDonald actually sent the "valentine" to Milroy. Like Mary Chesnut, and many other southern white women writers of the period, McDonald, despite her empathetic connections with specific black women, also participated in the white racist ideology of the culture in which she lived. At the same time, however, her relationships with specific black women within the domestic sphere (as well as her view of such matters from more than a decade's perspective) seems antithetical to that ideology.

Let us return to the textual history of Cornelia McDonald's life-writing. She first wrote her diary between the leaves of books, then a narrative based on its lost portions, then a memoir filling in the gaps. She put it all together and then copied and recopied over and over in a conscious act of tidying an untidy text—one that was squeezed into place, lost, and recreated. So a wife's historical text for a husband-reader is transformed into a mother's text painstakingly reproduced again and again for children-readers. Why was it so important for McDonald to inscribe and reinscribe her 491-page personal narrative for each of her eight living children? And how do we as contemporary readers read such a proliferation of texts? An obvious answer to the first question is that this white southern woman, in her early to mid-forties during the Civil War and having had nine children in fourteen years, believed in her own agency as a narrator of history as she herself experienced it. Most of that experience, whether it be her relationships with her slave women, her children, or the enemy at the door, occurs "inside the house." Again and again she fights the violation of her domestic sphere. Her greatest fear is finding herself evicted from her house: "Oh, the sad, sad time," she writes, "when in the still night I would lie awake, and all the distressing circumstances by which I was surrounded would rise up before me. Our home broken up, my husband and his sons exiles from it, and I and my children only tenants at the will and pleasure of our enemies; and then I would realize the terrible thought that at any time we might be driven out homeless" (**27–28**).

That time does come, but not before a long series of intrusions by soldiers who destroy property, steal food, and violate what little order she can preserve within the domestic sphere. The sense of encroachment pervades. Chaos reigns. McDonald finds a human foot in her garden. Her new potatoes are dug up and destroyed. She looks out the window to see fifteen hundred soldiers marching toward her house. On Christmas eve, 1862, hundreds of men rush into her house, some even snatching her cakes from the oven. She looks out her upstairs bedroom windows at night to see the faces of men in trees watching her. On Christmas day, soldiers break her windows with their fists. On May 22, 1863, she writes:

> I have had so many startling visits, and been so often summoned to surrender the house, and so often intruded upon by rude men, that if I hear a step on the porch my heart palpitates and flutters in a way to frighten me. It is often long before I can quiet its beatings. I am growing thin and emaciated from anxiety and deprivation of proper food and am weak; and now have become faint-hearted. So I fear if they make many more demands I must give up and leave all, for I do not think I can much longer continue the struggle. (**150**)

In these writings, the self's "house" is also capable of being overrun and torn asunder. At several points McDonald, deeply depressed by the deaths of her infant daughter, her stepson, and finally her husband, seems to be writing from a fractured psychic home. The house of the self and the actual structure in which Cornelia lives often seem conflated. The night after her Bess was buried, as she is lying in bed with "a perfect deadness of soul and spirit," she recalls that the real house was "shaken to its foundations, the glass was shivered from the windows and fell like rain" from the explosion of a depot (**73**). In her severe depression she becomes obsessed with corpses. She dreams of her husband's body lying with a wreath around his head—and that is how she finds it when she rushes to Richmond to visit him when he is ill. Over and over she describes the body of her daughter. In her descriptions the winter snow is "a winding sheet," and the spring brings only desolation and

Angus and Cornelia McDonald's home in Winchester, Virginia, photographed in 1914.

sorrow. She writes of eyeless faces, piles of amputated limbs, men choking in her arms from their own blood. On May 6, 1863, her entry begins: "The rain is pouring and the night dismal enough. I cannot quiet my excitement, or rid myself of a dreadful depression of spirit. 'For a field of the dead rushes red on my sight' . . ." (**143**). And later, in the memoir section of her narrative, she writes that she and her children are starving, and she is "seized with utter despair." She writes: "I felt that God had forsaken us, and I wished, oh! I wished that He would at one blow sweep me and mine from the earth. There seemed no place on it for us, no room for us to live" (**227**).

Eventually, through her talent for drawing and painting, McDonald makes a place—a new "house"—for herself and her children. Exiled to Lexington, Virginia, she takes up residence in part of a house and begins to give art lessons. Because of her lack of resources, she is released from domestic chores to draw and paint.

Though her children are in rags, there is no material to make them clothes. There is little food to cook. So, McDonald writes, "having much time at my disposal I spent it in drawing, so as to learn well what I might afterwards be able to teach. . . . I could take time to the task, for I had more of that than I wanted" (183). The lost harmony and order of the natural world, which she mourns throughout this narrative, she retrieves and recreates by drawing and painting "gloomy gorges," "purple peaks," and their reflections in "the smooth and placid river at their feet" (183). Ironically, therefore, it is only when McDonald is forced *out* of the domestic sphere, the "house" which she defends so staunchly, that she is able to create another kind of house within the self, one which allows her to begin to rebuild her fractured self and still take care of her children. As an extension of that self, McDonald's endangered, untidy autobiographical text may have evolved in her own mind, in the aftermath of the war's traumas, into a kind of shelter in which and for which her shaping and reshaping were a form of housekeeping or homemaking. Squeezed between the lines of books, lost, remembered, rewritten, recopied again and again, this text is, in the end, carefully and devotedly made into a home.

I want to return to the question of how we as contemporary readers read such a text. How do we enter such a "house"? This is a particularly pressing question for feminist readers. Women's autobiographical texts have much to teach us about history and women's lives—public and private—and about how we can begin to retrieve the female subject in history in all her specific detail and material reality. Instead of reading statistics about how many people have been wounded in war, we read about a real woman tripping over a bloody pile of real legs. As Bella Brodzki and Celeste Schenck point out, autobiography "localizes the very program of much feminist theory—the reclaiming of the female subject."[24] In Cornelia McDonald's narrative we read detail by detail an account of a woman's life in process and, through that account, the day-by-day progression of history. In this way we can recover what Bunkers calls "the distinct marks"[25] of the woman writer's shaping of a text of self in history. This effort primarily involves reading a text in process and about process; we cannot read Cornelia McDonald's "house" without reading her "housekeeping" as an intricate interface of female creativity and female reality with the unfolding of history. As we read McDonald's vision of history through the lens of female experience—hers and other women's—we construct new histories of reading and new ways of reading history.

The value of Cornelia McDonald's story of the Civil War, finally, lies not only in its textual production of history as a domestic subject but in her text's conflation of place and psychic space. For McDonald, history is what happens inside the "house," for it is there that she finds the voice to assert herself as cultural subject in the midst of chaos, fear, and despair. This woman's narrative and others yet to be pulled from their dusty library shelves thus force us to read from within the house of history—from the female subject outward—rather than from an ideological perspective that valorizes in cultural and literary studies the public over the private, the masculine over the feminine, the outside over the inside. Cornelia McDonald's "metaphor of self"[26] is indeed the house, her own often-lost, often-fractured *place*. Her woman's voice brings history into the house, and therein becomes history.

A DIARY
With Reminiscences of the War

Preface to the Diary

My Diary was begun at the request of my husband who was on the eve of leaving Winchester with the Stonewall Brigade, and in the expectation that the town would be immediately occupied by the enemy, he wished to be informed of each day's events as they took place during his absence.

The record was faithfully kept, and when I left Winchester, in 1863, I had it all with me, but in going from place to place, the first portion was unfortunately destroyed, or lost; That part extending from March to November, or nearly all of it.

Believing that my children will take interest in the record of that time, as they were all too young to realize what was occurring around them, and wishing them to remember the trials and struggles we endured and made, and the cause in which we suffered, I have tried to recollect the incidents recorded in the first part of the diary, and to write them again as nearly as possible like the original; that, though not all lost, was in many parts illegible, having been written some on blank leaves of old account books, and some between the lines of printed books. Paper being very difficult to get, any that could be made available was used.

Louisville, Ky., 1875.

A diary with reminiscences of the war

March, 1862—On the night of March 11th, 1862, the pickets were in the town; part of the army had already gone, and there were hurried preparations and hasty farewells, and sorrowful faces turning away from those they loved best, and were leaving, perhaps forever. At one o'clock the long roll beat, and soon the heavy tramp of the marching columns died away in the distance.

The rest of the night was spent in violent fits of weeping at the thought of being left, and of what might happen to that army before we should see it again. I felt a terrible fear of the coming morning, for I knew that with it would come the much dreaded enemy.

I laid down when the night was almost gone, to sleep, after securing all the doors, and seeing that the children were all asleep. I took care to have my dressing gown convenient in case of an alarm, but the night passed away quietly, and when the morning came, and all was peaceful I felt reassured, dressed and went down.

The servants were up and breakfast was ready. The children assembled and we had prayers.

I felt so thankful that we were still free, and a hope dawned that our men would come back, as no enemy had appeared. We were all cheerfully despatching our breakfasts, I feeling happy in proportion to my former depression; the children were chatting gaily, Harry and Allan rather sulky at not having been permitted to leave with the army, as they considered it degradation for men of their years and dimensions to be left behind with women and children.[1] Suddenly a strain of music! Every knife and fork was laid down and every ear strained to catch the faint sounds. The boys clap their hands and jump up from the table shouting. "Our men have come back!" and rushed to the door; I stopped them, telling them it must be the Yankees. Every face looked blank and disappointed.

23

I tried to be calm and quiet, but could not, and so got up and went outside the door. Sure enough that music could not be mistaken, it was the "Star Spangled Banner" that was played. A servant came in. "They are all marching the town, and some have come over the hill into our orchard."

I made the children all sit down again, and began to eat my breakfast, but felt as if I should choke with anger and mortification. Now, as I look back and recall this scene, I can be amused at the expression of humiliation on the small faces around me.

Tears of anger started from Harry's eyes, while Allan looked savage enough to exterminate them if he had the power. Kenneth looked very wretched, but glanced occasionally out of the window, as if he would like, as long as they had come, to see what they were like. Nelly's face was bent in the deepest humiliation on her plate, as if the shame of defeat was peculiarly hers. Roy's black eyes were blazing, as if he scented a fight but did not exactly know where to find it. While Donald, only two and a half years old, turned his back to weep silently, in sympathy I suppose with the distress of the rest. Presently a trampling was heard around the house, loud voices and the sounds of wheels and horses' hoofs. Suddenly a most unwonted sound! A mule braying; Nelly looked up from her plate where her eyes had been fixed in shame and distress: "Even their very old horses are laughing." That was irresistible. I was compelled in spite of all to join the horses in their laugh.

I was obliged to attend to my household affairs, and in passing to and fro on the porch and through passages, encountered them often, but took no notice, just moved on as if they were not there. Donald was sitting on a step very disconsolate looking, when one blue coat passed near him, and laying his hand on his head, said, "How d'ye do Bub." He did not look up, but sullenly said, "Take your hand off my head, you are a Yankee." The man looked angry, but did not try to annoy us because the small rebel scorned him.

Ten o'clock had come, and we were still undisturbed. Only men passing through the yard to get water from the spring; so I put on my bonnet and went to town to see what had befallen my friends, and to attend to some necessary business. As I approached Mrs. Powell's house,[2] I saw a group of officers standing at the gate, brilliantly dressed men who, as I could not help seeing as I advanced, were regarding me very curiously. I was obliged to pass very near them, but did so without being, or seeming to be aware of their presence. When I had gone by, I heard behind me a "Whew" and a little quiet laugh. I knew they were laughing at my loftiness, but tried to smother my resentment.

As I came near the town I encountered throngs of soldiers of different parts of the army. The pavements were lined with them, the doorsteps and front yards filled, and they looking as much at home, and as unconcerned as if the town and all in it belonged to them, and they were quietly enjoying their own.

Conspicuous above the rest were Banks' body guard.[3] A regiment of Zuaves, with scarlet trousers, white leather gaiters, and red fez.[4] I would not look at them, though I saw them distinctly.

Though they behaved well, I fancied they looked triumphant and insolent; it was perhaps only fancy.

As I passed Mrs. Seevers' beautiful house that was her pride and delight, I saw an unusual stir.[5] More Zuaves were on the pavement in front, many stretched on the beautiful lawn or smelling the flowers that were just budding out. Two stood, straight and upright at each side of the door, while sentinels walked back and forth outside the gate. That I afterwards heard was Banks' headquarters.

I passed some friends who looked at me with unspoken mortification and distress. All houses were shut, and blinds down.

Occasionally at a door might be seen an excited woman talking resentfully to one, or a group of men. I hated the sight of the old town, as it looked with strangers meeting me at every step, their eyes looking no friendliness; only curiosity or insolence. I finished my business, and without exchanging a word with any one, set out for home.

As I turned in at the gate at the end of the avenue, I beheld a sight that made my heart stand still. A number of horses were tied on the lawn, and in the porch was a group of men. I went straight up to the house, as I came near saw they were U.S.

officers. There they stood in all the glory of their gold lace and epaulettes, but I felt neither awed by their martial appearance, or fascinated by their bravery of apparel. I walked deliberately up the steps until I reached the top one, as I felt that I could be less at a disadvantage in an encounter if on a level with them. When there I stood still and waited for them to speak. One took off his cap and came towards me colouring violently. "Is this Mrs. MacDonald," said he. I bowed stiffly, still looking at him.

He handed me a card, "De, U.S. Army."[6] I bowed again and asked if he had any business with me, knowing well that he had, and guessing what it was. Another then came forward as if to relieve him, and said that they had been sent by General Williams[7] to look at the house, with a view to occupying it as headquarters, and asked if I had any objection to permitting them to see the rooms. I told him that I had no objection to them seeing the rooms, but that I had very many objections to having it occupied as headquarters. (This was said very loftily.) But that as I could not prevent it, they must, if they chose do it. This was meant to be indignant, but at the end, angry tears would come. One or two seemed sorry for me, but the others looked little moved. I went and opened a room for their inspection, but they declined looking in, and asked what family I had, and how many rooms the house contained. I told them there were seven children, and that the two youngest were ill.

They bowed themselves out but Maj. Wilkins,[8] the one who was the second to speak, turned back and coming close to me said, "I will speak to Gen. Williams and see if they cannot be accommodated elsewhere." Then they all left, but in a few hours a note came from Maj. Wilkins, saying that in consideration of sickness in my family, Gen. Williams would not inconvenience me. I was very grateful at being left to myself, but not glad to be obliged to feel grateful to these intruders.

For a week or more I was annoyed but little, though every day would hear tales of the arrest of citizens, and occupation of houses belonging to them, while their families were obliged to seek quarters elsewhere, so of course there was nothing like quietness or peace of mind. These outrages roused all our indignant feelings, but when we had a closer acquaintance with war, we wondered how such things could have disturbed us so much.

One morning, very early I observed a U.S. flag streaming over Mr. Mason's house.[9] Found out that it was occupied as headquarters by a Massachusetts regiment. The same evening I was waited on by an officer, very gentlemanly and officerlike (having been in the old army), who requested me to be perfectly easy, and to rest assured that the troops would not annoy me, or do any injury to the property, and he requested that if any of them misbehaved it should be communicated to him and that every offender would meet with speedy punishment.

I thanked him, and asked if stealing fowls would be considered an offense. He laughed, and said that the usages of war permitted these small depredations.

I told him that a steady course of slaughter had been persisted in till there were only few left.

He was sorry, but feared that nothing could be done, as the offenders would not be easily caught.

He was Col. Chapman of the Massachusetts regiment.[10]

That evening an orderly came to present the Col.'s compliments, and to beg that I would be so very kind as to send him a few gallons of wine, as they had found Senator Mason's cellars empty. I sent word with my regrets, that in anticipation of the occupation of the Federal army all my husband's wines and liquors had been sent off when Gen. Jackson's army left.[11]

In a week or two things had settled down, and anxiety had given place to a feeling something like peace and securing. I went about my daily tasks, and when anything annoying or distressing would happen, would try to find comfort in the thought that my children were all with me, and we had a home.

My blessed little Bessie, with her bright little face and happy smile, her looks of love following me wherever I moved, was a constant joy. How well I remember when on returning home from some fruitless errand, or annoying encounter I would be so cheered by the delight of the little creature at seeing me.

Oh, the sad, sad time, when in the still night I would lie awake, and all the distressing circumstances by which I was surrounded would rise up before me. Our home broken up, my husband and his sons exiles from it, and I and my children only tenants at the will and pleasure of our enemies; and then I would realize the terrible thought that at any time we might be driven out homeless. But I trusted in Him who is able to shelter and succor those who call upon Him, and felt tranquil.

One day in April I was returning from a walk in town, and on approaching the house saw a U.S. flag floating over the front door, and an orderly quietly seated under its protecting folds on the door step.

On asking the meaning of it all I was informed that Col. Candée of the 5th Connecticut regiment of infantry had taken possession of the house as headquarters, the regiment being encamped in our orchard.[12] I stood for sometime too indignant to fix on any course of action, but at last resolved on taking steps to get them away, I found the Col. had taken possession of my husband's room which he used as a study, and in which he kept his books and papers.

Knocking at the door I saw the Col. and asked him if it was not possible for him to find quarters elsewhere; as I was alone and my children sick it would incommode me very much to have strangers in the house.

He regretted being obliged to annoy me, but said very quietly that their presence would be a protection, and that as they wanted but one room they would annoy me less than others might do. I saw the wisdom of submitting, but could not accept the flag without a protest; so I ventured to say, "You will confer a favor on me Col. Candée if you will have that flag removed from the front door if you must remain, as while it is there, I shall be obliged to enter at the back of the house. He was standing with his back to the fire, and his officers were listening to what passed. The Col. coloured and hesitated for a moment. Some of the officers laughed derisively, others because they were amused, but all laughed.

I stood till the merriment had subsided and the Col. had regained his composure. Then he said, "I will do all in my power, Madam, to make our stay here as little unpleasant to you as possible." In the afternoon I noticed that the flag had been removed and floated some distance from the house to the left.

28

Things went on comfortably for a time, except that every day the cows were milked by the soldiers, and I took pains to have every offense reported to the Col. with the intention of annoying him, and disgusting him with his quarters. On each occasion he requested that the offender be pointed out in order that he might be punished, but the culprit in every instance escaped detection.

One morning, however, the children came in with the report that the cows had been milked, and the offender caught.

I lost no time in having the Col. informed of it; and in crossing the hall on coming down to breakfast I glanced out at the front door and saw a man mounted on a barrel with his hands tied behind him, and his face so miserable that my heart was melted.

He had such a human look, so dejected and wretched, that Yankee as he was, and milk the cow as he did, I could not help feeling self reproach at being the cause of his punishment. After breakfast I went to the Col.'s door and knocked; he opened it himself but I felt almost ashamed to speak. I managed to say, "How long, Col. Candée, do you intend to keep that poor man on that barrel?" "Until justice is satisfied, Madam." I saw his eyes twinkle as if he enjoyed the fun of seeing me take it to heart. "Do let him go," I said, "he may have all the milk rather than have him standing on that barrel any longer." "As you please, Madam, if you are contented he may go." I did not annoy the Col. any more with complaints—it was malicious in him to punish the man where I could see it. He knew I would not suffer it.

I omitted to mention that soon after Gen. Banks left Winchester to take up his triumphant march after the retreating Jackson, who had, as they supposed, fled to the mountains, Gen. Shields being in command, some officers came to search my house.[13]

Dr. Baldwin was in my room on a visit to the sick children.[14] I went down to the door to receive them, telling the larger boys to keep out of the way. It was nine o'clock at night, and as I went to open the door the old doctor came and in passing out said he was sorry to leave me, but had no fear, as he thought I could take care of myself. He looked very sorrowful, poor old gentleman, and mortified that he could do nothing to save me from their presence.

The officers came in, and I could see through the darkness outside that they were accompanied by a number of soldiers.

One of them was a tall man with quite an air of fashion but not at all military looking. He had large black eyes with so disagreeable an expression that I hated his looks. I felt an antagonism towards him perfectly independent of his character as a Yankee, or of his insulting mission.

The other was fair haired with a rosy face and blue, good natured eyes. In spite of his military dress, he looked and behaved like a country-bred man. The sight of him excited no irritation but that of the other did, with his insolent eyes and fastidious dress. He wore a rose in his buttonhole. I felt impelled to resent his intrusion with the greatest scorn, and as the door closed on their entrance, I stood silently waiting till Col. Clark disclosed his errand.[15] "I have been sent to search this house for arms and military papers," said he.

"You will find neither," said I, "for all have been taken away, where you will never find them." "I will search nevertheless," he said. "Very well," I said, "it may be interesting to you to look through mine and the children's wardrobes, so I have no objections, though I regret that in anticipation of the coming of your army, everything of value has been removed."

I led the way to the dining room where he pulled out a few sideboard drawers, rummaged the liquor case and wine cooler, turned out the contents of my writing desk, read some notes aloud in a mocking tone (for which I could have shot him), looked into the parlor and my husband's private room, and then demanded to be shown upstairs. I led the way and opened my room door for them. There sat my sweet Bess in Lethea's arms crowing and reaching out her hands after the light.[16] On the entrance of the strangers the little hands dropped, and the countenance changed from glee to wide-eyed astonishment. The three little ones were crouching by the fire, while poor little Hunter lay sick in his crib.

The search was begun by Major Stone, rather diffidently.[17] One or two drawers were opened, and closed again after being slightly examined.

He knelt to look into the bottom drawer in which were the baby's clothes. Clark stood by trying to give an air of pleasantry to the scene, tired, I suppose of playing the role of stern warrior. "I declare Stone," he said, "you seem to be all unused to business of that kind." "Oh no," said I, "you do the Major injustice. He acquits himself very creditably. I should think he had been long accustomed to examining ladies' and children's wardrobes; but if he feels unequal to the task, I will assist him." So I spread out a baby frock and little shirt, asking Clark if they did not look traitorous. And so they were disgusted, and went to other rooms to continue the search. While they were thus engaged, the three boys, Harry, Allan and Kenneth, had stolen out in the yard, and in front of the house and, in view of the soldiers were fighting a sham battle, two against one. When the one attacked, the two invariably took to their heels.

One of the soldiers asked why the two ran from one. "You two," said he, "ought to be able to whip one." "Oh!" said one urchin, one of the defeated, "we are obliged to run, we are the Yankees."

Clark informed me that they intended totally to demolish our army, and conquer the Southern people. "And what will you do with us when you have conquered us?" I said. "Make serfs of you," said he. "You will never see us conquered by such as you," I said. Then his great eyes flamed with anger. "Should the fortunes of war place your husband in my hands, Madam, you will wish you had used less intemperate language." "I do not fear it," said I, "from present indications your army will never get near enough to ours for that, as I see that they always keep at a respectful distance."

Clark was Col. of a New York volunteer regiment of infantry, and must have been a man of most vindictive character. After Banks' defeat he recommended to the returning army, that when they entered the old town it should be sacked and burned.

I had one other encounter with Clark. Some weeks after on Sunday, I learned that one of the horses I had left me, had been taken by some soldiers out of the stable. I was told to go to Gen. Sigel and he would see that it was restored.[18] It had been a good horse, and for a time was used in the cavalry; now I used it to drive in our little carriage. Being lame, and not fit for cavalry service, it had been left behind.

31

I went to the Hotel and saw Gen. Sigel.[19] He was quite elegant in manner, very polite, and seemed to wish to oblige me. He directed me to go to the Provost Marshal's office and he would see that I got it. I went, and while waiting in the anteroom I took up a newspaper. Being Sunday, and I having been to church, was rather more stylishly dressed than when Clark had seen me at home with my sick children. Soon I saw some one enter the door opposite where I sat, and looking up saw Clark resplendent in a fresh suit of citizen's clothes, with a fresh rose in the button hole. I gave only a glance, and dropped my eyes again on the paper. He advanced towards me in his most gracious style, and in a bland voice said, "What can I do for Mrs. MacDonald today?" He was perhaps influenced by the better clothes I wore to be polite, but I fastened my eyes on the paper I held and said not a word. He turned and walked off to a window, and the Provost Marshal came in. He told me there were a number of horses in a building near, and I might see if it was there. I had taken Tuss down to identify it, and bring it home in case I got permission to do so.[20] A soldier led me to a large building on Water Street that had been Mr. Baker's wholesale store.[21] At the large plate glass windows appeared the melancholy faces of a number of horses. I sent Tuss in to see if he was there but after a while he came out saying "They knowed that Burwell horse w'ant dar—and just made believe for us to go and see."

March

From the diary.

The Baltimore American, the only paper we see, is full of the amazing success of the "National Army" over the rebels. "The traitor Jackson is fleeing up the valley with Banks in hot pursuit. The arch rebel suffers not the grass to grow under his flying feet. There is perfect confidence in his speedy downfall." Gen. Shields is in command; Banks has gone—with nearly two-thirds of the army. Those that are here make a great display of their finery, and the grandeur of their equipments, but the people take no notice of them.

I meet the gorgeous officers every day in our hall, but I never raise my eyes.

As I came up the avenue a few days since, I noticed one of the beautiful ornamental trees cut down for fuel.[22] I was greatly disturbed by it; and as I entered the hall, still angry and excited, I met rather a fine looking officer coming out. He was a large man, handsomely dressed, and seemed inclined to be courteous. He raised his cap, and held the door open for me to pass, but remained standing after I had entered. I took the opportunity to speak of the trees, and asked that no more be allowed to be destroyed. He said he would do his best to prevent it; and as he still stood and wished to say something else, I waited to hear what it was. First he said he was astonished to see so much bitterness manifested toward them by the people, especially by the ladies of Winchester. "I do not think," he said, "that since I have been here I have seen a pleasant countenance; I always notice that the ladies on the street invariably turn away their faces when I look at them, or if they show them at all, have on all their sour looks. Do they always look sour and do they always dress so gloomily in black?" "As for the dress," said I, "many of them are wearing black for friends killed in battle, and others are not inclined to make a display of dress when those they love are in hourly danger; and they cannot look glad to see those they would like to have drowned in the sea, or overwhelmed with any calamity that would take them from our country." He said no more but passed on.

One day Maj. Wilkins called to bring me a written protection for the house and ground, consigning to death any who should violate it. Gen. Shields had given it. He also offered to take for me any letters to friends in the Stonewall Brigade, as he was to set out that day for the upper valley, and could communicate by flag of truce. I soon wrote one or two while he waited, putting nothing in them but that we were well, and in quiet, but anxious for intelligence of their well-being.

He sealed them in my presence, and when I asked him if it would not occasion him trouble he only laughed and said carelessly that it might cost him his commission, but that he would see that it did not.

33

I expressed great concern lest it should be a cause of trouble to him, and felt so grateful for his kindness, that I told him if he was ever sick or otherwise in need of a kind office to apply to me; he thanked me, and mounting his horse, galloped off to join Banks in his advance up the valley, as I was afterwards told.

The Baltimore American still continues to publish flaming accounts of the advance of the Union Army up the valley, and having no means of knowing their resources, or ability as a military body, except from their own boastful accounts, I was filled with apprehension. A feeling of utter despair would take possession of me when I saw their great army moving, or marshalled in all its pomp for parade or review. My heart would be filled with indignation and even rage, all the more violent because of its impotence.

Had I forgotten the gallant array and brave appearance of Gen. Johnston's army as they passed our house on their march to their great victory at Manassas?[23] The exulting strains of "Dixie" or the "Bonnie Blue Flag" almost giving wings to their feet as they moved triumphantly on, keeping time to the joyous music.

I could not recall any triumph of a former time in the humiliation of the present, and the apprehensions for the future which their power and strength would awaken. To hear their bands playing, as they constantly did, in our streets as if to remind us of our captivity and insult our misery was distracting, but Oh! the triumph of their faces when they had a slight advantage! It was maddening to see.

Though their papers were so noisy and boastful, it was observable that they continued to hover near Winchester, and as we could every day hear the sound of cannon not very far off, it was not easy to persuade us to believe that our troops were frightened away altogether.

For two or three weeks, on successive Sundays there was brisk cannonading near the town, and an evident commotion among the troops. One bright Sunday morning I was standing on the porch listening to the sounds of the cannon in the distance, when a Yankee approached and asked me if I expected "Old Jackson" that day, saying that "Sunday was the day he usually selected to come."

But a day came, a Sunday, when the cannonading did not cease after the usual annoyance of the enemy in the distance, but as the day wore on it thundered louder and louder, and came nearer and nearer. All the troops left the town, and we soon became aware that a battle was being fought very near us.[24] An intervening hill shut out the sights but not the fearful sounds, which, as the right of the enemy met our left became more and more dreadful and deafening till two o'clock in the afternoon; then the cannon ceased, and in its place the most terrible and long continued musketry firing, some said, that had been heard since the war began, not volley after volley, but one continued fearful roll, only varied in its distinctness by the swaying of the battle, now nearer and now farther away, as each combatant seemed to gain or lose ground. Harry and Allan had begged me to let them go to the top of the hill early in the morning to see what was going on. I had given permission, thinking of no danger other than occurred every day; but now, how I repented having let them go, and sat all that fearful afternoon in terror for fear my boys had come to harm.

I remained during all those miserable hours with my baby on my lap and the four little ones clustered round, listening to the dreadful storm of battle, and feeling, Ah! how bitterly, that at each shot some one of the flower of our youth was perishing, (for that Stonewall Brigade comprised the very pride and flower of the upper counties of Virginia) that they were being cut down like the grass. Oh the anguish of those hours! My little boys! How could I have suffered them to go away from me so thoughtlessly when nearly every moment brought danger?

At last the gloomy hours had all rolled by, and with the darkness came silence. All the turmoil had ceased, and in its place a dreary pattering rain was the only sound I heard.

As I sat there in the darkness my imagination painted the scenes behind that hill. The dead, the dying, the trampling horses, the moans, the ghastly forms of those that some of us loved, the cries for help when no help was near. I cried out in my terror, "Where are my boys?" and ran down to the kitchen in the hope of seeing some face that looked natural and reassuring. Aunt Winnie sat there by the fire with Tuss.[25] He was the picture of terror. His poor ugly face was ghostly, his eyes and mouth wide open and his hands clasping each other nervously. He looked up at me and asked in a husky voice, "Whey is dem boys?" I could not answer but went back and sat in the dining room with the little children and poor little Kenneth, who was grieving about the boys. About nine o'clock they came in, very grave and sad looking. Indeed they seemed not like the same boys, so sad and unnatural was their expression. Everything that fearful day seemed unreal. I felt as if a new and terrible existence had begun, as if the old life was over and gone, and one had opened, from the threshold of which I would if I could, have turned away, and lived no longer.

All the careless happiness had gone from the faces and manner of the boys, and though there was no sign of fright or of excitement, they were very grave and sorrowful; disappointed, too, as we had lost the battle, and they had been compelled to see the Southern troops sullenly withdraw after the bloody struggle. I could see that they had comprehended the situation of the contending forces, and had given a correct account of what had transpired under their observation.

They told of the prolonged fight behind the stone wall, of the repeated onsets of our men, and the rolling back of the blue columns, as regiment after regiment was repulsed by the Confederates, till at last, outnumbered and borne back, they had retired from the field, leaving behind the dead and dying, and even their wounded. When the boys told of the retreat their anger and mortification found relief in tears, but they were tears of pity when they told of the wounded. They remained for a while to give water to some, and would have gladly done more, but were hurried away by the sentinels. "I was mortified all the time," said Allan, "because we had to stay on the Yankee side." They had a position in the beginning of the battle near where a body of the Federals were awaiting an attack, and they, the boys, were perched on a fence for a better view, but the attack was made, and a man's head rolled close to where they were, and they prudently retreated to a more secure position.

Next morning, a worn and weary, ragged and hungry train of prisoners came in town under a strong guard. Throngs of ladies and poor women greeted them and cheered them with comforting words. Mothers at the doors of elegant houses waited to give these poor boys food. They were not allowed to stop, but were hurried out of sight without a word to the parents whose darlings they were. No one had been allowed to go to the battlefield the night before, though many had begged to be permitted to carry relief to the wounded.

No one knew who was dead, or who was lying out in that chilly rain, suffering and famishing for the help that was so near, and would have been so willingly given but for that barbarous order that no relief should be sent from the town. No eyes closed during those nights for the thought of the suffering pale faces turned up under the dark sky, or for the dying groans or helpless cries of those they were powerless to relieve.

Not until the Federal dead were all buried on the field, and their wounded brought in, which occupied nearly two days, were our people allowed to go to the relief of their wounded. Then, no doubt, many had perished who could have been saved had timely relief been given. Our people buried their own dead. Though, as we had no conveyances, the authorities had our wounded brought in.

Every available place was turned into a hospital, the courthouse was full, the vacant banks, and even the churches. I went with some refreshments as soon as I heard they were coming in. I first went to the Farmer's Bank, where I saw some ladies standing by several groaning forms that I knew were Federals from their blue garments. The men, the surgeon said, were dying, and the ladies looked pityingly down at them, and tried to help them, though they did wear blue coats, and none of their own were there to weep over or help them.

I went from there to the court House; the porch was strewed with dead men. Some had papers pinned to their coats telling who they were. All had the capes of their great coats turned over to hide their still faces; but their poor hands, so pitiful they looked and so helpless; busy hands they had been, some of them, but their work was over.

Soon men came and carried them away to make room for others who were dying inside, and would soon be brought and laid in their places. Most of them were Yankees, but after I had seen them I forgot all about what they were here for. I went on into the building intending to find our own men and give them what I had brought.

A long line of blue clad forms lay on each side as I passed up the room. I had not gone far before I saw a pair of sad looking eyes intently regarding the pitcher the servant carried. I stooped and offered him some: it was lemonade; he could not raise his head to drink, so I poured it into his mouth with a tablespoon. He looked up at me so thankfully. "It is a beautiful drink," he said, "for a thirsty man," and the poor fellow looked after me as I walked away.

The next day when I went he was past all succor in this world, he still lay in the same place and in the same position, with his head bent far back; he was breathing painfully and heavily, and after I had spent some time in another part of the room and was going out, I saw them carrying his corpse towards the door.

Many, many poor sufferers were there, some so dreadfully mutilated that I was completely overcome by the sight.

I wanted to be useful, and tried my best, but at the sight of one face that the surgeon uncovered, telling me that it must be washed, I thought I should faint. It was that of a Captain Jones, of a Tennessee regiment.[26] A ball had struck him on the side of the face, taking away both eyes, and the bridge of his nose. It was a frightful spectacle. I stood as the surgeon explained how, and why he might be saved, and the poor fellow not aware of the awful sight his eyeless face was, with the fearful wound still fresh and bleeding joined in the talk, and raising his hand put his finger on his left temple and said, "Ah! if they had only struck there, I should have troubled no one." The surgeon asked me if I would wash his wound. I tried to say yes, but the thought of it made me so faint that I could only stagger towards the door. As I passed my dress brushed against a pile of amputated limbs heaped up near the door. My faintness increased, and I had to stop and lean against the wall to keep from falling. Just then Mrs. Magill stopped by me on the way in, and asked me what was the matter.[27] I told her about the poor man whose wound I could not wash. "I'll wash him," she said, and with her sweet cheerful face she went in, and I saw her leaning over him as he laid propped up by a bench. Another poor man I saw who was well known to my family. Townes was his name; he had married a wealthy widow of Shepherdstown.[28] He told me his wife was away in Missouri and he should not see her ever again, as the doctor had told him that he could not live till night. It seemed dreadful to hear him say that when his face was full, and his eyes bright as if in health. His wound was in his neck or spine. He shook my hand as I left him and begged me to give his regards to my husband and family.

The regards of a dead man! but he was so polite, and such a gentleman he must send a message of remembrance even though when it could be delivered he would be in another world. He did not like me to see how he suffered, but tried to talk pleasantly, never mentioning his wound. He said he would love to hear some of the church prayers, but there was no book at hand, and it would have been impossible to read among all those sounds of war, for all the amputations were being performed in the room where the wounded lay.

The afternoon of the next day I went by the courthouse, the scene of so much anguish and despair. I could not believe my own eyes when I saw a flaming banner flying from the porch gaily painted and inscribed with the words, "Theatre here to night."

A gentleman told me that they had spent the night before removing the wounded and dying to make way for the theatre, as they said the men must be amused.

Soon after, the Baltimore American contained a paragraph to the effect that the ladies of Winchester evinced a very great unconcern for their people and the army as well as for their own situation as prisoners, as the theatre was nightly thronged. It was thronged with negro women and Yankee soldiers.

Some days after the battle of Kernstown I noticed unusual preparations going on by the officers in the house, and the soldiers outside. Sleek, splendid horses were brought from the stables, and gorgeously dressed officers came out and mounted them.

The band was playing "Hail Columbia" on the lawn. I felt curious to know what was the occasion of so much parade, and raised the windows to ask a soldier.

The Col. saw me, and after the patriotic strain was ended spoke to a soldier to play "Dixie," which was done, but always spoiled by introducing parts of other pieces, for fear that we, I suppose, should enjoy our rebellious pleasure unalloyed. So as the strains of "Dixie" floated on the air, the Col. and his officers rode down the avenue, their horses curvetting and prancing, as if to keep time to the music.

Those officers were very kindly disposed men. They seemed to feel for our forlorn condition, and had constantly refrained from any expression of triumph at what they thought was a great victory. One young man, The Adjutant, Lieut. Gwynn, was quite a gentleman, and did many little acts of courtesy and kindness.[29] He was a nephew of Judge McLean of Ohio.[30] He often brought some delicacies for the sick children, which he knew we could not get, oranges, lemons, etc., and many a morning hour he spent walking up and down in the shade with my little Hunter in his arms. I never asked him in the parlour, though I often stopped in the hall to talk to him.

One evening about dark, he was coming in as I crossed the hall. "Can you stop one moment," he said. "I have a letter I would like to show you." The parlour was lighted, and the hall was not. I stood, and did not offer to get a light, or to go where there was one. So he, seeming to understand, went into the Col.'s room and brought one.

He then began to read from the letter which was from his uncle, Judge McLean.

He said that there were old friends of his who were living, or had lived in Winchester, Dr. Maguire,[31] Mr. Robert Y. Conrad,[32] Mr. Joseph H. Sherrard[33] and others. "Are any of these families in Winchester now?" he asked. I told him they were all here. "Would you advise me to call on them and present my uncle's letters of introduction? He has sent letters to each of these gentlemen." I hesitated, but finally said, "They would not see you, coming with this army, and with that uniform on. If you had come a year ago, as Judge McLean's nephew, you would have met with a hearty welcome." "Is it possible," said

40

he, "that they can carry their political prejudices so far as to refuse to see me because I am on the Union side?" "Not a brother or a son would be received if he came with enemies," said I.

About sunset the bright cavalcade returned, and after dismounting, seated themselves on the front porch. I went and stood in the door, as I was consumed with anxiety to know the occasion of their gay expedition in the afternoon. Col. Candée, after saying good evening, soon remarked that they had had a most delightful time. Mr. Seward[34] and his daughter had come from Washington to see the battlefield, that all the troops had been ordered out to meet them at the depot, and escort them to the scene of their great victory.

The thought of their triumph, and of the glee of the heartless old schemer whose intrigues and falsehoods had done so much for our undoing, was more than I could bear. "Ah!" said I, forgetting prudence, "we can well excuse him for rejoicing as it is the first time he has had occasion to do so, but I must tell you what crossed my mind as you told of his visit to the battle-field. It was a short poem of Lord Byron's wherein he relates how Mr. Seward's great prototype once visited a battle-field:

> Then next he paused upon his way
>   To look upon Leipsic plain,
> And so sweet to his eyes was the sulphury glare,
> And so soft to his ears was the cry of despair,
>   That he perched on a mountain of slain
> And gazed with delight on its growing height
> Not often on earth had he seen such a sight,
>   Or his work done half so well.[35]

Some of them laughed, but the Col., with a very red face, sat silent for some time. I began to repent what I had done, as I felt that I might have to pay a severe penalty for my rashness, but soon the Col., addressing the Major, said, "Did the General give the order concerning the hospitals today?" And turning to me, "You will probably have to seek other quarters, Madam, for whenever I leave this house as I may do in a few days, it is quite likely it will be occupied as a hospital."

My courage had all oozed out by that time, so I silently withdrew into the hall, and standing by the window tried, tried to realize the probable consequences of what I had done. My troubled look, though, had softened some of them, for I heard a low conversation, and soon the Surgeon came into the hall, and coming to me told me not to be uneasy, that he would speak to the General and try to prevent my house being taken from me.

Two days afterwards, preparations were on foot for a march, and the Col. asking to see me for a moment after breakfast, I went out and found them all waiting to take leave of me before mounting their horses. All were politely and smilingly standing, and offered their hands which I was not quite sure I ought to take, but could not be rude enough to refuse.

The Col. thanked me for the civility I had shown him during his stay under my roof, regretting being obliged to leave his pleasant quarters, but they had orders to push on up the valley with the rest of their army. After they had mounted and were touching their caps gallantly as they turned their horses, I spoke to the Col. "I shall be very glad to see you Col. Candée on your way back if you have time to stop."

That last piece of impudence was cowardly, as he could not, as I thought, reply, but he did, saying, "Madam, Jackson is now pushed to extremities—three columns are now converging to crush him." My heart sunk, and as usual my courage melted away in a fit of weeping. In the light of subsequent events though, my farewell taunt to the Col. seemed prophetic. Mary and her children were now with us.[36] When the enemy had come, and things had settled down somewhat, I had sent for her. Harry went for her to Charlestown after getting a permit from the commanding officer, and also one to allow him to bring up his shotgun which he had left there when he had hastened away on the first entry of the Yankee army. Mary had been very uncomfortable since the occupation of Charlestown by the enemy, and it was better for us all to be together, as we could be a comfort to each other in our adversity.

May had come, and the trees were showing their young leaves, the lawn was a bright, vivid green, and the flowers were all out in the garden, and but for marching troops, and strains of martial music from the regimental bands, we might have felt like ourselves again.

One rainy afternoon, I was looking from my chamber window at the lovely fresh green of the grass and the dripping trees, and thinking how beautiful everything was, and how they seemed to rejoice at the refreshing rain. Smooth as velvet was the turf, and neat and trim the walks and drive. The exuberant Spring had covered up all traces of the mischief done in the month of March, when the enemy first came.

The orange blossoms and syringas were bursting out, and sweet violets were lurking in every nook and corner, and all had on their loveliest looks.

It was the last look of beauty that scene ever wore, for as I stood by the window, the large gate opened and troop after troop of cavalry entered and wound along through the cedars that lined the drive. They did not keep to the drive, but went on over the grass in any direction they saw fit to take. Fifteen hundred horsemen rode into the grounds and dispersed themselves, tying their horses to the trees and pouring out grain for them to eat. As I looked a party tore off the light ornamental wooden railing on top of the stone wall to kindle their fires. A crowd soon collected around the house demanding admittance.

I told the servants to close every door and bolt it, and to answer no knocks or calls, that no one must go to a door but myself. For some time I took no notice of any knock or summons to open the door, but at last the calls became so imperative, that I, fearing the front door would be broken in, went and opened it. I only opened it a very small space, but saw three men holding another up between them, they requested permission to bring in a sick comrade. I suspected a trick and closed the door again. They retired, but soon another party came, more earnest and determined than the other, as their man was hurt, and was their Captain. His horse had fallen down a stone wall with him as he rode to the stables, and had broken his leg. It was no use to refuse permission as I was sure they would take it. So I had to open the door, and they brought him in and laid him on a lounge in the dining room.

From that moment such confusion reigned that it was impossible for me to do anything to stem the tide of those crowding in. The hall, the rooms and even the kitchen was thronged. I tried to get into the kitchen to get some supper for the children, but had to give it up. So Mary and I took our little ones and went up stairs for the night, leaving the invaders possession of the lower floor. I took very good care to see Harry and Allan safe in their own room, lest, if left in contact with the soldiers they might talk themselves into trouble, as I was very sure they would not be able to hold their peace.

The next morning I went down, determined at all hazards to have some breakfast for my family. My heart sunk as I beheld the scene that awaited me down stairs. Mud, mud, mud—was everywhere, over, and on, and in everything. No colours were visible on the carpets, wet great coats hung dripping on every chair and great pools of water under them where they hung. I went to the hall door and looked out at the lawn. I would never have recognized it; a sea of deep mud had taken the place of the lovely green—horses and mules were feeding under the trees, many of which had been stripped of bark as far up as the animals could reach; wagons were tilted up with lazy men around them laughing and joking. I turned from the sight and went into the dining room where was a scene almost as irritating and wretched.

Stretched on a lounge, pale and ill, lay the man who had been hurt; the lounge was drawn close to the fire, and seated around were several more men who never moved or looked up at my entrance. One had hung his great coat on the back of a large rocking chair before the fire to dry, and another was scraping the mud from his boots over the handsome bright carpet, or what had been so the day before.

I knew it would not do to give them quiet possession, so I took the great coat, and threw it out on the back porch, turned the chair around and seated myself in it by the fire.

The men, upon this, got up one after the other and left the room.

After a moment's silence the man on the sofa spoke and attempted to express his regret at my being so incommoded; saying that after his own admittance he tried to keep the others out, but that he could do nothing with them as they did not belong to his own company.

44

I asked him if nothing could be done to compel them to leave me my fireside for my family. He made no reply, and I went out to see if there was a chance of getting some breakfast for the starving children.

The kitchen was so full of men that for some time I could not get in. When at last I succeeded I found the stove covered with pots, pans, kettles, griddles, and every conceivable utensil that food could be cooked in, but as I soon saw, there was none on it for us. Old Aunt Winnie had been ignominiously driven from her throne, and her place had been filled with a mocking crowd that irritated her to look at. I at last prevailed on some of them to make room for our cooking, and before I left Aunt Winnie was installed.

In about an hour and a half our breakfast was ready, and the prospect of a comfortable meal did a great deal to make us forget our surroundings, and as I poured out the nice fragrant coffee my heart melted towards the pale man on the sofa, and I offered him a cup which was thankfully received.

Mary was so sympathizing with the suffering man that she was induced to speak kindly to him, and so he joined in the chat at table, and seemed to try to make himself as agreeable as possible.

Some of the incidents that had taken place during my struggle for breakfast were related and excited much mirth. It seemed wise to accept whatever offered of gaiety to make us forget even for a moment our distresses.

While we sat at table a tall, large man opened the door and walked in without ceremony. He was arrayed from head to foot in India rubber, a cap of which, with a large cape, almost concealed his face.

On seeing us, the cap was removed, and when Capt. Pratt[37] (the man on the sofa) introduced him he advanced with quite an air of ease and held out his hand to shake mine, at the same time bowing low, he begged permission to thank me for the hospitalities of my stone fence, on the north side of which he had slept to keep off the rain. He had a merry, good face, and his fun was so effective as to turn our wrath away from him as a new intruder, and make us rather enjoy him.

He amused us for an hour and when he rose to take leave, Capt. Pratt whispered a few words to him, and in half an hour after he went, the house and kitchen were free from soldiers, and during the day the horses, mules and wagons were all removed from the grounds immediately around the house. But the mischief was done, the wreck only remained of all the beauty I had so delighted in the day before. Our visitor, Capt. Pratt told me, was the Lieutenant Colonel of his regiment, the 7th New York cavalry. He was an Englishman, his name was Johnson, and he had engaged in the war merely for something to do.[38] In other words, he was a mercenary, and an adventurer.

He had during the conversation at the breakfast table informed me of his nationality, and I had asked why he fought against us, with whom he could have no quarrel. He said that all his life he had delighted in something big, and could not remain idle while so "big" a nation was being split asunder. I told him that his motive did not justify him in meddling in a quarrel that was not his own, and especially in assisting the stronger in putting down the weaker.

After some days we became accustomed to the condition of things around us, and began to pick up a few crumbs of comfort in a state of existence that at first seemed unbearable.

Pratt was still there, though his regiment had left. The surgeons said he ought not to be moved, and for fear he would be too comfortable, I would not give him a chamber up stairs, but still permitted him to occupy the lounge in the dining room.

He was therefore present at the family gathering around the fireside, and as our talk was unreserved, he acquired some knowledge of our feelings for Yankees in general, though he hoped we did not entertain the like kindly sentiments for him in particular. We gave him to understand, however, that though as a man we might show him kindness, as a Yankee we would feel it our duty to withhold from him our mercy, should an occasion arise when we had the opportunity so to do.

This state of feeling was illustrated one evening in rather an amusing manner. We were all around the fire, my children, Mary Green and her two, and myself; Capt. Pratt occupied a corner with his sofa. He was showing us a pistol, very finely mounted with gold, which he said a friend had sent him. I had

46

taken it in my hand, and was turning it around to examine it, when my little urchin, Donald, three and a half years old, who was leaning on my lap, touched my hand and said, "Take care, Mama, you will shoot Captain Pratt." "Well" said I, "ought I not to shoot him, he is a Yankee?"

Capt. Pratt had petted him, and seemed to like him, and his liking was reciprocated to such a degree that he had never thought of his being a Yankee. He turned his blue eyes on the Captain sadly and reproachfully, with a look that seemed to say, "My idol has been shattered"—gave a deep sigh and said, "Well, shoot him then."

One morning in May, Pratt rode away to join his regiment. He took leave very politely, and hesitatingly offered me a crisp bank note. It had "United States" on it very conspicuously, as I could see at a glance, but I proudly ignored the note and the offer also, and merely shook hands with him. If I had known then how much more efficacious a U.S. bank note was, than a stock of lofty pride and independence to secure comfort and comparative ease of mind, I should have cast aside the latter and accepted the former. But in those early days of our adversity we had only tasted our bitter cup, and not till we were draining its dregs did we forget our pride, and thankfully accept favours at their hands. Besides it seemed to me then like faithlessness to our cause and people to accept their money, as it implied a belief in their ability to hold our country and keep our army out, and in that case only would the money be of use.

The town was now emptied of troops, all having pushed on up the valley after Jackson, but in a few days a regiment from Maine, very fresh and clean, with perfect neatness displayed in all their appointments, occupied the town.

Comparative quiet reigned, and but for the separation from our friends and family, and the remembrance that those in the army were hourly surrounded by dreadful dangers we might have had some happiness. Our church, Christ's, was occupied by Yankee preachers, so we went to the Kent Street Presbyterian Church, where we could have the comfort of hearing God's word from the lips of a friend, and of knowing that every heart there joined in the prayers for the safety of our army, and the success of our cause, though their lips must be silent on that subject.

Of our army we knew nothing except what we could learn from the papers of our enemies, and they with exulting joy and great flourishing of trumpets published flaming accounts of the advance of their conquering hosts, and of our poor, ill-clad rabble, humbled, flying, disheartened, and in a short time to be wiped off the face of the earth.

McClellan was advancing with a grand army ("the finest army on the planet"), they said.[39] McDowell[40] pressed on through Fredericksburg, while Shields and Banks pushed up the valley. Frémont was coming from the Northwest to join the forces in the upper valley, and nothing awaited the traitors but destruction or submission.[41]

But though sometimes our hearts sickened, they did not altogether fail for we believed in our people, and trusted in God to deliver us.

News of victories for us would sometimes reach us, too, and we would feel glad and proud, but no good news, or anything served for a moment to drive from the faces of the older people whose sons were in the army, the look of anxious care; and constant anticipation of evil gave them a sad and weary expression that was painful to see.

In those anxious weeks and months they grew old, old— and before the struggle ended many had dropped out of sight, and were spared the anguish and humiliation of defeat, and despair at loss of all, children, home and friends.

On the evening of May 22nd, 1862, a guard of soldiers from that triumphant army rode into town at a gallop.

Orders were hurriedly given, and preparations for something important set on foot. I had been in town on business and was hurrying home when I first saw the commotion. As I came up to Mr. Patrick Smith's house, an officer was dismounting at the gate.[42] I do not know what prompted me to do it, but I stopped and asked him where Gen. Banks was. He looked at me for a moment very angrily and suspiciously, but in a little while said that he was near the town and would be in that night. I never could imagine why he told me unless he thought I was a Union woman. His information was sufficient. I knew from it that they were retreating because they were beaten, and I went on home quietly, and slowly, with an air sad and subdued, but those I passed could see the triumph of my heart in my face and manner. I got home, whispered it to Mary, and quietly sat down to supper without a word of what I had heard to the boys and children.

Soldiers were constantly passing about near the house as if to observe what went on.

I sent all the children to bed early, put out the lights, and fastened the doors in the lower story, then took my seat up stairs by my chamber window to await whatever might come.

About nine o'clock I heard the sound of a horse's feet rapidly galloping along the turnpike road leading from town. I listened, and knew that the horseman had, on reaching our gate, turned in there, for the footsteps were heard softly on the grass or the tanbark drive. Soon from out of the shadow of the trees on the lawn a man galloped and stopped at the front door.

I asked from the window who was there. "A friend," was the answer. "Please open your door," was added in a low tone. I went down and opened it, and by the light I carried saw, sitting on his horse, a dust-covered, smut-begrimed man, who I with difficulty recognized as Maj. Wilkins. "May I beg a night's shelter and something to eat, Madam," said he. "You once told me that if I was in need of a kindness and you were near, to apply to you." I consented, and he came in, leaving his horse at the door with the reins on its neck to go its own way.

When he went in he told me that the Federal army had been for three days flying before the Confederates, that in that time he had not slept and had scarcely eaten anything. "I may be taken prisoner here tonight," he added, "but can go no farther. Our retreat is now a rout and I will take care of myself."

He spoke of the conduct of our men, of the gallant stand they made at first; of their splendid advance, till my eyes filled with tears of joy and pride. He described one regiment which he said was newly uniformed in grey trimmed with dark blue. He said there was a wide space that had to be traversed under a terrible fire from their batteries, but that that regiment had preserved an unbroken line in marching across it, though its ranks were every moment thinned—that they came on with even step till their opponents retreated before them and left their battery for them to take.

He supped and I sent him to a room up stairs where he could sleep without disturbance. In less than two hours after he had retired, as I still sat at my window, I saw a line of armed men approach the house, coming from the shadow of the trees. They soon surrounded it, and some came up on the porch and knocked loudly at the door. I went down again, and found several officers standing on the porch and a large number of men fully armed surrounding the house.

The first officer said he had come to arrest a man who had passed through the pickets about nine o'clock, giving the name, and merely saying he was an officer, in reply to the picket's challenge.

My repeated assertion that he was a Federal officer had no effect. With an incredulous smile the officer insisted on having him brought down for inspection. So I went to wake him. Knocking at the door did not rouse him from his deep sleep, so I had to go in and shake him. The poor tired man woke at last, and stared around as if bewildered.

I told him that men waited in the hall for him, for by that time the hall was lined with armed men, and he seemed greatly concerned at the information, thinking, as he afterwards told me, that they were Confederates. They were not at all ready to believe, even when they saw him that he was not a rebel, as his coat was off, and he wore only a blue flannel shirt and pantaloons without any military mark or trimming. So they made him go up and get his coat, and certain papers to prove that he was all he ought to be. After his examination he retired to finish his night's rest, but not till the men were withdrawn, and the door again closed. He told me before he went up stairs that they suspected Col. MacDonald had taken the opportunity to visit his home, and had come with the hope of taking him prisoner. He laughed and said that the authorities supposed as the Confederate forces were so near the town it would be too great a temptation to a man whose home was so near, to be resisted. Soon all was quiet, and I betook myself to bed.

At dawn the next morning we were awakened by cannon close to the town. I got up and while dressing, Lethea told me Maj. Wilkins had gone. He told me the night before that service in that army was most distasteful to him, that belonging as he did to the regular army, he could not help being disgusted at the mismanagement and mistakes of the civilians who were in high and responsible positions, placed there by political influence, and who could only lead their armies to disgrace and defeat. He said they could at least have held their ground, if the troops had not been overcome by fear.

Through the early morning hours the din of the musketry and cannon increased and came nearer and nearer. Federal troops were moving in all directions, some scudding over the hills toward a point opposite to the place where the battle raged.

Mr. Mason's house had been long occupied as headquarters by the Maine Regiment, and their camp was in the grounds.[43] Those gallant fellows had fled early in the morning, leaving their breakfasts cooking on the stoves, savory dishes that the hungry rebels enjoyed greatly. Harry and Allan ran in to say that they could see our flag coming up from behind the hill to the south, from the top of the house, where they had posted themselves.

I could see from the front door the hill side covered with Federal troops, a long line of blue forms lying down just behind its crest, on the top of which just in their front a battery spouted flame at the lines which were slowly advancing to the top. Suddenly I saw a long even line of grey caps above the crest of the hill, then appeared the grey forms that wore them, with the battle flag floating over their heads! The cannon ceased suddenly, and as the crouching forms that had been lying behind the cannon rose to their feet they were greeted by a volley of musketry from their assailants that scattered them. Some fell where they had stood but the greatest number fled down the hill side to swell the stream of humanity that flowed through every street and by way, through gardens and over fences, toward the Martinsburg turnpike, a confused mob of trembling, fainting objects that kept on their mad flight till they were lost in the clouds of dust their hurrying feet had raised. Nothing could be distinguished, nothing but a huge moving mass of blue, rolling along like a cloud in the distance.

At different points the battle continued, and through the streets the hurrying masses still rushed. Occasionally a few would pause to fire at their pursuers, but all were making frantically for the one point of egress that was left open to them. Arms, accoutrements, clothes, everything was thrown away as they sped along, closely followed by their victorious foes, who never paused except to give a word or smile to the friends who were there to greet them.

I put on my bonnet and went in town, and the scenes I there witnessed I could not describe to do them justice. Old men and women, ladies and children, high and low, rich and poor, lined the streets. Some weeping or wringing their hands over the bodies of those who had fallen before their eyes, or those who were being brought in by soldiers from the edge of the town where the battle had been thickest, and others shouting for joy at the entrance of the victorious Stonewall Brigade, and exultation at the discomfiture of the flying enemy. All were embracing the precious privilege of saying what they chose, singing or shouting what they chose.

People in different spheres of life, who perhaps never before had exchanged a word, were shaking hands and weeping together. All seemed as if possessed by one heart and one mind. Baskets of food were brought from the houses and passed hastily among the thronging soldiers, who would snatch a mouthful and go on their way.

I was told that as the columns were hastening by, Mrs. Barton[44] stood at her door with baskets of food, distributing to the hungry men, and while she did so some one touched her and told her that her eldest son, Marshall, had been shot not far from her house. "Bring him to me," she said, and went on distributing her bread to the men.

Soon a squad of men came up with the body of her son. He was already dead, shot in the neck. She led the way into her house, and directed them where to lay him. "He was born in that room and there he shall lie," she said. Then all day she sat by him, wiping the blood that oozed from his wound. He was an accomplished young man, had just a year before graduated at the University of Virginia, and married his cousin, Ellen Marshall.[45]

I met Judge Parker,[46] and he asked me if I and some other lady would go and see to the proper caring for the body of an officer of a Louisiana regiment which had just been carried into Kerr's building. I spoke to Betty, Angus's wife, and we went.

As we passed in we saw a poor corpse with the cape of his great coat thrown over where his head had been. As I glanced fearfully at it I caught a glimpse of his hands, dyed deep with blood as if they had been dipped into it. He, we were told, was a Hardy County farmer's son, a member of one of the boy companies that had been formed and drilled at school.

A sad sight met our eyes when we went into the room where the dead man was.

I could not at first believe he was dead—so natural were his features and so easy and restful was his posture.

He was dressed in a beautiful new uniform, grey and buff; a splendid red silk scarf was around his waist, and his sword was lying by his side. He was very tall and slender with regular features and dark hair—very fine soft hair—his face was noble looking and must have been very handsome. I took one of his hands (such small white hands). It was still warm and it was difficult to believe he was not asleep. No wound could be seen, and not a drop of blood stained his clothing. The poor soldier who watched him, and who wept constantly, showed me a small gun shot wound in his chin hidden by the long jet black beard. But that was his death wound. He was the Major of his regiment, the man said, and was shot while leading his men in pursuit of the fugitives as they poured down that hill side in the morning. It was his regiment that I had seen charge and take the battery, and I remembered having heard my boys say that they had seen an officer of the regiment as he galloped over the crest of the hill, fall backward from his horse. They described the splendour of his equipment, the beauty of his horse which had stood still after its rider had fallen, and I doubted not it was the same.

Betty and I wept over him tears of sincere sorrow, the more so as we thought that perhaps ours and those of the poor soldier would be all that would fall on his lonely bier. I wiped the pale forehead, and smoothed the hair and the man arranged his dress with some articles we had brought. In the afternoon I brought some white roses and laid them in his cold hand. By his side sat four or five rough looking soldiers, men of his regiment.

They, his regiment, had raised money enough among them to buy an elegant metallic coffin for him, and were about to put him into it. That evening he was buried, and a small board placed at his head was inscribed:

ARTHUR MacARTHUR
AGED 27

We planted some violets and lilies of the valley at his head.

The next day General Jackson sent in four thousand prisoners, captured on the retreat. They were collected in different parts of the town, some in the courthouse yard. I had some business near there, and in passing was stopped near the gate by the crowd. The yard was filled with them, and as I stood waiting to pass I heard a voice call out, "Good morning, Mrs. MacDonald," and looking towards the crowd of blue creatures, saw one push forward to the fence. Touching his cap he spoke again, giving me the information that he was one of the Connecticut men that had occupied our ground when the army first came. "Ah, indeed!" said I, "you are then one of the party to whom I am indebted for stealing my chickens."

He laughed and said "yes." A redlegged Zuave commended himself for having offered me some of my own early May cherries which he was stealing.

They both wanted something to eat, which I could not give them being too far from home.

By noon they were on their march to Richmond, a large army, guarded by a handful of the much-despised Confederates.

We were all full of joy, and felt too triumphant to even think of a change—but the change nevertheless came, was coming even then swift and sure. Edward, Wood[47] and Will all came home in high spirits, and all most confident that we would hold the lower valley. Wood told of the battle of Port Republic where our army had turned back the Federals; he showed me a cut on his left ear made by a passing bullet. His horse had been killed under him there, the pretty blooded Kate that had been the family pet. Wood looked so hopeful and bright, much more so than when he had left the autumn before to join Elzey as aide-de-camp.[48]

That was the last time I ever saw him, the last time he was even under his father's roof.

My husband did not come. He wrote saying that he was on duty in Richmond and could not leave then; but if our army held the lower valley he would come in a few weeks. Ed and Will urged me to go if the army did, or even if it did not, as I ought not to stay in Winchester to run the risk of being again cut off. I did not agree to go, for my plans were none, and Ed's were very vague. But he urged, and in his earnestness declared his intention of sending vehicles and seeing that we went.

He finished his argument with "I know it is best, and I am going to see these children taken care of; I have as much interest in them as anybody else has." Of course we laughed at that and he did too. Days passed, and I had not made up my mind, when a sudden change in the aspect of affairs decided the matter for me.

One morning as I went into town I noticed an unusual stir and every one I met looked anxious and troubled. I learned that Jackson was on his retreat and that we would be probably left that day. Returning I met Edward riding from our house to meet me.

He said they would all be gone before night, and that he was in search of me to say goodbye. We parted and he was off at a gallop to join his regiment which was then moving.

I went sadly on home with the bitter thought that the army had come and gone and I had not seen my husband. By night all had gone, but an occasional squad of Ashby's cavalry passed by lingering near to make sudden dashes on any rash Federals that might come within their reach. They, the Federals, did not come in force, however, for a week, when a small detachment marched in under Col. White,[49] took possession of the hill close behind our orchard, and began to fortify.

The main body of Federals had gone on after Gen. Jackson without passing through Winchester, though they did not follow him very far, and only at a safe distance.

Some prisoners had been sent in, poor tired, sick men, some of them, who could not keep up with Jackson's retreating army, and were picked up by scouting parties. They placed them in different church yards, and so guarded them that no one could approach or speak to them. In passing, I saw the face of a soldier who had been for some days sick at our house before the army marched, but had gone when he heard the army was about to march. He was leaning on the fence, very pale and pitiful looking, and I wanted to speak to him, so attempted to go near when a bayonet interposed.

I quietly turned it out of the way and passed by. The man told me he had given out before he had gone many miles, and that he felt very ill, begged for a towel and some soap and a change of clothes. I told him to stay just there, and I would send them, which I did by the boys, as well as a warm cup of tea and some toast.

From the Diary.

1862 June 4th—The army has increased a great deal, several German regiments are here. Blenker's Brigade among them, that famous brigade that fears not God, neither regards man.[50]

Among the Federal officers who have called to pay their respects or show their spite was Capt. Pratt. He was by no means the meek sufferer that I remembered him, but a grim warrior armed with sword and spear and burning with vengeance.

To wipe out the ignominy of that rout down the valley, and the disgraceful flight from Winchester, was his and their inflexible purpose. We would be overwhelmed, he declared, and that in a short time. I presumed on his obligations to me to reply as the occasion seemed to demand, and said we did not fear, were perfectly confident of winning our cause.

He laughed sardonically. "I know," said he, "that one Southerner is worth six Northern men in a fight, but we will win." "And," he added, "it will be a terrible day for you when we do."

I hated the man for littleness in trying to scare me; but he did it effectually for a while.

One thing though always made me think well of him. He had in his youth seen and loved a pretty, graceful girl, and before their engagement had been fulfilled she had met with an accident that compelled her to lie on her bed for years, and all her life to go on a crutch, but he had married her, cripple

as she was, and seemed to love her dearly. He told me that part
of his history when he was lying on the sofa with his broken leg.

June 8th—My garden looks well, and we have an abundance
of raspberries and some early vegetables which I have managed
to get planted and cultivated. I have a good crop of early
potatoes, and also some late ones, enough I hope to serve the
family for some time. We have many provoking, and some
amusing encounters with our neighbors, the Yankees. Senator
Mason's house being the next one to ours, and that and its
ground very much like ours, the soldiers, who I suppose having
heard of the Trent affair, and the Commissioners Mason and
Slidell, always connect the two.[51] As that was Mr. Mason's
house, they fancy this is Mr. Slidell's, and often stop and ask
if it is. Some come mere civilians "to look around," they say,
which they do with the utmost composure, sitting on the porch
where they post themselves without hesitation, and with an
air of proprietorship in perspective.

One day lately, a rather impudent looking elderly man in
a shabby suit of clothes and looking like a half Methodist
preacher and half sharper, with long hair and lantern jaws, and
an unmistakable Connecticut twang, stepped up on my back
porch and walked unceremoniously up to the door as if about
to come in. I had a rather independent feeling at the time, and
stopped him, asking what he wanted. "I am a gentleman," he
said, "and I am only looking around." "I was not aware that
you were a gentleman," said I, "as they do not usually come
to the back door." At that he grew very angry, and said he was
looking at those two places, Mr. Mason's and ours, as he had
some view to settling in the valley when the rebels were cleaned
out. I laughed partly in derision and partly from amusement,
then, quoting Mrs. Barton, told him that he was entitled to
six feet of Southern land if he needed it, and that we would
joyfully give every one of them, but more than that they never
would have. He turned pale with anger, and bending his
wrathful looks on me, asked savagely if I had any rebel flags.
I never had one, but did not choose to satisfy him, so informed
him that that was a matter with which he had nothing to do.
Just then Mary, who was very much afraid that he could or

would do us harm, came behind and pulled my sleeve and begged me to tell him we had no Confederate flag. "How do you know," said I to her, "what I have." So I defied him, knowing perfectly well that he dared not enter the house without authority and a search by authorized parties I did not dread as I was used to them and prepared for them. So I enjoyed his rage and his discomfiture and saw him walk away.

Blenker's amiable brigade is encamped in our orchard, and we cannot avoid frequent encounters with them. Whenever I send out to gather raspberries there are two or three Dutchmen already. One day last week, Mary was in the garden gathering them with some of the children helping her, when several Dutchmen came in and began to talk to her in rather an excited manner; not a word they said could she understand, and she became frightened and sent for me. When I reached the scene of action about twenty were assembled, and more were still climbing the garden wall. They looked at me defiantly, and pouring forth a volume of Dutch, began to pull up the potatoes. I thought they wanted only enough for their dinners, and stood on the terrace looking at them. But they did not stop after getting enough for dinner, but continued amid roars of laughter and defiant looks at me to pull them till all were lying on the ground. I looked on, intending to have them picked up and put away as they were nearly ripe, but they gathered them all up, and with infuriated looks began to pull up and cast aside the second crop to wither in the sun. They were no larger than peas, and the destruction seemed so wanton that I was provoked beyond enduring. However, I could only content myself by retiring to the house where I could hide my anger and distress for the loss of my crop of potatoes was a real distress. They soon became so audacious that they came constantly about the windows and doors, annoying us in every way. So at last I determined to appeal to the commanding officer to interpose and keep them away.

I was under the impression that Col. Sweeny was in command, for last week when the army came in he was with that brigade.[52] As they marched by our gate I happened to be there, and an officer rode up and spoke, and introduced himself as Col. Sweeny. I stood and talked awhile with him as I had learned by experience that it was much better to be civil to the commanding officer than otherwise, and as the band came up he ordered them to play "Dixie." He enquired if I lived at the house, pointing with his whip towards it as it stood among the trees. When I told him I did he said he expected to encamp near there, and it would give him pleasure to be of use to me. So I determined to make an appeal to him.

June 11th—I wrote my note to Col. Sweeny, begging him to use his influence to have the Dutchmen kept off our premises, and telling him, not that they had destroyed the garden, for that was but the fortune of war, but telling how they annoyed us otherwise.

June 12th—This afternoon I was called on by an officer, very short in stature, very gorgeously arrayed, and very red in the face. He walked up to me quickly as I appeared in the hall and presented his card, "Col. D'Utassy."[53]

I bowed, and he then held before my eyes a paper, so close that I could see the writing with difficulty, and asked if that was my handwriting, speaking in very broken English. I was frightened at first, as I did not know of what treasonable practice they might judge me guilty, and visions of the old Capital Prison, where the recalcitrant Southern women were imprisoned rose up before my mind's eye, but on looking closely at the paper, recognized it as my note to Col. Sweeny and said "Yes," that it was my handwriting. He stood still for a moment, his face glowing with gathering wrath, and at last gasped out in his anger, "You call my men Dutchmen." His rage and his broken English excited my risibility so that I burst out laughing. His anger then knew no bounds, and almost dancing with excitement, he averred that they were no Dutchmen, adding a great deal that I did not understand. I said nothing till he had finished, and then politely asked "Of what nationality are you, Col. D'Utassy? I could see at a glance that you are no Dutchman. I should have taken you for a Hungarian." This was said at a venture, but it had a wonderfully modifying effect. His face instantly changed; a bland smile took possession of his little grey eyes, smoothed his forehead and puffed out his fat cheeks. "Dat ish me, Hungary is my country." He assured me that his men should trouble me no more and took his departure in a very stately manner with his Adjutant, a tall, good-looking young American, whose countenance all the time we were talking had been full of suppressed laughter, following.

June—My flattery of Col. D'Utassy has not saved me from the tender mercies of Blenker's brigade, for every day and hour if I look out I can see them in the plum trees helping themselves to the green plums, or taking whatever else they have a fancy for. A plum tree grows close to one of the chamber windows, and often we are startled by seeing a face peering at us from among the branches.

Col. Sweeny, I understand, has nothing to do with that brigade or with any troops near our place, except those employed on the fortifications which he is building on the hill next to our orchard. It is the very same place where old Capt. Canfield[54] planted his Columbiad to command the approaches to the town when Patterson and Cadwallader, those two valiant militiamen, threatened a descent.[55]

June—More forces coming in and fortifying going on on the hill. Our stone fencing is being carried away to aid in the work.

They have begun to tear down Mr. Mason's house. All day axe and hammer are at work demolishing that pleasant, happy home. I saw the roof taken off today—that roof, the shelter of which had never been denied to the homeless, and whose good and gifted owners had never withheld their sympathy from the sad and suffering, or their generous hospitality from any who had a claim on it. Dear and lovely Mrs. Mason, what a friend she had been to me, so kind and gracious, so elegant and accomplished, and so unpretending and simple hearted! Last autumn after the Romney disaster, when my husband was reported killed or captured, how soon after hearing it she was at hand to encourage, hope, or soothe distress. And in the following winter my husband's brother[56] was brought to our house ill, how she stood by his bed side when he was suffering the agonies of death, all that long dreary day, his last on earth; how his hands clung to her dress and would not suffer her to leave till his poor agonized form was still in death.

How bright and happy their home was. The young ladies, her daughters and her young sons with their companions made such a bright and attractive circle. Now they are all wanderers, she and hers, with no place to call their own, and their home a desolation.

June—In spite of sorrow and distress, the birds will sing and the grass and flowers will grow. Every day Margaret[57] brings my sweet Bess from her walk in the garden with her little bonnet all dressed with the Persian lilac or other flowers. Today she came in and how sweet her bright eyes looked peeping out from under the blossoms. The children are happy, and though not all well, we are at least peaceful.

Nell delights in her little sister, puts on the woman and tries to nurse her, looking much like a cat carrying a kitten. Donald, fat, white and rosy, gets sweeter every day, and Roy with his black eyes and yellow hair is a most attractive little creature, though those black eyes more often look stormy than sunshiny.

A day or two ago I felt a longing for a walk to the top of our hill just where the orchard climbs it. There the air is always stirring and always fresh. About sundown I went out and began to climb the hill; the air at every step grew sweeter with the fragrance of the fields and wild flowers. I had just gone up far enough to have a view of the Blue Ridge with the tops of the hills just touched with the parting sun's ray. The Alleghanies in the distant landscape, and the hills at the west all black and purple against the sunset sky.

The old town spread out below looking so peaceful and lovely. I stood and looked long at the scene, and had for a moment forgotten everything disagreeable in the contemplation of the varied landscape, and listening to the many sounds from the town, made soft by the distance, and those of the twittering birds, seeking their night's resting place, and enjoying the sweet summer scents that filled the air. But my quiet was soon rather rudely interrupted, for I heard the trampling of horse's feet behind me, and turning beheld an officer in full uniform who I thought would pass on. But his errand was to me, as he peremptorily announced that no one should come to that place. I told him that I was merely taking a walk on our own ground, and had no idea of encroaching on any one's rights. In a passion he loudly cried out that no rebel woman or any one else should spy out what they were doing. I turned from him, but stood still till he rode away, then quietly went home. It was the first time I had felt that I could be restrained from going as I pleased to any part of our own grounds, but they did not look upon it as ours. In their eyes we had forfeited every right but those of prisoners.

June—We hear no news of our army except rumours. Some say Jackson is in the valley. Others that he is not. McClellan is steadily advancing towards Richmond and is, as he says in his dispatches, "pushing the enemy to the wall." He may find the wall himself before his enemy does.

We have not much though to encourage us, as they are so powerful and have all the resources of what once was the nation at their command. Many fears are felt for the result of the struggle before Richmond, and our people seem more despondent than they have ever been.

Maj. Whittlesey,[58] a Federal officer, a son-in-law of Col. Fauntleroy, is here. He has remained during all the changes, sometimes a prisoner on parole of the Confederates, and again with his own army around him. He is a kind man and loves our people, but of course does his duty to the government in whose service he is. In a conversation with me and some other ladies a day or two ago, he said he did not see how it was possible for Richmond to stand when McClellan made his final attack; that as far as he could see there was no hope of a successful issue for the Confederates, and that when Richmond was in their hands the Confederacy was over.

I felt greatly discouraged at this and went home thoroughly miserable. No one seemed to hope much. It was so dreadful a picture which he had drawn to us of our weakness and their strength that we almost gave up hoping.

June—A day or two ago a Yankee cavalry man came to the house and asked to see me. I went down and he asked me if I would promise not to betray him if he made a communication to me. I told him I would not if it did not affect me or mine in any way.

He said he had made up his mind to leave the Federal service, and wished to know where our troops could be found if he made his escape. I said I knew nothing, and could tell him nothing.

He then said that the service was odious to him, that he had been willing to fight for the Union, but that now he saw their object was to free the negroes and he would fight no longer. He said that Gen. Jackson, in his opinion, was not in the valley, that the Federals did not know where he was, but that an able general like him would do the one thing that would totally discomfit the Federal army of the Peninsula. That he would quickly cross the mountains and flank McClellan.[59]

June 20th—We have just heard of the death of Ashby,[60] fallen at the head of his brigade while leading a charge at Cross Keys. Ashby, the gallant soldier, that the enemy so dreaded. How often have I seen him dash in town with a few men when the enemy were advancing, and carry off prisoners while our army was slowly retreating.

He generally picked off some of the vanguard. Once, some ladies told me, he was under their window talking to them when the Federals were coming up the same street. He waited, standing by his horse with the bridle in his hand till they came within half a square, then sprang on his horse and dashed out of town to join his men who had gone before. The Federals stood very much in awe of him and greatly desired to capture him. One day as I walked down the street with Virginia Sherrard, a covered wagon was driven up and stopped at the Provost Marshall's office. Two soldiers sitting in front of the wagon tauntingly asked us who we supposed was in the wagon. We did not reply, and they shouted after us that it was the _____ rebel Ashby, and pointing to a led horse, said that was Ashby's horse.

We found out afterwards that it was one of their own dead cavalry officers who was in the wagon, and his horse they led.

Some amusing incidents were related after the return of the Federals when they had recovered after Banks' discomfiture.

When that hero first took possession, an old pieman had established himself in business on Loudon Street in a little shop. He could be generally seen standing at his shop door with his sleeves rolled up and clothes covered with flour, enjoying the military shows that were constantly going on, or obsequiously inviting in customers. He suddenly disappeared as Jackson entered the town, as suddenly as if he had melted into thin air, and nothing was seen of him during the occupancy of the Confederates but empty counters, and flour covered shop, the door of which stood open as he had left it. But simultaneously with the first sound of the Yankee drums in the streets, appeared the old pieman, in his accustomed place at the door with sleeves rolled up and face smiling serenely as usual.

On the approach of Jackson the negroes, who had, many of them left their homes and were living in the town, began a flight that was only equalled in speed and madness by the Yankees themselves. A terror-stricken mob pushed out of town in the rear and in advance of the flying bluecoats and many were overtaken and turned back by our men, who had to assure them that they would not all be killed, and that their babies especially would not be thrown to the dogs to be devoured. They had been told by the Yankees that Jackson's men would have no mercy on them but that they would be put to the most cruel death. A week after our army had come, some one told me that a negro man of ours, Manuel, who had left the place when Jackson evacuated Winchester in March, and had since been acting as teamster for the Federals, was lying ill and starving at the back of a cottage on Piccadilly.

I went to the place and found all the windows and doors fastened down so that it was impossible to get in; but after securing the services of a black boy and going around through one or two back gardens, I succeeded in entering the house by a window. There lay the poor creature, emaciated almost to a skeleton, and greatly frightened at our entering the house. When he saw me he burst into tears, and amid his sobs told me that he was not concerned now for himself, but for Catherine and her babies.[61] I asked where Catherine was, and he said she had been frightened at the accounts they had heard of the cruelty of Jackson's men, and had fled to save her children, leaving him to his fate. I was deeply distressed as I was in some measure to blame for his misfortunes, for when Jackson was leaving, I was advised to send Manuel away with the army for fear of his going to the Federals.

Mr. Brown had agreed to take him as a teamster, and I had told him that I would take care of Catherine and her children. I had a great regard for her, as she had been so long my children's nurse, and had only left me when her first child was born for a home of her own.

When I told him, he assented to all I said, but when the teams were ready to set out Manuel could not be found.

I went to see Catherine but she knew nothing of him, thought he was going with Jackson, and was grieving greatly.

The poor fellow seemed very repentant, said he never would have left me if he had been permitted to stay at home, but that he knew if he went into our lines he would never see Catherine again. He had hidden in a field under a haystack, and remained there till the Yankees came in, when stiff with sleeping in the wet hay, and with a violent fever he had made his way home to Catherine. I got Edward to take the carriage and have him brought home, and comforted him by telling him that I would send and try to find Catherine, which I did. Some one found her making her way painfully along the road from Harpers Ferry, with her baby in her arms and little Manuel following her, the picture of famine and grief. Some gentleman took her in his buggy and brought her to our gate, and when I saw her gaunt figure approaching the house with her poor baby on her arm and the other little one clinging to her ragged skirt, I could not believe the starved, forlorn creature could be my trim-looking, neat nurse, who looked so prosperous when she left me. She said she had had only three hard crackers in the three days past, and that she had turned back because she saw women drop by the roadside with their babies to die. The Federals had induced them to fly, but could not succor them in their distress.

June 21st—We have heard that an attack is very shortly to be made on our lines at Richmond and we are trembling at the thought of the possible result. It is heart-sickening to think of the carnage which will be the result, which ever side wins. We have plenty of spirit and bravery, but they have the men and means.

25th—Fighting on the lines before Richmond has been going on, but no large bodies of men as yet have been engaged, at least as far as we can hear.

30th—Fighting, dreadful fighting before Richmond, but nothing certain as to results. Every one is sad and anxious. We have our secret prayer meetings where we can pray for the success of our arms and the safety of those dear to us. The battle is over, but who are the victors, or who among the dead we know not.

July 4th—We have heard the result. We were victorious. McClellan driven back, driven away! The whole town is rejoicing, if we dared we would illuminate. The Sherrards are coming to tea tonight, and I am to have a small Confederate flag on the tea table to celebrate our 4th of July.

We learn that the Federals were driven in the greatest confusion till they reached the James river, and got under cover of their gunboats. Some wag said that their joy was so great, when they saw the gunboats that officers and men embraced each other, and that one officer cried out as he clasped another in his arms, "Every man ought to have a gunboat in his family."

The defeat was due to Jackson's stealthily crossing the mountains, and suddenly appearing in McClellan's rear just when they were doing their best to beat the enemies in their front. Gen. Johnston, we hear, was wounded the third day and General Robert E. Lee is in command.

July 5th—We did celebrate our fourth, and had a happy merry time. The little flag waved over the table; but little we dreamed that at that very moment the folds of the stars and bars wrapped the corpse of our dear Wood, who had perished in that battle.

In one moment he was taken out of life. A grape shot struck him, and his cousin who was near him, the accomplished young Will Bronaugh,[62] and young Frank Sherrard.[63] All were brought into Richmond together.

Many, many others we know, but we cannot think of others for our own loss. The whole town is in mourning, but still we are triumphant; the hateful, boasting enemy are driven away.

The last time Wood was at home, except when he stopped as Jackson's army passed through, he was in the room where Ida Mason,[64] the girls and myself were rolling bandages for the hospital. He looked on for some time as we worked, and

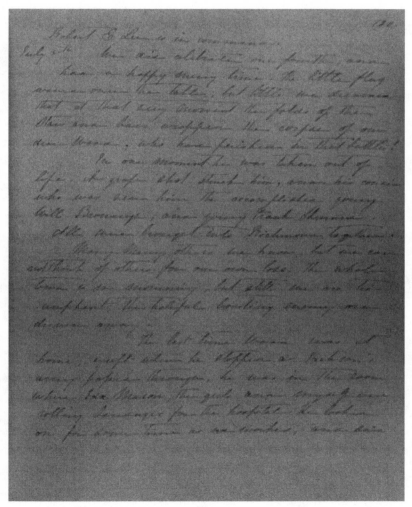

A page from Cornelia McDonald's diary

said very sadly that if he were to be struck in battle he wished to be killed immediately, as he did not wish to live if mutilated. He had his wish, for his agony lasted but a moment, and those who saw him say that a calm, happy smile was on his face, and that every white feature looked peace.

July 10th—No troops in possession now. Ours are too busy; there is work for them, dreadful work. We only know that they are pursuing, and that the enemy retreats before them. Every day disappears our stone fence. They are carrying it away for their fortifications. The days are all sad and the nights so lonely.

A whippoorwill has come near and is singing his melancholy song in a tree. It is the loneliest of all sounds to me now, but in happy days I liked it. A night or two ago, my little darling Bess was restless in her crib. I heard her up stairs fretting, and went up and saw her sitting up in her crib with one little hand holding to the bar, and the moon shining full on her. I brought her down and sat in the porch with her in my arms, and she fixed her sweet eyes on the moon as it was "walking in brightness" and did not close them till I took her up stairs again and shut out the light.

25th—A regiment of infantry and one of artillery is here. One is encamped in Mr. Wood's grounds,[65] and the other on our orchard hill where are their fortifications. A Capt. Hampton[66] commands the artillery and Col. White the infantry.[67] Every day there are more depredations, and less left us to furnish food. Besides that the injuries done to the property are great and will take thousands of dollars to repair.

July 28th—To day a messenger came from Mrs. Dailey saying she was in great trouble, and asking me to come to her.[68] She had left her home, Cumberland, Maryland, on a short visit and while absent had learned that her husband had been obliged to leave the town and the state, as there was great excitement against him on account of his attachment to Southern principles. She had therefore not been able to return, but had to make her way as fast as she could, leaving behind her furniture, bedding and everything she possessed but a few clothes they had taken for their visit.

They had secured a small unfinished frame house in a field belonging to Mr. Wood and had furnished it with such rough furniture as was available, pine table, stools, beds, etc., besides a few cooking utensils. Dr. Dailey, having established them in their rustic home, had gone with Jackson as surgeon to a regiment, and with such surroundings Mrs. Dailey went through the household duties with quiet contentment, and so happy to have her children with her, and her husband in a place where he could earn money for their support, she enjoyed the little pleasure left her, and did not at all complain of her rough life.

When I went over I found her very much distressed and excited. All her furniture had been carried off except her bed and the chair she sat on. Not a cooking utensil or a drinking vessel left. I told her to send a message to the commanding officer. She said she had done so, but without effect. "Let us go then and see him," said I. "If he is a gentleman or a man either he will make the soldiers give them up."

We went, and when we arrived at the camp were told that the Captain was in his tent,[69] and would see us directly. As we had to wait, we availed ourselves of chairs that were near, and which having a familiar look we felt at liberty to occupy. Soon the Captain made his appearance, and bowing politely, asked what he could do for us.

We told him what the soldiers had carried away, and he expressed some surprise that we should think they had been taken there, saying that he was confident none of the articles were there.

"At any rate," said he, "if you will be good enough to point them out, it will give me pleasure to restore them. At this invitation I pointed to the chairs we had been sitting on. "Here are two of the chairs, and there is another on which the Captain's coat is hanging to dry," said I. "That table set for the Captain's breakfast is Mrs. Dailey's front door; those cups are hers, that coffee pot," and after I had enumerated all the articles in sight he looked at Mrs. Dailey and asked if they were hers.

She said they were, and he, looking much annoyed, told her he would send them over to her. He then bowed and bade us good morning and was about to retire to his tent, but I thought if we trusted to promises we would in all probability be disappointed. So touching Mrs. Dailey I said, "With your permission Captain Hampton, we will remain until they are sent away, as you may not be able to identify them all. He looked vexed, but we resolutely seated ourselves again and waited. He stood for a while as if undecided, then called two soldiers, ordered them to gather together all the articles designated, made them heap them all up on the door, chairs, pots, pans, pillows, beds, cups, saucers and spoons, and then told them to carry it where we wished. We waited till the door had set off, and four more soldiers loaded with heavier things had gone after them, and then we turned to thank the Captain. The whole scene was so ludicrous that we could not suppress a smile even in the presence of the great man, but when we observed in his face an answering one we laughed outright, he joined heartily. Taking a card from his case he handed it to me and said that he was sorry his men had annoyed us, and that it would give him pleasure to be of use to us as long as he remained near us.

He asked if I lived in the house in the grove, pointing to Hawthorn, and asked if he might call, which he did in a few days. He was a Virginian I learned from his conversation and consequently more bitter than a native born Yankee would have been.

He said he knew my husband by reputation but had never met him.

A few days ago I was walking from church with a friend and noticed two officers riding along the street, one of them much embarrassed with the movements of his horse, which seemed to be entirely in a sidelong direction, and with such mincing steps as to take a very long time to get over a very small piece of ground. The efforts of the rider to get him along were so great, and that together with his embarrassment at being the target for so many eyes, that his face had reddened to almost a purple hue; and though too stately to beat and ill-treat his horse, his blazing eyes showed his rage, and the effort it cost him to look unmoved. The churches were just out, and the streets full of ladies, and that made the obstinacy of the horse more unbearable. I looked up to see what was going on when I saw so many people staring at the spectacle, and encountered the eyes of Col. D'Utassy.

He saw me and touched his cap, trying to look benign, but his fury was not appeased. The Adjutant toiled painfully after his Colonel, obliged to keep the same pace and step that his superior did. I did not feel at all sorry, for the officers were in the habit of displaying their gorgeousness in the streets when the ladies were there to see.

No knights of old were ever more gorgeously arrayed then D'Utassy and his Adjutant, and they could not but be aware that the glances cast at them and the smiles bestowed were of derision and not the admiration they expected to elicit.

Sept. 26th—Two months since I wrote a line, and oh! the sorrow they have left me. They have taken away my flower. My sweet blue-eyed baby has left me forever. I saw her fading out but never dreamed that she was dying. Though for many nights I have sat with her in my arms soothing her restlessness, the day time would come and bring smiles and happy looks, and I had not a thought of danger.

After a time the smiles were all gone, and the little face was sad and grave.

> Just as if her soul had tasted
> Drops of death's mysterious wave.[70]

Her head drooped and her little round limbs grew thin, and her eyes followed me wherever I went. Then I held her night and day and I clung to her as if I could not give her up.

One evening as the sun was going down I held her in my arms, and as she breathed out her little life her eyes were fixed in my face with the shadow of death over them. The children stood around sobbing. The little breast heaved and panted, one long sigh and all was still; her eyes still fixed in my face. Ah that fearful shadow! How I saw it flit over that lovely countenance, withering all its bloom and leaving its own ashen grey to remain forever.

I felt as if my heart was lead, I still held her but could see or feel nothing but that it was only her lovely clay that I held, and that I must let go my hold.

Soon Betty came in, and leaning over looked into the sweet open eyes. "Oh Bess!" she said, "what visions of glory do your

71

eyes behold now!" Almost instantly my thoughts were lifted up from the pale form in my arms to the bright home to which she had gone, and as I looked involuntarily at the evening sky I could almost see her glorified form floating away in the brightness to her Father's throne.

How often since then have I thanked Betty for her timely words, for I have never thought of her in the dust, but always as I believe she is in the home of her Father, and always beholding His face. Mary dressed her in her pretty baby garments and laid around her sweet flowers, "roses pale and lilies fair," and I sat by and looked at her till the little white coffin came. I slept by her side, and dear, good Mrs. Conrad came to comfort me.[71] She read "And the small and the great are there."

Her words I can never forget, "God will preserve your precious handful of dust, and will restore in His own good time, and in perfect beauty."

You may live to thank Him for taking your precious little babe from the sorrow and evil to come.

Friends were kind, but few could come to me, as I was outside the pickets. Judge Parker and Mr. Williams[72] kindly took the arrangement of everything on themselves.

Mrs. Conrad and I carried her on our laps to the cemetery, and there Mr. Williams tenderly took her from us. I gazed after her till she had gone down to her rest, and the "doors were shut about her."

Sweet voices had sung over her, "as the sweet flowers that scent the morn." Lute and Lal Burwell, Miss Nett Lee and others, and all seemed so touched and sorrowful.[73] My house and my heart were desolate for the sweetest joys of life were gone from me.

For days after she left me I felt as if my heart was dead. Nothing could interest me and it was vain to try to occupy myself with any thing. All seemed unreal, as if it was slipping rapidly away. The world was a dream, and a troubled, sorrowful one. Eternity appeared so near that earth and its concerns were being absorbed in its light.

On Tuesday night, August 26th, after she was buried, I was lying in bed with a feeling only of indifference to everything, a perfect deadness of soul and spirit. If I had a wish it was the world, with its fearful trials and sorrows, its mockeries and its vanishing joys, could come to an end. Suddenly the house was shaken to its foundations, the glass was shivered from the windows and fell like rain all over me as I lay in bed; a noise, terrific as of crashing worlds, followed, prolonged for some fearful moments.

My first thought was that the world was really in its last convulsion. I could not move, but lay fixed and paralyzed. Then a cry, and my room door was burst open. "The town is on fire!" screamed Betty, rushing in. I got up and running across the hall to where the windows looked towards the town, and then saw the whole eastern sky lighted by the blaze of burning buildings, a long line of which was in one huge conflagration. We learned the next day that the enemy had evacuated during the night, and had fired the depot, and the buildings where were government stores and army supplies, many other buildings having taken fire, a large hotel among them.[74] Their great magazine had been blown up, which had caused the fearful noise.

On the 3rd of September our troops came in, they secured many prisoners who had been unable to escape from the town. A battle had taken place a short distance off, and many killed on both sides.[75]

My boys in looking over the field for whatever they could find of arms or any thing else left behind in the haste of the fugitives, came across the mutilated remains of the poor creature who had been sent back to see if the fuse was burning. One foot was found in our garden. Our army is nearly all marching north. On their entrance we first learned of the victories and steady march of Lee from the Peninsula, the flight of McClellan, the battles of Cedar Mountain and Second Manassas, the rout of the vaunting Pope and the crossing of our men into Maryland.

My husband came home and stayed ten days—has gone back to Richmond. He was deeply distressed at the baby's death, and troubled at the sickness of the other children. Hunter has been very ill, was taken with a convulsion.

He is a poor little shadow, his father scarcely knew him. The place has been made so unhealthy by the nearness of the camps that there is a great deal of sickness in the family.

There has been a terrible battle in Maryland.[76] A hundred and fifty thousand Yankees engaged. We have lost eight thousand in killed and wounded.

The wounded are being brought in town. I saw such fearful sights in town today that I turned sick; long rows of wounded men sitting on the curbstones waiting for some shelter to be offered them, the wagons still unloading more. Ah! their pitiful faces, so haggard with suffering.

Some with torn and bloody clothes, and others with scarcely anything to keep their wounds from the hot sun, their shirts having been torn partly off in dressing the wounds.

I saw a pale face looking out from a pile of straw in a wagon and went up and asked if he had a place to go to. He said "No," and I told the driver to take him to our house, which he did, with another who was in the same wagon. They were Capt. Clarke of the New Orleans[77] and Lieut. Richardson[78] of his company.

Sept. 21st—Sunday and communion at our own church—again we were allowed to join in that sweet service, and in our own church, to thank our Heavenly Father for the comfort He had sent us in the deliverance from our enemies, and the presence of those we love even for a little while.

Just at this hour four weeks ago we laid my darling in her grave; and just at this hour I used to stand with her in my arms at the door, waiting for her nurse to come from her Sunday walk. How her eyes would beam and her little voice chirp with joy when she would see her coming through the trees.

Morning, noon and night I think of her; every object reminds me of her, and at every turn as I go about the house I am thinking I shall meet her smiling face. And Oh! the struggle against distrust and unbelief. I try to think of her as clothed with that body that shall be, as God has said he would do it, and not as a disembodied inpalpable spirit. There is no comfort in the thought of that tomb. And I know that He can restore my precious handful of dust as beautiful and substantial as before, only adorned with a diviner beauty. He has promised and He will do it.

As he has called out of the dust this rose with all its beauty and fragrance, so can he clothe with beauty those that are his. "Awake, arise! Ye that dwell in dust, awake and sing, for the dew is as the dew of herbs, and the earth shall cast out her dead."

Sept. 22nd—No news from the army. The report is that the enemy is at Martinsburg.[79]

Wounded men coming in town all day. I gave breakfast to some, one a black-eyed Alabamian. He had no shoes, but old Aunt Winnie gave him a pair that Tuss had secured when his friends took flight.

Went this evening to my baby's grave. She lies close to her Uncle Edward. We laid him there last winter.

He had fought from the first in Price's army,[80] then came to Richmond on military business; had come to Winchester to spend his Christmas with his brother, and within a week from his arrival died of pneumonia.

He had when a boy left Winchester to go to West Point; after he resigned and left there he spent most of his youth and early manhood in an expedition to New Mexico, was with Kendall in his Santa Fe Expedition.[81] Spent some years among the Indians in the Territories, and returned to Winchester to be married. After twenty years or more, he returned to his birthplace to die.

His wife, my poor sister,[82] remained in ignorance of his fate for months.

I used to hold my little beauty by his bedside for him to play with her. How little I thought that so soon they would be lying side by side in that cemetery.

Not far from where they lie in what was the Roman Catholic graveyard lies my husband's grandfather and grandmother, both Catholics; Highlanders and Jacobites. They had escaped from Scotland after the rebellion of 1745 was crushed.

23rd—The bands are playing in the streets their lively airs. It seems such a mockery, so much suffering and those mirthful strains.

Reports say that our army occupies Arlington Heights, and that Gen. Lee has crossed into Maryland again. It is scarcely possible but nothing can be learned certainly. Will the winter come again and find this dreadful war still raging? Our poor men will suffer more than they have yet done, for there is less to be had of that which they need for their comfort in their hard, hard life. "But the Lord is King, be the earth never so unquiet," and He can bring us peace in His own good time, and in His own way. We must learn to trust Him, and believe that He will do all things well.

Mr. Buck came today.[83] Told us of Capt. Hampton's sojourn in Front Royal. He wished to have the town burned. He telegraphed to the War Department that the Colonel commanding the Post had refused to do it.

He spoke of Gus. Tyler,[84] said he had been in all the battles before Richmond, and along from the Rapidan to the Potomac.[85] His shoes gave out on his arrival at Potomac, and some one gave him a pair. They being too hard and stiff to march in, he went on barefooted, preferring that to remaining behind.

Mr. Thomas of Maryland[86] called with messages from the girls. They are at Charlottesville and will soon be at home.

Mary has taken Mrs. Hopkins' house in town,[87] and gone there with her children. She will take officers and boarders as Mr. Green's pay,[88] as a private would be of little avail to supply their wants.

No glass to be had to supply the broken panes, so I will have to use old oil cans to shut out the cold. Whole windows were shaken out by the explosion.

27th—Three days and so many interruptions that I have written nothing. Thursday Sue and Flora arrived, and ever since there has been a constant coming and going and seeing company.

Had a letter from Mrs. Pleasants of Richmond, formerly Sally McCarty of Washington. She wrote on Maj. Wilkins' behalf, as he was an old friend of hers. He was taken in Pope's army and put in irons, as all his officers were.[89] She had received a note from him saying that he had known me in the Valley, as well as Mrs. Parker,[90] and he thought if we could be induced to write a line to the authorities in his favor, to say that he had behaved well to the people of Winchester while there with Banks, perhaps his confinement would not be so rigorous. I wrote and soon after heard that he had been released on parole. They say that we are to be left again to the enemy. They have recrossed the Potomac at Leesburg. Some say indeed that they are at Harpers Ferry. My officers are doing well. Lieut. Richardson can go about the house, and Capt. Clarke can get out of bed.[91] Lieut. Richardson is only twenty-one, is remarkably handsome. The girls begged me to invite him down stairs, as they were anxious to see for themselves if the report I gave of his good looks was true. I went and told him we would be glad to see him down stairs.

He and Capt. Clarke began to laugh, and the Captain explained that Lieut. Richardson had no coat, no linen, and only one boot. I told him I might be able to supply the deficiency, and after a search in the drawers and shelves in the room of the older boys, I found a black swallow-tail coat from Bond Street, London, which I recommended, a pair of doe skin pantaloons and some shirts.

These I sent him, and after a while a message came that on account of the wound in his neck he could not wear a cravat or collar, and would I be so very kind as to lend him some kind of handkerchief or scarf to tie around his neck. I sent him a scarlet China crape scarf, about three yards long. This he disposed around his neck, and when I met him on the stairs I laughed at his ludicrous attire. Swallow-tails have not been seen since April, '61, even in evening attire. Nothing but grey is worn, and nothing else would be respectable. He was not at all abashed on appearing in the presence of the young ladies. Some others besides Sue and Flora were here.

He was sitting on the porch bench with the setting sun shining in his face, lighting up his brown hair, the scarlet scarf making his eyes a deeper blue and his face a more brilliant fairness, and he seemed utterly unconscious of what a beautiful picture he made.

"Why did you not tell me how handsome he is," said Flora that night. "I would have tried to look prettier myself." "I did," I told her. "Yes you did but I never believed any one could be so good looking." We were talking of the different states, and of those of the South we liked best, when some one asked him which state he was from. He looked very much vexed and unwilling to tell. At last he said, "I was born in Maine and I am sorry to live to tell it. My parents moved to New Orleans when I was a child."

Of course we pitied him for his misfortune in having been born in a Northern state.

The girls have had some amusing adventures. While boarding in Lynchburg with a party of refugees, they began to perceive that the people were not as kindly disposed to refugees as they were in other places, and even displayed their disapproval when the wanderers ventured to occupy their pews in church.

One Sunday in the Rev. Mr. Kimble's church[92] a party of these girls had seated themselves, when the pastor rose and said that the congregation were incommoded by having their seats occupied by strangers, and that for the future the refugees would find seats in the gallery. On this they all rose and went to the gallery.

After they were seated the pastor gave out the hymn. His selection proved a very unfortunate one, being "Rise my soul and stretch thy wings," when the two last lines of the first stanza were read.

> "Haste my soul; Oh! haste away
> To seats prepared above."

There was a titter in the gallery, and the faces of pastor and congregation reddened perceptibly.

The next Sunday a church warden met the refugees at the door and invited them into the pews, but the girls told them they preferred "The seats prepared above."

28th—Went to church and heard Mr. Scott of King and Queen county preach.[93] At night to Mrs. Tooley's to our Sunday night prayer meeting.[94] Mr. Meredith preached a short sermon.[95] Mr. Scott also spoke. I heard for the first time that Mr. Meredith had been serving as a private ever since he left Winchester with Jackson. He is now Chaplain. Nothing of interest except more news of the falling back of the army.

29th—Assurances that we are to be left to the tender mercies of the Yankees again.

The merry sound of voices in the parlor recalls the old happy time when we were at peace, and when none of our circle was silent forever. I can never forget the tones of Wood's rich, sweet voice singing as he generally was when in the house, or walking about the yard. Sitting alone, I can almost think I hear him singing among the trees, and expect to see him lolling on a bench with his books, or playing with the children on the grass, when at home during his vacation.

I had never understood him well till he became a man. When a boy he was wayward, as all boys are, had his sharp angles. Only when he was grown did I understand him fully, and know what a noble affectionate character he was, and what a good, warm heart he had. The boy's roughness had all gone and given place to a manly grace, and a tender gallantry that became him so well.

That last summer when he was at home from the University none of the family were here but he and me and the children.

I enjoyed so much the sweet summer nights sitting on the porch with him, talking in the dim starlight of all the beautiful things we had read or seen in poetry or in nature.

I repeated one night an old fragment of a poem I had seen somewhere long ago, not remembering where, or by whom it was written.

> We parted in silence, we parted by night
>   On the banks of that lovely river,
> Where the fragrant limes their boughs unite
>   We met, and we parted forever!
> The nightbird sang, and the stars above
>   Told many a touching story
> Of friends long gone to the kingdom of love
>   Where the soul wears its mantle of glory.
>
> We parted in silence—Our cheeks were wet
>   With the tears that were past controlling
> And we vowed we would never, no never forget,
>   And those vows at the time were consoling.
> But the lips that echoed that vow of mine
>   Are cold as that lovely river,

And the eye, the beautiful spirit's shrine,
  Has shrouded its fires forever!

And now on the midnight sky I look
  And my heart grows full to weeping,
Each star is to me a sealed book,
  Some tale of the loved one keeping.
We parted in silence—We parted in tears
  On the banks of that lovely river,
But the colour and bloom of those bygone years
  Shall hang on its waters forever![96]

He admired it very much and seemed much moved by it. I remarked that it was possible its beauty consisted more of the melody of the verse, the peculiar rhythm of the measure, than in the poetry itself. He said no, that it was poetry, beautiful and touching, and asked me to repeat it again. How little I thought that the verses that had no associations for me then, would be from that time freighted with memories of him. I never think of them, or look upon "the midnight sky" without seeing his image as he then was before my mind.

He was so sad when he went away from home the last time. He looked back at the house often as he went till he was out of sight.

I could not help recalling how dejected he was, and how silent he sat as I made the preparations for his departure. His wistful glance around at everything as he was leaving.

He often went to see his sisters at Charlottesville while the army was in that neighborhood, and the last evening he spent with them he proposed singing some hymns and began himself to sing—

"My days are gliding swiftly by."

Anne followed him down to the gate.[97] He said good bye, and looked long and earnestly in her face; went some distance and returned to where she stood in the moonlight, and kissed her again.

In three days from that time he was lying a corpse on the battlefield.

The many voices in the parlour, the laughter and chat of the young people make me remember all I have lost. I miss the sweet blue eyes that sparkled with joy to see me; the outstretched arms and lovely smile. The white baby face hid in the coffin and the smell of those fading roses I can never forget. That odour seems always to linger near.

A bitter grief it was to my husband to lose at the same time his young soldier and his pretty baby girl, who, he had said, was to be his old age's darling.

General Lee is near town, and they say his army has been divided. There has been a great battle but we have heard nothing certain. Capt. Murray[98] and Lieut. Thomas of the Maryland Line are here. They say there is no likelihood of the army leaving us again.

Oct. 1st—No news from any quarter. We cannot learn definitely where our army is.

Some days ago there was a cavalry skirmish near town, and Edward and Holmes McGuire were reported killed or captured.[99] We were nearly distracted at hearing it, but about nine o'clock Edward rode up safe and sound. He had been cut off from the others in a charge, and found himself confronted by three Yankees who all rushed at him. He fired his revolver at them till the balls were spent, striking two of them, and throwing the pistol in the face of the third, turned and galloped off.

2nd—Negotiations between the two governments for peace talked of, for peace or an armistice. It is difficult to believe that. It is much easier to credit a second rumour that Lincoln has proclaimed that if the "rebels" do not lay down their arms by the 1st of January, slavery will be abolished in all the states.

Night:

The low moon is shining brightly, casting long black shadows on the ground. The whippoorwill has come again, and is making the night sadder with his melancholy call.

I sit at the window late, late when every body else is asleep, to think of the past, and try to live over again the pleasant days that are gone.

The Maryland line has its camp near us, and we see them every day. Some of them accomplished young men of the best families of Maryland. They are all cheerful and merry in the midst of their hardships.

12th—Sunday. Heard Mr. Robert Baker preach in our own church.[100] Had Mr. Iglehart and Mr. Thomas to dine.[101] The owner of Lethea has been here several times to persuade me to give her up. He wants to sell her to prevent her leaving with the Yankees.

She has already been tried and found faithful, for she never offered to leave me when they were here before and it would be cruel to reward her with such treatment. It is downright perfidy to deceive the poor creature into consenting to go. He does not tell her there is a negro trader coming for her, though I am sure she suspects it. I have refused to give her up, but am not sure that I have the right to do it, or that if she is lost we will not have to pay the owner for her. If I had the money to buy her, or if Mr. MacDonald was here she should not go. I cannot endure the thought of her grief; to be torn from her husband and perhaps from her children. Her image will be always associated with that of my lovely baby. She held her in her arms when she was first born, she fed and cared for her, and my darling loved her. Her bright face was always brighter when she saw her. It is like giving up the last of her. To me it seems as if all the flowers of life are withered, and nothing left but the bare, bitter, thorny stems.

13th—A little soldier from the Maryland camp came this evening—a mere boy, but with his black eyes full of fire, eagerness to join the flag. He had just come from Paris, France, where his family are living, to join the Maryland line. He said his father wished him to come; did not think it honourable to remain in a foreign land while Maryland struggled for her freedom. His mother was not so anxious.

He spoke gaily and enthusiastically of the life in the camp, and the battles he expected to take part in; and I did not like to be a prophet of evil, and tell him about the dark side of war that I had seen. So he talked on about Maryland, and I asked him what he would do if, when the Confederacy was established, Maryland was left in the hands of his enemies.

"They cannot keep her," he said. "No peace will be made that leaves her with the North."

14th—More solicitations to give up Lethea. Her tears and grief make me wretched. They say our army cannot remain here for want of supplies. News of the defeat of our army at Corinth. Our forces under Van Dorn.[102]

Heard today that Gen. Stuart had gone all around McClellan's army, gone into Chambersburg, Pennsylvania, and brought away two thousand horses, and a large quantity of specie.

The English papers are full of expressions of admiration at the courage and genius of the Southern people. But they do not recognize us. Though tonight there is a report that commissioners have arrived in Washington to arrange a plan of intervention.

It is said also that Lincoln's proclamation has had the effect at the North of creating such alarm among those who are not abolitionists, as to cause serious apprehension of disturbance among themselves.

There seems no doubt now that the Yankee army is disgusted with the war, now that the real object of it has been made manifest, and many go so far as to say that they will fight no longer if the fight is for the freedom of the negroes. Some of their soldiers have said that in my presence.

McClellan has found it necessary to issue an order to the effect that no discussion of politics will be allowed in the army.

15th—Another painful scene with Lethea's owner. Poor Lethea must go. It is dreadful to see her tears and distress. I went up stairs into a room where she was busy tacking down a carpet. Her tears were falling on her hands as they held the hammer. That I could see though her head was bent down so that I could not see her face. I could not tell her she had to go, dreading to witness her sorrow, but turned away, and waited for some other time.

19—Poor L. has gone. When she saw there was no hope, she submitted humbly and quietly.

She came to my bedside in the early dawn to say "good bye." She wept and wrung her hands.

Margaret was with her, but her other child was not to go. She did not wake Hunter but looked sorrowfully at him. "Poor little fellow!" she said. To think of her pitying him in the midst of all her woe!

20th—Hunter wanders about the house calling for "Margy;" "where are you Margy" and in the early morning when he wakes, he lies and listens for Lethea's footsteps. This morning I heard him. "Did you call me Edy? Where are you Edy?" I would not have believed that the sorrow of a poor servant and her departure would have made me so sad. I thought of that beautiful and sad lament of Jeremiah. "Weep not for him that dieth neither bemoan him; but weep for him that goeth away, for he shall return no more, nor see his native country." Intelligence has come of a great victory over the Federals by Bragg in Kentucky, and the capture of 26,000 prisoners. Buell commanded their army.[103] Some say the chances of peace are greater because of dissensions among the Federals themselves. The Lincoln government's throwing off its disguise seems to have a bad effect.

21st—The autumn winds are whirling away the leaves from the trees, the sunshine looks cold and sad. Only a feeble chirp of a poor insect is heard now, of all the summer voices. Since last autumn what a harvest Death has reaped! Where is the home that is not shadowed by grief, or the heart that has not received a blow?

The difficulties of life are increasing manyfold. The inconveniences and troubles of the past seem now all so trifling.

Besides increased anxiety and responsibility, with the burden to bear alone, there are unaccustomed tasks to be performed. Such tasks as formerly fell to the lot of the servants; but they are gone, and we have to make the best of a very unpleasant state of affairs. I have though so much to be thankful for; so much to bless my daily life, in the presence of my children. One great difficulty is to preserve patience amid so many provocations, and not be irritated at the mischief it is their nature to do. Such an imp of mischief is Roy that it is a difficult task to preserve an unruffled front with him; especially as he heeds no rebuffs, but his black eyes look up through his yellow curls with so much fun as well as impudence in them that he is irrepressible. And who could say a hasty word to Donald with those mildly reproving blue eyes looking wonderingly at you, and the lisp of that sweet mouth. There is a dignity in his face, if he is but three years old. My little Bess had his blue eyes and sweet mouth.

Went this afternoon to see Mrs. Dailey. Found the D. there. Poor Tom Dailey[104] is at Mr. Wood's and is near his end; near the end of a useless and ill spent life. Mr. Thomas and Mr. Iglehart spent the evening with us. From late accounts we have reason to believe that the battle of Boonesborough was not a success for us. Wounded men have been pouring into the town all day and for some days past, and are moving on to Staunton. Today it is said that the Yankees have crossed the Potomac in pursuit of our army, but have been driven back with great loss, many having been drowned in attempting to recross the river. The engagement took place near Shepherdstown.

We have heard that Gen. Lee and Gen. Jackson have both been wounded.

I dread to hear of Edward and Will. Where are they in all this dreadful confusion? Set out to go to prayer meeting at Mrs. Williams' tonight; got as far as the Episcopal Church and saw three wounded men lying in the churchyard. One had very recently had his arm amputated. They had had no food all day, but spoke cheerfully and did not seem to think their case a very hard one. I could not see them lying there hungry and so forlorn, so turned back, and went home with Harry and Allan and sent them some supper. They were all Virginians.

Oct. 25th—No news from our army, and no further indication of a falling back.

Report says that a change of public opinion is rapidly progressing at the North. A defeat always creates a change of opinion. Gold steadily rises, and treasury notes decline as steadily.

Nov. 1st—Went last Thursday to Warren and enjoyed the drive so much.[105] The more so from having been shut up so long at home. I began to feel a lightness of spirit, and exhileration as we approached the mountains, that I had not felt for a long, long time.

First came the pale blue, faintly defined against the sky. Nearer and nearer as we came, they reared their rough, shaggy sides just before us; great mountains upon mountains piled till they seemed to shut us in on all sides. The foliage of every brilliant colour, variegated with the dark evergreens, and now and then a farm with its brown fields and pleasant looking homes was a lovely picture. Soon we came to the grim hills where there were no farms or peaceful homes, with gardens and orchards and fields dotted with sheep. Steep precipices, deep gorges, where the sunlight seldom comes, high peaks covered with thick foliage nearly to their rock summits. No sign of human foot having ever trod those lovely steeps and hollows. No sound reached us but that of a mountain stream dashing down among the rocks, or the scream of the wild birds sailing above our heads. The quiet and rest was so delightful to me that I felt as if I would be willing to leave the sweet home, much as I loved it (so changed it was, and so troubled was life within it) and live there in the peace and rest that I could find among those shades and nowhere else.

I remember a sojourn in the Alleghanies once in my early married life, and it is a part of my experience that I never could forget. I went on horseback with my husband, Angus, and Anne to a mountain where he owned some land and was then surveying it. We took up our quarters at a country house, a poor one as far as external appearance went, but abounding in all the most delightful and precious things of life. Cool delicious air, fragrant with the breath of the pines and hemlocks, and the fresh earth that plow had never touched, and within, the warmest welcome I ever remember to have received, for the host was a tall old mountaineer whose heart my husband had won when employed as Commonwealth's Attorney, he prosecuted a man who had killed the son of the old man— Mr. Dixon. His manner of conducting the case, and the speeches he made so won the old man that he was ever after his willing slave, he and his six other sons, all nearly seven feet high.

When we sat down to our meals we were waited on by the host, his wife, and some of his sons; they never sat down with us. And oh, the delicate, rich food! Cold milk, thick with cream, from a dairy on the side of the mountain, fresh venison steaks, the whitest bread, and tenderest broiled chicken revelling in the sweetest butter. No king ever fared better than that; and then every day the rides through the mountains, the views from first one point and then another; the deep glens we visited, the dark hemlock groves we peered into, but could not penetrate except with our eyes. The heights we climbed to see spread out before us billows of mountain tops below us and far away from us, green lanes through the thick trees, and above all we had the joy of youth and love to make every scene lovely. One day in those mountains I can never forget. We got off our horses at midday by a trout stream in which we, the ladies, were to fish, and on the banks of which we were to dine. The bank of the stream was very steep and leaning over it and looking down we could see down in the deep water, six or eight feet deep and clear as crystal, the brightly speckled trout darting about, the red, green, gold and blue spots glittering in the sun as it shone down over our heads. On the sides of the stream the pink laurel bloomed in such profusion that the reflection in the clear water made it a vivid pink, and all up the high mountain sides, and all around us the flowers hung; the lovely pink bell-like flowers with the delicate specks of black inside, and the glossy, deep green leaves.

We fished for trout and when the gentlemen joined us we dined, and that dinner, nothing on this earth of food was ever so sweet. The midday sun was not hot as it shone directly down on us, and the leaves waved up and down over our heads in the gentle air, and we all enjoyed so intensely, that after a time we had nothing to say.

Presently the gentlemen dozed on the soft grass, and Anne and I went off some distance down the stream where was a waterfall of about five feet high. We took off our dresses, put on wrappers and went in and sat on the rocks under the fall. It poured its clear cold water over us and we were young and strong and had never a rheumatism or any ill consequence. We rode back in the shadow of the mountains and sat down to our trout for supper; sat out late after listening to the sighing of the night wind through the tall trees, and the lovely notes of some nightbird. Went to bed and slept sweetly.

That was a day of days. Well, on this November day we kept on our winding way along the shelving road till we came out on the bank of the Shenandoah. I looked long at the smooth peaceful water, at the shadows of the trees and clouds reflected on its shining surface.

When a child I spent a few years in the neighborhood of the Shenandoah, and nothing ever so fascinated me as it did, either afar when its glassy bosom mirrored the blue sky with its garments of white clouds, the fringe of thick trees or its brink, and the large wild birds sailing serenely over it, or when near enough to look down into the clear green water. I used to spend hours gazing on it and fancying, as I often did when suffering from a childish trouble or disappointment, or from that heart-sickness that only children feel, that weariness and disgust for the sordid things of life; that down there in those blue depths was a world of sweet repose, a blissful, fanciful world peopled with beings different from, and more delightful, than any that I knew.

A little story of an Indian maiden and her brother, Hawkseye, had I suppose, given the fancy, for I remember well that for days after I read of her plunge into the still waters of the lake of Canandagua I wept and grieved at her fate; and that of her brother, turning sadly away from her watery grave, and the bones of his fathers to pursue his lonely journey towards the setting sun, whither his people had already gone. Two years after we left the neighborhood I met some children in traveling who belonged to a family living in the town of Canandagua and near the lake.[106]

I remember the deep interest with which I regarded the favored children who had dwelt by that enchanted lake, and my asking one of them if she had ever seen the place where the maiden had sprung from the rock into the lake, and if she had known Hawkseye.

Coming home Tuesday evening we met all of Longstreet's division, marching along in the chilly twilight.[107] I felt so sad to think there were no pleasant firesides for them, but that on they must go through the weary night, or lie down to rest on the cold earth. Many of them were very poorly clad, even barefooted. We had to stop on the roadside for the column to pass. Some one ran out of the dusky line to the side of the carriage. "How do you do, Aunt Cornelia." It was Gus. Tyler, the little hero of so many battles. He looked well and was comfortably clad. Dear Charley also came yesterday.[108] He has been exchanged, and has been appointed Inspector of Cavalry.

He was in Fort Warren with Mason and Slidell and the Maryland Legislature[109] says he had a casemate for his apartment shared by one of the Marylanders, who was a delightful companion. Indeed he says that of such a quality was the society in the prison that he never spent a more agreeable time, in spite of his feeling himself a captive. They were most of them elegant, cultivated and agreeable men, and their mess table was like a charming dinner party.

All of our army have left but Jackson's corps; have just heard it. They have been passing through town for two days. Mr. MacDonald has written me to prepare to leave Winchester and go to the neighborhood of Richmond. I cannot see how it is to be done, and I hesitate to leave my home till I know there is another provided. Besides there is no one to manage the details of such a journey for me, and where are the conveyances to come from? It is not an easy matter to move about the world with seven children in the best of times, and the most quiet, but now it seems next to impossible. If I do not go though, I am certain to be separated from him all the winter.

6th—Last night Charley came again; had been to Front Royal; said the enemy were near there, perhaps had possession of the town already.

Our army is still falling back, there are a very few here now. Northern papers say General Burnside expects to occupy Winchester during the coming week.[110] I scarcely have time now to think of them, or of anything but caring for my household which is more difficult to do every day as servants are not to be had, supplies are scarce, and Confederate money of little value.

13th—Nothing written since the 6th, Sunday, we were in great distress caused by the report that the enemy was advancing. Farewells were said, haversacks were packed, and all ready for the order to march, but it did not come. Night passed, and the dawn of the next morning saw the army marching back to its old camps. The intention now is to take up winter quarters here. Gen. Jackson has his headquarters in town, and the "Stonewall" is not far off.

Poor Tom Dailey was buried today. A sad old house that is of Mr. Wood's with the family graveyard not a hundred yards from the yard gate. A straight walk leads from a door in the back of the house to that solemn grove of pines that wave their branches over the generations of the family sleeping beneath. Last night as I sat at a window in the room next to the coffin, I looked out at the shadowy forms of the trees in the starlight, and as the wind swayed the heavy branches up and down, they seemed to be beckoning for the one that was coming. It will not be long before they are all laid there, for the three that are left of the family are old and feeble. How dreary it must be for them to sit and wait.

16th—Went to the Kent Street church today and heard a beautiful sermon from Mr. Graham.[111]

General Jackson was there. He sat quite near where I was. He had on a splendid new uniform, and looked like a soldier.

He looked, too, so quiet and modest, and so concerned that every eye was fixed on him.

His manner was very devout, and he attended closely to every word said.

No one would have thought one year ago that his fame would be spread the wide world over as one of the greatest of Captains. He may well be fearless, as he is ready to meet his God; his lamp is burning, and he waits for the bridegroom.

Stories of intervention again. The papers say that Lord Lyons is to visit Richmond in ten days.[112]

Went to prayer meeting at Mrs. Hugh Lee's.[113] Had a pleasant chat before service began.

Heard that Mrs. Peyton Clarke[114] had lost her little Lulu. I feel so bad for her. She was her constant sweet little companion. I should have lost mine if God had taken my Nelly instead of the baby.

18th—Rain all day and every thing looking dreary and disconsolate. Why is the November rain the dreariest of all? It comes when it can refresh nothing; it seems like the grief of old age when there is no hope of renewed freshness and life from it, and the tears are so useless. I try to drive away the cheerless feeling by thinking how much I still have to bless and give me life and energy, and I think of my children needing so much care and toil, and take heart for what is to come. No letter from Mr. MacDonald yet. It is wearying to expect every day and every day be disappointed.

Whenever I come into my room at night my eyes always first rest on the spot where sat the cradle with my beauty in it. I lent it to Mrs. Dailey after she went, and whenever I go there and see it with her baby in it, I try to cheat myself with the idea that it still holds my treasure; that her tiny, delicate face is there nestled in the soft pillows. I sit often in the twilight and think I hold her in my arms.

I kiss the sweet lips, and smooth the pretty head.

"You may thank Him for taking her when He did," Mrs. Conrad said. I thought of that when I looked at old Mrs. Dailey's face when she stood by her son's corpse. Would my darling's forehead ever have had such lines? Would her eyes ever have looked so dim and weary? Her work was finished and she went to rest "while yet 'twas early day." I would not bring her back if I could to resume the burden her Savior removed that day when she fled from my arms as the sun was setting.

22nd—Days pass and the promise of a daily record not kept. Cares and heavy tasks all day, and when night comes such weariness that I can only go to bed without touching pen or paper.

Today went in town to make some purchases. Lost my pocketbook with all my money in it. Have worried about it a great deal. Sue and Flora came today. Sue to stay some time.

23rd—Sunday

Have felt so disturbed all day about my purse that I could scarcely give attention to Mr. Graham's sermon. His description of the second coming of our Lord was glorious, but it was so because the words employed were almost the same sublime and expressive ones the Bible itself uses; the splendid imagery all its own. I am thankful that I can see in its beautiful and simple language, each day a new and better meaning. His glory and greatness shine brighter in His book than even in the works of His hands, because it tells, not only of His power and wisdom, but of His love, and His pity and pardon.

28th—At the dentist's all the morning. Not in the best of humour because of the toothache.

Saturday, I forgot to mention Gen. Hill's division passed through town.[115] They were very destitute, many without shoes, and all without overcoats or gloves, although the weather is freezing. Their poor hands looked so red and cold holding their muskets in the biting wind. Such delicate, small hands and feet some of them had. One South Carolina regiment I especially noticed, had hands and feet that looked as if they belonged to women, and so cold and red and dirty they were. That last must have been the hardest to bear, the dirt, for gentlemen, as most of them were. They did not, however, look dejected, but went on their way right joyously.

25th—We heard to-day that the enemy's gunboats had appeared before Fredericksburg, and demanded its surrender of Gen. Lee. This he refused, whereupon notice was given that the town would be shelled in one hour. The women and children had left at last accounts, but we have not heard yet if the shelling was begun.

Donald was brought in to me this evening with a frightful gash cut in his head, three inches each way, forming a triangular-shaped wound. He had fallen down a terrace in the garden, and cut it on a large broken bottle. He behaved so well, was not crying at all, though the blood poured all over him and his lips were pale and blue, and he trembled a little. That was the only sign of suffering he showed. Dr. Maguire pressed it together, washed and sewed it up, and he never complained, but bore it manfully.

I stopped at Mrs. Dandridge's to get Willie[116] to go home with me as it was late. Found Mrs. Dandridge very sad and lonely. Her husband is away. It is a great change for her, the once admired and distinguished daughter of the President of the United States who, as the wife of Maj. Bliss, the President's aide, graced all the gay scenes at the Capital. Not only then but always she was, and is distinguished for her grace and elegance, as well as her amiability. She now sits lonely, and her little son is her only companion and protector.

Tears gathered in her eyes as we talked there in the twilight, but she never alluded to her own sorrows.

To-night Mr. Thomas and Mr. Leacy came.[117] Mr. Leacy said he thought they would be ordered from here very soon. My heart sinks at the idea of having the enemy again this winter and seeing all hope cut off of seeing my husband again before Spring, if then. A fear haunts me that I never will see him again—nothing can be counted on now; we cannot look forward with certainty to a single day.

Nov. 26th—From home all day at the dentist's and at Mrs. Conrad's, found her better than I had hoped she would be.

Heard that the military authorities had seized a large quantity of tobacco in the hands of persons in town who were holding it in the expectation of trading with the enemy on their next entrance. Some had it in store, and others hidden in their houses. It is hard to imagine how people who seem to have all their hearts in the cause of the Confederacy, could betray it so shamefully. But perhaps that is the only way they can procure necessaries for their families, and they scarcely realize that the possession of the articles so much desired by the enemy would ensure their coming again to enslave and oppress the people of the town. They burnt all the tobacco out in the suburbs.

27th—Spent the day at Mary's. Had a pleasant time with the girls. Poor things! They are merry though there is little now to contribute to their enjoyment. Read some letters from Marshall from Vicksburg.[118] He is on Pemberton's staff.[119] He writes a great deal that is very interesting and exciting of his adventures, and believes the town will hold out. The uncertainties of life now seem to have aroused him to the thought of the things that belong to his peace. Oh! That they would arouse us all to greater diligence and faithfulness. My husband, too! I feel constantly as if some great change was at hand; a change that shall alter our whole future. I feel a great anxiety for the welfare of the family, but with it a realization of the insignificance of all things earthly.

I saw today in one of the children's books a picture of the "round world" enveloped in its garment of great waters, surrounded by clouds and darkness on all sides but that reached by the sun's rays, and I thought of that outer darkness that the rays of no sun could ever dispel. Those outer regions where no light comes, and where the glory of the Lamb can never be the light thereof.

Took a long walk this evening, returning found Sue, Flora and the Tidballs,[120] they are full of their fun and seem to extract all the enjoyment they can out of the present state of affairs.

28th—To day a snow storm and an alarm about the Yankees; Saw the Maryland Line march out to fight them; they returned before dark.

There is now almost a certainty that they will leave us again.

The cedar trees in the grounds look so lovely covered with snow, lovely in the day-time, but at night by the clear moon, so sad that I shut the windows and will not look. The snow seems now like the winding sheet of the two who were here a year ago.

29th—Went to church to day and heard Dr. Boyd preach.[121] His subject was "Christian Steadfastness." That which makes a man adhere to the right in defiance of danger or opposition. The determination it gives to obey God and leave results to Him, knowing He is faithful who promised.

I was so shocked to hear this evening at prayer meeting of the death of Virginia Gilkinson.[122] We were talking of her illness when some one came in and said she had just died. Had a letter from my husband, a long one but not a cheering one.

30th—Went to walk this evening. Met Sue and Mr. Thomas on their way to dress parade. Joined them and went too. It was a melancholy spectacle, such a parody on a dress parade. The poor fellows looked so cold, and their ranks so thin, that I could not help thinking that in case of an onset by the Yankees, our defenders could be easily put to flight. Major Herbert met us and walked with us, and we had some pleasant talk.[123] I could scarcely help laughing to see some of them cooking their suppers. They were boiling their beef in a coffee boiler, and afterwards no doubt used it to boil their coffee. They were making up their dough in one corner of their oil cloth blanket, and baking it by holding it in the fire on the end of a stick. They are a nice set of young men, and some of them have beautiful voices.

When the girls are with me they often come to serenade them, singing out in the cold moonlight their pretty love songs.

We are paying one dollar a pound for salt, two dollars for brown sugar, and a dollar and a quarter a yard for very poor calico, and glad of the privilege of buying it.

Dec. 1st—Went to Virginia Gilkinson's funeral. Felt very sad when I remembered what a gay girl she was so short a time ago. She leaves a little infant three weeks old.

A great alarm at the reported aproach of the enemy. Our defenders, the Maryland Line, are preparing to depart. They all came to bid us good bye. Mr. Iglehart, as he left, asked me to keep his Bible for him.[124] I saw the poor fellows march off sadly enough.

Our fartherest pickets have been in town all day. This evening two videttes rode in to say that all soldiers must leave.

I saw the last cavalry picket ride off sadly enough, for I knew that with the morning might come our enemies. I have always had a dread of their entering the town at night. and breaking into the houses.

Dec. 3rd—Last night our poor town was left to its fate and all expected the enemy this morning. Nine o'clock, and a flag of truce from Gen. Geary,[125] saying that if he was not molested the town would be taken peaceable possession of; if otherwise, it would be shelled. The troops were all gone, and the Mayor, Mr. Reed, sent word that the town would surrender.[126]

On came the host of Yankees filing through by one street, first cavalry, then infantry. They sent around to all the hospitals to parole the sick and wounded, rode up to their deserted fortifications from whence they shelled the woods where our men were supposed to linger. Then filed out of town by the Martinsburg turnpike and were gone. So harmless now are the Yankees considered to be, that when Geary approached the town a deputation of boys met him, self-constituted, Allan among the number, and escorted him in. While the shells were whizzing over the house the little boys were playing in the yard. As soon as Donald perceived what was going on, he made a run for the house, and bursting into the dining room where I sat, said "Just let me in here," and seating himself by the fire, in a few moments his blue eyes looked as placid as ever, and in half an hour he was securely asleep in the corner, and oblivious of all the commotion around. Went in town and saw one of our cavalry men returning from following the retiring enemy, a prisoner walking by his horse, he holding a cocked pistol to his head. In a few moments another came by with a Yankee woman mounted on his horse behind him. He had captured her while she was trying to keep up with the retreat. She was fashionably dressed and looked a person of some consequence; and the contrast between her genteel apparel and the very dingy outfit of her captor, together with her pendant limbs as he trotted solemnly past all the principal residences had something in it ludicrous indeed. Next came a body of the returning Marylanders from the opposite direction. Everybody was out of doors, handkerchiefs waving, voices cheering, and full of exultation. I did not return home till nearly dark, was with Mary, Sue and Flora.

4th—The Psalm for to day begins, "The Heavens declare the Glory of God and the firmament showeth his handiwork." So does everything; the beautiful soft snow as much as any other thing. It looks so lovely from this window; the dark cedars with their heavy green branches covered with the white wreaths, and on its smooth white surface every branch and twig is marked distinct and clear in the moonlight. Always I am thinking of the soldiers sleeping out in the winter nights without shelter or anything to keep out the cold. I have seen them sleeping out in the yard by the side of their cannon in the chill autumn nights and now, nearly two years since, and they are no better off. One was frozen to death here last winter on his post. How different it all is now from the old happy time that seems so far away now that it is like a dream. The sleighbells tinkling, and the happy voices ringing out on the cold, still air. All is past now and gone, I feel, forever. It is a sad time to have fallen upon; even if my own sorrows seem to lighten I cannot feel happier when I see and know of so much misery. Scarcely a household that I know but has a vacant place, and a fireside but where there are breaking hearts and want. Actual want sits gloomily in homes where all before was peace and plenty.

We have heard of a great battle at Fredericksburg; that Burnside was taken prisoner, and his army defeated, a large part being captured. That was perhaps the reason for the sudden departure of the Yankees yesterday. At least that furnishes some evidence of the truth of the report.

It is a weary, weary life, the hope, the fear, and sometimes the despair that crushes the heart, all that, and the hard work, the unusual tasks, the anxiety about food for the morrow. All this seems to be wearing me out. But our God is a strong rock and house of defense, and I feel comfort in the thought that all happens by His permission.

When I look at the happy faces of the children I can almost forget grief and care, for they do not grieve long and though they feel, sorrow sits lightly on them, as it should. If my little darling had lived she would now be running about, and how much brightness would that sweet little face have shed around. The twilight always brings her back, and it seems as if the shadow of death was over our house.

"When will the mournful night be gone."

8th—Four days and no diary. No quiet all day, and no repose of body or spirit; nothing but weariness unutterable when night comes; but my promise must not be forgotten, my daily record must be made as nearly as possible.

Will came to-night and brought intelligence of Edward's capture. He was in Hampshire county and was taken there and carried to Windlea and there placed in the cellar of his father's house and guarded by negroes.[127] Tonight two gentlemen called to see the girls. Major Howard and Captain Williamson of the staff of Gen. Jones.[128] Apprehensions of the Yankees again. Have been reading today Cummings' lectures on the prophecy of Daniel.[129] Heretofore I have read the Prophecy without much thought, and even with a sort of unbelief. Now I can see the meaning partly, and I can perceive that the Unseen is the reality. Daniel was a man faithful, true and upright, but how exalted his character must have been when the Ancient of Days whom he saw on His throne, who saw into the depths of his heart, could call him "greatly beloved."

12th—Work all day—in the evening Key Buchanan came, his boyish face looks pale and altered.[130] He came to ask permission to play on the piano as he feared he would forget all his music. I cannot bear to look at his childish figure, and fair forehead for always comes up to my mind the dreadful battle scenes, with the bloodless boys' faces turned up to the sky, and the lonely wayside graves. I did not know when I saw Maj. Howard that it was with him that Wood rode when he went to the battle that day, the last time, that it was to him as he went on by his side that he confided his foreboding that his life would be given up in that battle; and him that he begged that when he fell he would have his body removed from the turmoil and taken out of reach of horses' or trampling men's feet.

15th—Saturday morning I went in town and found the streets full of moving troops. No one knows the meaning of it. Some thought the enemy were approaching, others that the troups were going to Fredericksburg, where our army is waiting for the enemy. We heard yesterday of the bombardment of the old city, and of the attempt of the Federal forces to cross the

Rappahanock. Report said that when the attempt was made yesterday that several bridges were swept off with their living loads, and that thousands were drowned; that we were each day successful and the enemy's loss very heavy.[131]

Fearful stories of suffering in the town have reached us today. Families flying in the midnight darkness and bitter cold, after being all day in their cellars to avoid the shells.

Women, and many children were killed in their flight through the streets, and thousands houseless, shelterless and starving are wandering in the woods, there to abide the frost and cold of the winter days and nights. The old, the sick and the young children, all alike, driven out from their homes. May God look with mercy on them, for there is no other arm to save, or eye to pity. Stories are told of fearful fighting in the streets and many on both sides killed.

Like Jeremiah I must weep for the slain of the daughters of my people. We cannot tell who are among the killed that we know, or whose names will appear in the ghastly list. I am so sickened with horror and harrowed by the tales of suffering that I could willingly say "good night" to the world and all in it. It is hard to believe it the same in which I have lived and enjoyed so many happy years. The evil days have indeed come.

Christmas is but ten days off, the blessed time that used to be so joyous. It shall have something bright and cheery in it for the children. They shall hang up their stockings, poor little things, even if I have to manufacture the things to put in them.

16th—Another son of Mr. Barton has slept his last sleep since those dreadful battles at Fredericksburg began. Poor David, cut down in his first youth, and from such a loving household. He died alone and far away from all who loved him. Many noble and brave hearts beat their last that day. Many bright heads are laid low, and many hearts are mourning now over the news of that bloody fray at Fredericksburg. There is a report that Gen. A. P. Hill is a prisoner, and Gen. Stuart killed.[132] Henry Buck came today, and is I believe on picket duty near this place.[133] We see no papers and can hear nothing reliable.

17th—Our weekly prayer meeting had been appointed to be held at Mr. Barton's, and when we all assembled it was as if the corpse of the dear boy was there in the midst of us. Every eye wept, and every voice was hushed. Mr. Barton himself prayed, and though his voice trembled and often ceased altogether from stifled sobbing, he uttered words of comfort and hope that no one could have given voice to, but one who in the deep waters found that his God was with him.

"The morning flowers display their sweets" was sung by sweet girls' voices, for there were no men to add their steady tones. Mr. Barton gave out the words standing by the hearth where all his life his boy used to sit and laugh and chat with his brothers and sisters in the pleasant firelight. How his face and form must have been present to his mind, and how his sad thoughts must have wandered away to the silent traveler who was then on his way to his home.

18th—Read an account to day of the battle of Fredericksburg. Twenty-five hundred of our men wounded, and five hundred killed.[134] Some of those very ill-clad, eager faced fellows that I saw pass through the streets. All their bravery, all the sharp hunger, all the cold and the suffering borne in vain. A bloody death, and an unknown grave at the end of it all. Not all those I saw on that march looked hopeful and eager; some of the most dejected and hopeless looking faces I ever saw were among them. Poor men, perhaps with not much desire for glory, or interest in the issue of the contest, except to have peace.

Perhaps they thought as they plodded on their weary way through mud and snow, of the little faces at home, pinched and pale; the poor home; perhaps some hut on the mountain side; of the want and hunger; of the poor over-tasked wife whose lot was hard in the best of times, now toiling indoors and out, trying to fill the places of both father and mother.

Those are the thoughts that take away the strength from the men's arms, and the hope from their eyes. Those poor, sad ones and the gay and happy hearted, the rich, the intellectual and accomplished all have gone down together and the long trenches have received them and hid them away.

Many of the flower of the country fell there.

General Cobb and General Gregg among them.[135] So many are the fearful battles that have been fought that we can scarcely remember them all. The catalogue increases fast. Bethel, Manassas, Belmont, Lexington, Springfield, Elkhorn, Donelson, Corinth, Fair Oaks, the dreadful battle of a week before; Richmond, Kernstown, Winchester, Crosskeys, where Ashby gave up his life; Port Republic, Cedar Run, the 2nd Manassas, Sharpsburg, where we lost ten thousand men—Where will it all end? Can nothing stop the dreadful havoc?

23rd—Every day an alarm that the Yankees are coming. Yesterday it was said that they were a few miles from town. Shops were shut up in a hurry, straggling Confederates sought safety in flight, and the commotion was general. I was at Mary's spending the day. I first thought of flying home to my nest, for fear the spoiler would enter in my absence, but concluded to wait and see what should "turn up." The day wore away and no Yankees. But this morning as I was dressing I heard a clatter as of cavalry on the march, and looking out beheld the blue coats, five hundred strong.

They posted pickets at our gate and rode on through the town. All was soon as quiet as ever. Went in town in the evening and on the way met some girls with angry brows and pouting lips. They were chagrined at the advent of the enemy, so they said, but I knew well that they did not take that to heart as much as they did the scampering of their beaux.

My two boys have set out for their Christmas visit to their Uncle Fayette which they expect to enjoy greatly. Poor little fellows, they have been for weeks cutting and hauling a supply of wood for our use during the winter. There was no other way to get it, and fortunately we had old Kit left of all our horses. I hated to see them go out to such rough hard work, but they liked it, and have already brought in ten cords.

24th—In the kitchen all day making cakes for the children's Christmas, labour by no means light with only a young servant to assist, but as Aunt Winnie was there to direct and retrieve errors, all went on right smoothly.

In the afternoon I saw from the door a cavalry regiment ride in and take possession of Mr. Wood's yard and beautiful grounds, attracted no doubt by the grass which is still green in many places. I was pitying them from my heart as Mr. Wood and his sisters are such old people and have always been accustomed to quiet and comfort; but my pity for them was suddenly displaced by anxiety for myself, for I beheld two cavalry men on their way through the yard stop and take the Christmas turkey that had been dressed and hung on a low branch of a tree for cooking on the morrow.

He had walked with it a few steps before I realized what had taken place, and with the consciousness of the loss came the remembrance of the straits to which I was reduced before that turkey could be obtained; how I had spent six dollars, and sent a man miles on horseback to get it rather than have nothing good and pleasant for our Christmas dinner. With the recollection of all that, came the inspiration to try and recover it, so I flew after him, and in a commanding tone demanded the restoration of my property.

The man laughed derisively and told me I had no right to it, being "secesh" as he expressed it, and that it was confiscated to the United States. "Very well," said I, "go on to the camp with it, and I will go with you to the commanding officer." He gave it up then and I returned triumphantly to the kitchen with it. Just as I got back I looked and saw a regiment of infantry, "foot people," as old Aunt Winnie calls them, filing into our orchard. In five minutes the garden fence had disappeared and the boarding from the carriage house and other buildings was being torn off. Some were carrying off the wood that my poor little boys had cut and hauled. It made me almost weep to see the labour of their poor little hands appropriated by those thieves. How thankful I was that they were far away. I permitted them to go to their Uncle Fayette's some days ago to spend the Christmas with his boys.

They went off so happily, both riding on Kit, with ammunition enough for a good long meet of shooting. While I was trying to arrest the work of destruction, someone told me the robbers were in the kitchen, carrying off the things. In I went, and found it full of men. One took up a tray of cakes, and as I turned to rescue them, Mary, the servant, pulled my sleeve to show something else they were carrying off, and when I turned to him another seized something else till I was nearly wild. At last Mary said, "Miss Cornelia he's got your rusks." (Those rusks that I had made myself and worked till my wrists ached, the first I ever made.)

A man had opened the stove and taken out the pan of nice light brown rusks, and was running out with them. A fit of heroism seized me and I darted after him, and just as he reached the porch steps, I caught him by the collar of his great coat, and held him tight till the hot pan burnt his hands and he was forced to drop it. An officer was riding by, and beholding the scene stopped and asked the meaning of it. Explaining, I lost my gravity, and so did he, and there we laughed long and loud over it. It was so perfectly ridiculous that I forgot for the time all the havoc that was going on. The officer went away, and soon a guard came and quiet was restored, at least near the house, but all night long the work of demolition of buildings went on.

A surgeon came and asked me to give him supper and a place to rest for a while as he was sick and weary. I dared not refuse, so consented. He went in and seated himself in a rocking chair in the dining room. I had to go in town on some business, but told him I would return by tea time, and would then let him have supper. He seemed satisfied, and settled himself comfortably to rest. Nelly, Donald, Roy and little Hunter all huddled in a corner fartherest from, and opposite to him, looking at him with no kindly eyes, as I was amused to remark.

I went away, and on my return found him gone; asked the children why he went, if they had said or done anything to offend him. They said "No," but one observed that "Nelly had tucked her frock up close around her." I asked her if she had done it to show her dislike to him, and though she said nothing, I knew how scornfully the little lady could look and act if she cared to do it, and I felt much afraid that he had been offended. Flora and Sally Conrad had come during my absence, and seeing him in the dining room did not come farther than the hall, but turned and went away. All remained quiet that night, however, and we slept and dreamed of the pleasant things of tomorrow.

25—The day has been too restless to enjoy, or even to realize that it was Christmas. All day reports of the advance of the Confederates, and our consequent excitement. Just as we were sitting down to dinner, we heard repeated reports of cannon. We hurried from the table and found the troops all hastily marching off. They expected a fight, I was told by one, as the Confederates were near town. We could eat no more dinner, the girls and myself, so it was carefully put away till we could enjoy it.

In the evening I went over to Mr. Woods' to see how the old people were bearing their burden, and to take them something nice from the dessert we could not eat. Found them all very quiet, but sad enough. The poor old gentleman's head looks whiter, had his forehead more wrinkled than before they came to intrude on his sweet, quiet home. As I returned home I saw the troops marching back again, like the King of France. The guard was withdrawn at night, which was rather singular, but all is quiet, and so "I will lay me down to sleep and take my rest, for it is Thou, Lord, who makest me to dwell in safety."

26th—All day distress and misery. As soon as I was up, and before I was dressed, some officers came to search the house. They found poor Harry's gun which, with his toy pistol, they took of course.

That was scarcely over and we were about to sit down to breakfast, when the house was surrounded by men who, with their fists began to break in the windows, and also threatened to come in and break up the furniture if breakfast was not immediately given them. I rushed to the front of the house, and shut and locked the hall door, but on opening the study door found that they had entered there by breaking in the windows, and were carrying off the few stores I had which had been put there instead of the usual place for safe-keeping. I locked that door, shutting them off from the rest of the house, leaving the things there to their mercy, and returned to the other part of the house where were assembled at least a hundred desperate and furious men. We fastened down the windows and tried, Sue and I, to keep them from coming in at the door. In the midst of it all a deputation of surgeons arrived and there was a pause in the havoc for a while. They came to inform me that they should that day take the house for a hospital, and would give me a few hours to find quarters elsewhere.

I stood in the door, and they around it, with fierce, resentful faces. Not a look of kindliness or pity did I see on a face in the group. All around were the soldiers, impudent and aggressive, and not one word was said by any one of them, who no doubt thought themselves gentlemen as they wore shoulder straps, to remonstrate with the men for their behaviour, or to interfere in behalf of a helpless woman and a young girl.

I asked them as calmly as I could why they must take my house. They replied that it was a good "location" and that they would have the best places for their men who were sick, they would not allow them to occupy places that had before been used as hospitals while rebel women and children slept under comfortable roofs, and in clean beds. I was looking helplessly around to see if I could see any gleam of kindness in any of their countenances, and my eyes rested on one of the party who I recognized as the surgeon who had asked me for supper and rest the evening they came, and had left so suddenly and unexpectedly. I turned to him, and thinking to soften him by an explanation, asked him why he had left, and telling him that I was ready and perfectly willing to oblige him. Very angrily he said he "would stay nowhere to be insulted." "By whom were you insulted?" I asked. "By your little children, Madam. They spoke of Yankees in my presence, by which term they meant contempt for me." He had reported that to headquarters and then came the order. No one made an effort to disperse the hordes who threatened the house at every door and window. Some had effected an entrance into the pantry, and during the parley with the surgeons were jumping out of the window, one with a cut glass decanter full of wine, prints of butter and everything that could be carried off, including the remains of the Christmas dinner. As the surgeons departed a rush was made for the dining room where Sue and I were with the little children. A hundred heads looking over each other seemed to be clustered about the door. I told Sue if she would try to keep them out, I would, as a desperate venture, go in town and see the commanding officer. I went, and met Mr. Williams near there, and he went with me to see Cluseret.[136] At first he was indisposed to listen to me, but Mr. Williams kindly helped me to lay the case before him. He was very polite, listened to the end, and taking his cap requested me to lead the way to the scene of the commotion. When he arrived at the house, he looked around at all the havoc and destruction, knitted his black brows, and told a man to disperse the crowd, and send a guard. That was done and we were once more left in peace. When I left, Sue told me, the crowd had continued to push in, and that for some time she, with Kenneth's assistance, small as he is, was able to keep them out by standing in the door and holding to the sides of it. Even they were not brutal enough to push her away, but presently she saw a powerful man with a pipe in his mouth pushing his way through the crowd, and elbowing his way up to her, and with oaths and curses declaring his determination to enter in spite of her. Then she cried aloud, "Is there not one man in that crowd that will keep that Dutchman away from me?" One tall fellow seized him from behind, another, and then another, and between them they turned him around and put him out on the porch. The rest then quieted down a little, and she maintained her position till I arrived with Cluseret. Tonight, thank our Father, we have a shelter left.

28th—Sunday. Have had a guard of Yankees for two days, and have enjoyed the peace and quiet. Went to church to hear Mr. Graham. His text was "He came unto his own, and his own received him not."

Donald is sick, and I am left with him. The children are all out with Sue, and I sit beside him in the darkening room. Images of the past come crowding, as the shadows fall around.

There used to sit Wood for his favorite place was the nursery playing with the children, they climbing over him, and he singing them songs. And here I used to sit with my beauty rocking her to sleep—my pretty bird that has flown. Only for a moment do the sweet pictures remain for the bitter present comes and blots them all out. My thoughts are not free to wander long away from the cares, fears, worries and distresses of this sad time. But God is near to sustain and comfort.

Before I went to the Yankee Colonel to beg the privilege of living under my own roof with my poor children, I snatched a hurried moment to ask His protection and assistance, and felt sure as I went on my errand that He would help me and He did.

January 1st—Another New Year's day, the anniversary of so many happy ones that seem now so far away, as if they belonged to another life. The time when we had peace and plenty, friends and neighbors were near us, and what we had was our own. No exiles from home, and no insolent enemies looking taunts at us when they do not utter them. Lawley, the Correspondent of the London Times, is here. He writes "It is hard to expect that a state which like Virginia has borne the burden and heat of the war, which has laid bare her bosom to the smites, and submitted to sacrifices scarcely paralleled on earth, should look with patience on the lukewarm zeal of other rich and powerful states, and accept their lip-service as equal to her heart's blood. In the annals of the Old Dominion there will be no loftier pages than that which tells of how month after month the war which established the independence of the South was fought on her willing soil; How Lee and Jackson and Stuart, and a hundred others were among her chosen sons; and how upon every battlefield rivers of the best blood of Virginia has been freely shed, rather than abandon the title to independence which finds its expression in her fierce motto, 'Sic semper tyrannis'."

This was said in remarking upon the conduct of those border states, Kentucky among them, which delayed taking any decisive action till they were bound hand and foot, and could only applaud while Virginia stood and fought the battles for them all. I am proud that all my people are Virginians; father, mother, husband, and children, were all born on her soil; and I feel as if for love of her, and to defend her honour I would give all I have; I think even my six boys if they were old enough to go to the war. Any thing rather than see her subject to an impudent upstart race who have heretofore been content to follow her lead.

Jan. 1st—My boys got home today, were detained all day outside the pickets for fear of rebel muskets concealed somewhere about them. They enjoyed their trip, for to be out of Winchester was to be free once more. As they were going, both riding on one horse, they flanked the pickets and got out of town triumphantly, but twelve miles out of town they encountered the Vanguard of the Yankee army.

They were stopped till the Commander could come up and were searched, and all their powder, caps, etc., which they had provided for shooting game in the country was taken away from them, as well as a beautiful powder flask Maj. Howard had given Harry, and their father's game bag which they had been so proud to have possession of.

Milroy arrived to-day with flying colours and a flourish of trumpets.[137] He will take his departure as Dr. Baldwin predicted Banks would, with flying coat tails. From their papers we learn that "the whole nation is filled with grief and shame at the disaster before Fredericksburg. Shouts of execration against them come up from one side, wails of despair from another, cries of vengeance against treacherous Europe, and a voice above all, as of one trying to pour oil on the troubled waters—crying cheerily "The Union is not lost yet." It is a comfort that they are obliged to confess that it is nearly lost, a comfort to us. But how does all this contrast with their savage cry, "Crush the Rebellion," draw the cords, tighten the folds of the Anaconda (their imagery) till the rebellion is strangled. They can now say in the words of the Hero of yore—"We have met the enemy, and we are theirs."[138] They seem to be at odds among themselves like others of their character, so honest people may get their own. Seward the wily, has resigned, for reasons best known to himself; perhaps from mortification at being obliged at England's bidding to disgorge the prey he stole from the Trent.[139] Never was a transaction more full of meanness and duplicity than that whole affair from beginning to end.

In the first place when Wilkes[140] sent his dispatches to inform his government that he had stopped the British ship, and taken the Commissioners of the "rebel Government" from it, he was graciously rewarded with the unqualified approval of the President and Cabinet. The whole nation rung with his praises, and he was promptly rewarded with promotion. The prisoners, Mason and Slidell, were committed to Fort Warren, and all was nicely settled, but when England began to shew her teeth, a general growl went up from the whole Yankee nation, and though Seward was willing to apologize, nothing would satisfy the offended pride of the Mistress of the Seas but the delivery into her hands of the Commissioners, and an humble apology from the prompters of the outrage. Seward's letter to the British Government consenting to accede to the demands of England was the most transparent piece of hypocrisy I ever read. He meant it I suppose to be diplomatic, but it was very much the reverse.[141]

He began by not only justifying the act, on account of its expedience, but because, as he tried to make out, it was not unjustifiable under the circumstances, in short that it was what they had a perfect right to do, but towards the close of three columns of a newspaper which the document filled, he expressed his pleasure at being able to accommodate England in the matter, and confessed that he had done what he ought not to have done, and promised not to do so any more. Poor Wilkes was reprimanded at England's bidding, and his exaltation ended in his being disgraced. His act was disavowed, and he deprived of his command for the time, for that was part of England's demand.

The representative of Washington has now an opportunity of displaying his Washingtonian attributes; but poor creature, if he was not in a place where he has such dangerous power, his perplexities and bewilderment would be ludicrous.

He is between Scylla and Charybdis dreading the monster on one side to which his allies, the Abolitionists, would lead him, and yet afraid of the rocks on the other side on which he must split if he forsake them. Ah! how many desolate homes have been made so by his crimes and folly, and to what a condition of anarchy and confusion has he brought a great country.

Vicksburg is again to be assailed by the fleet. Great threats are made, and loud boastings as usual, but our hearts will not be like melting wax as long as we hear of Morgan's raids in the West; and of Stuart gaily cantering around the Federal army twelve miles from Alexandria, and last, though not least, of Wheeler with his cavalry capturing the enemy's gunboats on the Tennessee river.[142] A report today that Jackson is on his way to this place.

8th—Nothing of interest for some days. Sue and Flora have determined to leave the enemy's lines and go to Charlottesville. Today I went with them to get a pass from Cluseret, the General commanding the post. He was not in but an adjutant gave it to us quite readily; too much so I thought. I asked if there would be no difficulty, reminding him that Harry had had such a pass to go to Front Royal on business for me, but was nevertheless stopped and turned back.

He assured me there would be no trouble but I still feared a little, and warned the girls as we walked back, to take nothing in the shape of letters to any one.

9th—This morning the girls were off at daylight in high spirits, and full faith in the potency of their pass. They were in a comfortable carriage driven by a trustworthy white man who we knew would take good care of them. They had gone but six miles when suddenly a troop of cavalry dashed out from a lurking place and surrounded the carriage, stopped and turned it back. An officer dismounted and entered the carriage. When the door was shut and they had set off on the way back to town, he asked the girls if they had any thing contraband, and begged if such was the case that they would confide it to him and he would conceal it. He also admonished them that if any thing was found, they would be sent out of the state and imprisoned. They were frightened as was natural under the circumstances though they were guiltless. After a little hesitation Flora produced a pistol about six inches long, and a military cap she had made for a friend. The man smiled when he saw the pistol, but grew serious as he regarded the cap. He asked if these were all, and again earnestly entreated them to give them any letters they might have. They assured him they had none, and very soon they and their escort stopped before Milroy's headquarters. They were taken to an upper room and their persons searched by a negro woman. Their trunks were taken into Gen. Milroy's office where they were opened, and their contents passed in review before Gen. Milroy and his staff, the room being full of officers and men.

Finding nothing, the girls were called in before the General, and told that as they had nothing contraband in their baggage they were at liberty to depart. They all seemed ashamed of the transaction, of having laid a plot to entrap two helpless girls. Gen. Milroy explained to them that he had heard they were to take mail out, and that was the reason he had them stopped.

One of them asked if that was his reason for giving them the pass. He said No, but that no one under the circumstances would have hesitated to avail himself of such an opportunity to take letters or other things out of the lines.

"We would have hesitated a long time," said one of them, "before we would have done so, for we have been taught that it is dishonourable to give our word and break it, and we considered when we accepted your pass that we had given our word not to violate it."

He expressed his regret for what had happened, and offered them a pass to go out whenever they desired to do so, as well as an escort. They thanked him but declined his offer.

When they were about to leave Flora went up to Gen. Milroy, and holding out her hand said, "Please Gen. Milroy, give me my pistol." He looked at her for a while, and remarked that it was not a suitable plaything for a young lady but (with a smile) that as it was not very dangerous she might have it. She then preferred her request for the military cap she had made. He seemed about to refuse, but she told him it would do him no good, and that if he kept it she would make another. So he quietly surrendered it.

I have spent the day sewing. In the evening went to see Mary and the girls, and hear the account of the capture. Went to Mrs. Dandridge's for Willie to escort me home as it was nearly dark. Heard that Cluseret had resigned. Perhaps it had something to do with the girls' pass. He had given it, or rather his adjutant. He was, it is said, a French barber. He may have been, but he has very good manners.

10th—Hard at work all day mending clothes for the children. Had an invitation in the morning to spend the day at Mrs. Conrad's, Mary and the girls to be there. Had a bad headache, and in the afternoon was lying on the lounge before the fire, feeling very comfortable in contrast with the storm of rain and sleet on the ice, when a knock at the door of the room, and a vulgar looking man presented himself, and informed me that he had orders to take my house for a hospital, or at least part of it. I felt almost too helpless and wretched to resist, but as nothing was left to do but resist, as we had only the roof over our heads left us, I resolved to defend it, as I could not consent to share it with sick men, and the alternative was to leave it. I went to get my bonnet and wrapping to go to headquarters and found as I looked out that there was already a wagon full of sick men drawn up before the front door, and a large cooking stove unloading to be put up in the dining room under the fine black marble mantlepiece.

Through the sleet and rain therefore I made my way to Milroy's headquarters, so full of distress that I neither saw nor noticed any one as I passed through the streets. Excitement and apprehension had so wrought on my mind as I went, that without knowing how I got there I found myself in Milroy's presence, with the room full of men, his staff and others. He looked surprised at the apparition, and sternly asked me what I wanted. I told him the business on which I had come, at the same time painting to him my helpless condition, telling him that I came to him for protection, as he had the power, and I was sure could not want the will to protect a woman and children who were as defenseless as we were. With an ironical laugh, echoed by some around him, he asked where our natural protectors were. I told him they were in the Confederate army. "Yes," he said, "they leave you unprotected and expect us to take care of you." "We would not need your care, if we were allowed to take care of ourselves," said I. "It is only from the army you command that we want protection." He then asked if my husband was not Angus MacDonald, and if he had not several sons in the Confederate army. I told him yes, and in a loud tone he said, "There is not a greater rebel in the South." "That may be," said I, "but he is fighting for what he considers the right, Gen. Milroy." After a pause he said, "There is a gentleman in my command who is a relative of your husband I believe. We have been in Hampshire County where he once lived, and have heard all about him. There is not a greater rebel

112

in the South." A tall red faced man had risen as he spoke and I not replying to the last part of his remarks asked, looking at the man, "Where is Capt. MacDonald from?"[143] Milroy had spoken his name, so I knew his title. "From Indiana," was the answer. "Oh no!" I said, "he can be no relative of ours, for we never had any in Indiana, besides my husband had only one brother, and they were children of Maj. MacDonald of the U.S. army who lost his life in active service during the war of 1812.[144] He was the only son of his father who fled from Scotland after the rebellion of 1745, the last effort in the cause of the Pretender. So you see, Gen. Milroy," I said turning to him, "rebellion, if it is rebellion, is in the blood of the race." "Ah," said he with an interested look, "my ancestors came from Scotland, too, at the same time, and for the same reason." "Then," said I, "have you no sympathy for us, our ancestors having suffered in the same cause."

He turned away without replying, and said to Capt. MacDonald, "Go with her and see what can be done." I set out with the gallant Captain holding an umbrella over me, and was so elated at my success that I never felt the effect of the multitude of eyes looking through the windows as I passed, and looking wonder, too, at the unwonted spectacle of so stout-hearted a rebel as I, walking with a Yankee in a fine uniform. When we reached home the wagon was still there, and the cooking stove in the hall waiting to be put up. They were soon all cleared out and we were once more at peace. Capt. MacDonald imparted to me on the way that his name was Isaiah, which piece of information confirmed me in my belief that he has no relative of ours; for who ever heard of a fierce Highlander named Isaiah?

While I was in Milroy's room Capt. MacDonald asked me if those were not my daughters who were captured with a mail. I had heard that they had let it be understood everywhere that the girls were taken with a contraband mail, so turning looking full at Gen. Milroy I said, "It is true they were overtaken and turned back after having had a pass given them to go out of the lines, but they had no mail, as Gen. Milroy can tell you." "No, no," he said hastily, "there was nothing found."

They had allowed it to be so understood to cover up their own dishonourable behavior to the girls. So now the hard, hard struggle is over, and the night is come, and I am still under my own roof, thanks to my Heavenly Father whose goodness has never failed me.

11th—Could not go to church for fear of intruders while absent. Sent the older boys, and spent the time quietly with the little ones. Read St. Paul's epistle to the Galatians. Was struck by what he said about St. Peter's indecision of character, in eating with the uncircumcised Greeks until the visit of James and John from Jerusalem, and then withdrawing himself from their company. Could it be that the fault of character for which our Lord rebuked him, clung to him for all that he was the chosen one on whom his church was to be founded, and for whom such love was manifested by his Master, and on whom those loving eyes rested when he asked, "Lovest thou me?"

I do not know why I have failed to record the great victories at Vicksburg and Murfreesboro. Vicksburg has held out gallantly; Marshall was there, and we may well tremble to hear who are slain. The Yankees claim the victory at Murfreesboro, but the truth has not as yet come out. Banks failed to cooperate with Sherman in taking Vicksburg in the rear, and the gunboats played an insignificant part.

12th—Spent part of the day in town; heard that Cluseret had been arrested for sending in his resignation; and because he was disgusted at the part he had to take in persecution of women and children.

To use Harry's not very elegant expression, "Bully for Cluseret!"

Lincoln's proclamation flames at all the street corners. They say the population interested are jubilant, but I have seen no indication of such a state of feeling among them. I observe an unwonted display of white petticoats brought into view by holding up the outer skirts, but that signifies that somebody's sheets have been abstracted to manufacture the luxurious garments, nothing more. It is said, however, that there is to be a grand procession in honour of their freedom.

13th—More particulars of Murfreesboro'; and it proves not such a victory as we had supposed. In consequence of Bragg's communication being cut off either before or after the battle in which the railroad was destroyed, he was compelled to fall back, and thus lose the advantage gained, besides giving the Yankees the opportunity of claiming a victory, and exalting Rozencrantz into a Hero.[145] The triumph at Vicksburg has been complete. The enemy has been entirely driven away.

The papers are full of accounts of vessels fitting out in England to open the blockade, of peace propositions coming from the North, and various other rumours that serve to keep our spirits up, and our hopes alive. Cluseret resigned because his pass was not respected in the case of the girls, and that he was required to do unmanly things. It would be well if he had so wholesome a dread of doing immoral things, for his character is not the fairest, according to the report of a lady in whose house he had a suite of rooms. I heard he said that no one could be a United States soldier without being a rascal.

Went to town this morning with Mrs. Dailey. Was so grateful for the sympathy shown me in my persecutions and troubles. Dr. Boyd was particularly kind, as also Judge Parker and Dr. Holliday.[146] The latter tried to console me by telling me that I would live in history.

14th—A gloomy day, clouds above and mud beneath. Heard that there were letters for me at Newtown. I think tomorrow I will try to get out there to see. Perhaps a note to Capt. MacDonald may get me the pass.

15th—Failed in getting a pass. Could only be allowed to go out of town with an escort of cavalry, the *éclat* of which was not to my taste. This night last year my husband's poor brother died. It all rushed back to my mind as I went in the room tonight, and stood for a moment by the bed from which the poor weary soul fled to its rest, after that terrible day of suffering. Mrs. Mason had stood by him all those weary hours, and held his head on her arm, or supported the pillows where in his agony he would throw himself. No human care of sympathy could avail him, his agonized frame sought ease in

115

vain, till at nightfall he tossed himself over for the last time (and the hundredth that day), and moved no more. One gasp, and the features settled with the shadow of death over them. How well I remember that night! The windows open, and the curtains flapping in the winter night wind, how I mourned for the desolate widow and orphans far away, and how I could not bear the grief and melancholy and fled from it into my own room where was such a sweet picture of happiness and baby innocence. There bloomed my rose, and stretched out her arms to me to take her, while the other little ones were preparing for bed, unconscious in their careless mirth of the dread shadow out of which I had come to hear them say their prayers and see them safe in bed. They are all around me now; but when they gather at the fireside in the evening my precious little one is there, too, in my heart, and before my eyes often, for she comes in between me and their faces, and often her face fills the page of the book I am reading. The winter is so sad and dreary, that it would seem unnatural if she were here to partake of its dreariness and privation. But when the flowers come again, the lilacs that Margaret used to fasten in her bonnet, and the birds are singing, and the lawn green with the tender young grass, I shall be watching for glimpses of the little wicker carriage with my treasure in it moving about among the trees as I sit at work by the window, and never remembering how I laid her away from my sight, with the brown hair parted from her forehead, and the long lashes drooping over the half open blue eyes.

20th—It is a great effort to bring myself to write to overcome the listlessness and want of interest in things that sometimes tempts me to give up the task I have undertaken. Our victories at Vicksburg and Murfreesboro are confirmed. A few Northern papers seem to be violent against the Lincoln Administration, and it is said go so far as to demand that Lincoln and his cabinet shall be hung. The draft has aroused their ire, it has just begun to hurt them, this war, and they want it stopped. The Government is accused of fraud and dishonesty as well as crimes of every description. The Fort Wayne (Indiana) Sentinel is especially bitter against the administration. I had one this morning, procured by an accident. The thought of peace seems to be entertained by them very seriously. Governor Seymour seems to promise well.[147] If all the Western Governors act as he says he will do, the power of Lincoln's administration will soon be broken.

To day the walls of Mr. Mason's house were pulled down; they fell with a crash; the roof had gone long ago. The house has disappeared now, and the place which knew it will know it no more. I suppose if I were not in this house it would share the same fate. Every outbuilding is gone, the carriage house was pulled down over the carriage, and crushed it of course. Nothing is left of them all but heaps of logs which the Yankees carry away for firewood; and I, I can scarcely tell it, help them to burn it, for they have taken all our wood and we can get no other supply, but they graciously permit us to share with them, and my boys and the Yankee soldiers stand side by side cutting up the logs and boards of the houses; and I sit by the fire, and though I know that the crackling walnut logs are from my own hen and turkey houses, I must say I enjoy the cheerful blaze. They have taken the stones of Mr. Mason's house as well as many of our stone fences to build their fortifications. Snowing all day and could not take my walk.

21st—Sue and Flora came. Snow and rain all day. Saw the Baltimore Sun, now a violent administration paper. It gave an account of a raid of Van Dorn to Holly Springs Mississippi where a large amount of war materials and provisions were destroyed, the Commandant of the Post, Provost Marshal and a number of prisoners taken.[148] Van Dorn is highly spoken of. The Yankees put him on a level with the ubiquitous Morgan and the renowned Stuart.

The Yankees seem to be really bent on peace. I hope it may come, but do not want it at the expense of our honour or independence. We have the game on our own terms; we have only as Bishop Meade said in his dying message to his people, "to stand firm and think of our Dead." Great accounts of the exploits of our navy come to us over the water. The Alabama has made a name for herself, and a name to be dreaded, and several more of her style are coming. One iron screw steamer is ready for sea, armed with the most approved guns, and manned by a crew of picked men.

The account said that Maury is in command of her.[149] Officers of the Confederate navy are showing themselves in Liverpool ready to take command of the new vessels. They sport the naval uniform of the Confederate States of America.

The Yankee Government seems to be alarmed as to Louis Napoleon's intentions in Mexico. They seem to think he is about to help himself to a slice, or all of Texas. They need not be apprehensive about Texas. The Confederate Gov. will take care of her. Whatever Napoleon may do, I hope he will make those cunning and unscrupulous spirits at Washington tremble for their own safety. They know well that they will have to answer to the people they have duped for plunging them into two wars at the same time. The reins are being tightened over us every day. We can buy only the barest necessaries of life, and only they from people who have taken the oath.

They would not be allowed otherwise, to sell. I bought a quarter of beef, a great and unwonted luxury, from an old woman from the country. Her husband would not take the oath so she did it, and brought in her marketing. She says it was the only way they could get the means of living. I had to have it carried up stairs and deposited in one of the chambers to keep from having it stolen.

We would be badly off indeed if by a lucky chance I had not had a field of wheat sown while my husband was in Europe. When ready it was taken to Legg's Mill, and has been there ever since, and not called for. I thought the Yankees had taken it, but Legg sent me word that it awaited my order. There are ten barrels I am thankful to say, enough for a year's supply; but I will have to exchange some of it for other things.

Feb. 2nd—Nothing written since January the 21st. No news except that Burnside has been displaced in favour of Hooker.[150] No movement yet towards Fredericksburg. The capture of Arkansas Post seems to afford some cause of gratulation to them.

Vicksburg is again threatened, I hope it may be to as little purpose as heretofore; Our condition is not enviable, the rein is as tight as it can well be over all but the coloured population. We can buy nothing from the sutlers and shopkeepers without taking the oath. I have succeeded in buying a cord of wood from a countryman, and to keep the Yankees from taking it my boys have had to carry it, stick by stick, to the garret, three stories, and there saw it up for use. There is a great exodus of negroes; every day some government wagons depart laden with them and their effects; on their way to the land of Promise; where that happy country may be we know not, though some say it is Central America that they are turning their eyes to.

Their great Patron and fellow citizen, Abraham Lincoln, has, however, told them in the frankest manner imaginable that the governments of those states were not very willing to receive them; and that it was also true that many of them would die before being there very long. Another small inconveniece he touched on was, that "the political condition of those states was not very well settled, and that commotions were frequent in which the rights of the weak were disregarded, and their gains often appropriated by those who at the time were most powerful."

Still the far seeing and self sacrificing Sons of Ham were to rush upon all these uncertainties for the sake of the welfare of their posterity, as in the country they must ever be the inferior race.

3rd—Tried in vain to get a pass for Harry to go out of the lines to Warren, where he could communicate with his father. Today he set out to "make a flank movement" as he said, and get outside the pickets by strategy. His confidence in the success of his scheme was perfect and he seemed delighted at the prospect of the adventure; but I was not so sanguine as to his success, for I knew that to "flank" the pickets was a serious and dangerous affair; and more so in this instance, as they are within call of each other all around the town in three lines. But he went, and I am fearful of danger and of the cold for him, for he did not even take the great coat as that would have looked like preparing for a journey. He walked out of town with a whip in his hand as if he was looking for the cow. He carried his trap ball, throwing it as he went, as was his habit, boy like. The weather is very severe and he goes all the way on foot, twenty-five miles. Not a great distance if traveled by a straight road, but he must take a circuitous route to avoid enemies who are all over the country. He must go through fields and over fences, and perhaps hide in holes and bushes. So I am fearful, but there was great necessity for his going as we had no money, and not much of anything to eat. I have great confidence in his energy and ability, and I know he never shrinks from any task he undertakes because of its difficulty.

But I trust him to our Heavenly Father to guide and keep him from harm.

9th—One week ago our gunboats ran out of Charleston and destroyed the Federal fleet. All the blockaders took to flight! We have good reason to be proud of our achievements, and it is farcical to hear the Yankees talk of crushing a great nation with a navy before which their old vessels fly or go down, and any army against which they dare not come unless they out number it fourfold.

Milroy is screwing the engine tighter every day. One day he will not let us buy anything; another he forbids more than two female rebels to talk together on the street. He now employs spies to enter houses and report what the women talk about or if the children play with Confederate flags, or shout for Jeff Davis.

I sit every day and see this lovely place converted into a wagon yard. The smooth green turf has disappeared, and roads go over and across in every direction. Under the dining room windows runs one, and mules and horses continually pass, driven by men cursing and swearing, uttering oaths that make my blood curdle. I used to love to sit at those windows at sunset and watch the yellow glow fade away from the green fields, and from the round top of the "Round Hill" as it is called, and listen to the peaceful sounds of our own cows lowing as they came through the pasture, the calves calling for them; and oh! how sweet the air was, how fresh and pure; a very delight it was to breathe it. Now I turn away in disgust from the view, and the odious, odious smells would drive me away if the sights did not, and the sounds more dreadful than all.

120

Under the parlour windows goes another road. Those windows used to look out on a sweet shrubbery of syringas, mock orange, white lilacs and purple; white and yellow jessamine; red roses and white, sweet brier and eglantine; everything old fashioned and lovely that I delight in. Beyond the shrubbery is a deep hollow, where there are rocks steep and high, and deep green grass and tall maples that used to burn in the autumn sunlight, and shine with the bright glow of summer sunsets. Now as I said, a road goes through it under the window. The shrubs are there but their bare stems and branches, the pretty dell is there with the rocks and trees all bare and melancholy enough, but that is nothing compared to the sights and sounds that go by all the long day through, wagons, artillery horses, large droves of them three times a day to get water, soldiers and camp women, gay officers on foot and on horseback, and most sickening sight of all, Yankee "Ladies" in dainty riding habits, hats and plumes, pace by as if the ground they passed over was their own; and chatting with their beaux, glance around at us if they chance to see us as if we were intruders on their domain. I confess I feel wicked then, resentful and revengeful. I would be glad at those times, if our artillery could, from some near point, sweep them all away.

To day I saw one of the prettiest trees cut down for a camp woman to wash her clothes with, and when washed they were strung out in a line just before the front hall door, blue shirts and red ones, ragged women's clothes and all kinds of rags flap in the wind for me to see as I pass; and I have not the spirit to resent it, or the pride to be offended at the degradation. Think of how a year ago, I resented having a flag to wave over my front door. All my indignation would have been aroused if they had dared to hang their clothes in my sight.

My heart is too heavy now for any such resentments. My boy has not come back, and I am full of fears.

19th—Daily, hourly there is something to annoy. Soldiers stalk in and out of the house, at their pleasure, for in the front room that was my husband's, a meek eyed old quarter master has his abode; an inoffensive old creature that I permitted to come in the hope of keeping away the offensive ones; but the strain, the excitement and irritation is so great that if I hear a footstep on the porch my heart palpitates violently and I tremble all over in apprehension of intrusion, or of something being done to offend or irritate; or worse, that messengers are come to force me to leave my house.

We hear rumours of peace from over the ocean where our expectant eyes have been turned for so many weary months, during which we have battled and endured and suffered so much. Our people have made for themselves a great name, no people ever made a more glorious record. All the world sees with astonishment their successful struggle against a boastful, powerful, and unscrupulous foe.

Alas! though the rumours are of peace, preparations for deadly strife are still going on; the enemy are gathering strength for a grand attack on Charleston and Savannah, and from there we hear of the determination of the people to resist to the utmost.

Charleston deserves great honour. It was there that the first notes were heard calling the people to resist oppression; there the banner was first unfurled and the battle cry raised that aroused the nation to fierce contention for right and liberty; from her soil the armed men sprung like those from the serpent's teeth of old, and they have made their enemies cringe and grow pale with rage and fright.

Last Saturday I was in company with some girls, cousins and friends, at Cousin Mick Tidball's. One of them proposed to send Milroy a valentine. He had been rude to Mrs. Baldwin, ordering her from his room, and at the same time asking two coloured, and gorgeously dressed ladies to be seated.[151] They entreated me to paint them one to send him. So I made a grey headed officer in uniform seated in a chair, and inviting two negro women to take seats, while with a frown he was repelling a handsome young lady (not Mrs. Baldwin) dressed in stripes of red and white, with grey muff and tippet. I heard he received it, and he might have done so, for he ordered a search and prosecution immediately.

20th—More rumours of the approach of the Confederates; it can be scarcely true, for they would not uselessly expose themselves to the risk of battle, and the town to be shelled merely for the sake of a short sojourn here, for it could be nothing else if they came. We find it so hard to live. So hard to get anything to eat. The soldiers would willingly exchange meat, sugar and coffee with us for fresh bread or flour, but are not allowed. The prohibition, however, does not prevent me from getting Aunt Winnie to bake bread and give it to them surreptitiously as they pass on their way to the spring and receiving from them in return things which we can get in no other way.

Sometimes I sit in the dining room reading till midnight, and a low knock on the door. I get up and admit a Yankee soldier with a black camp kettle and a bundle in his hands. I take him to the pantry, lock the door on the inside and inspect the contents of the kettle and bundle. The kettle has coffee and sugar in it with a paper between to keep them apart. The bundle has a piece of fat bacon, but it is very welcome to us who have nothing but bread. I fill his kettle with flour and let him out to go his way back to the camp, while I lock myself in and hide the things. If they suspected him they would punish him as he is acting without permission. Many times I have done that and still must do it for it is the only chance to get anything to eat. A few days ago we heard that there was a man who had permission to sell molasses to the people. I went in town directly with Kenneth carrying a small jug. A great crowd was at the door and inside. So I had to wait my turn to get in, standing outside with a crowd of men and women, many ladies, all in the mud and rain waiting for their jugs to be filled, but I waited and got some molasses for my little ones.

Oh if our army could only come to bring in relief! We are oppressed on every side, even the little school girls are dispersed if more than two stop to talk on the street on their way home. Negroes can assemble in any numbers, and if they choose can jostle and crowd ladies off the pavement into the gutter as may suit their convenience. They are the only people who have any rights or liberty, and of the latter they have an undue share. In every instance they are preferred to the whites. If they had their just rights they would be on a cotton plantation in "thirty days," as Abraham would say in his business style when he fixes a period for our subjugation.

21st—I scarcely dare to hope that peace is coming: that the dawn is approaching after our night of sorrow. That the sun is about to break through the dark clouds that have hung over us for two long years. When the happy time comes, and our sun once more shines it will be on a desolate waste, vacant hearths, and broken hearts. It will be as when after a tempest the sun looks brightly out on a scene of havoc and destruction, and none the less brightly because of it.

Who can help asking why it must have been?

If we do come out of these trials and our nation is established in security and peace, will we go back to the old corrupt way, will we be money-loving, courting power, and striving for the things which in all ages have been the ruin of nations, till God shall again lay his hand upon us and we be again plunged into war and misery? God grant that we may have virtuous rulers, those that oppress not the helpless, that "shake their hands from holding bribes," that "keep innocency and take heed to the thing that is right." Spent the day with Mrs. Dandridge. Had a quiet pleasant time. Heard that great preparations were making for an attack on Vicksburg.

22nd—Sue, Flora and the Tidballs and Hollidays spent the day here. They all seemed merry and happy. They sang and played over all their old songs, both merry and sad, and it seemed a little like old times. We have quite a snow storm, and I have been sick all day. News of a certain prospect of breaking the blockade, and a recognition of the Confederacy. The Alabama had made a name to be dreaded. I saw a piece in the Baltimore American headed "Tracks of the Alabama." Four burning vessels, names all given. Another column gives an account of her reception at Jamaica. A dinner was given her officials by the authorities, and toasts and compliments freely offered. Her whole history was sketched, how she was built by the subscription of 290 merchants of Liverpool and presented to President Davis, and how that circumstance accounted for her being sometimes called the 290. The papers say that there is a pause in the attack on Charleston and Savannah, but do not give the why or wherefore.

24th—The snow is a foot deep and everything would look lovely if the scene was not marred by the groups of bluecoats passing to and fro.

26th—Have just learned that more of the beautiful cedars have been cut down. Those lovely trees that adorn the place so much. It does seem like sacrilege to destroy them for such base purposes as they put them to.

26th—Sitting wearily and sadly this morning, the door opened and on looking up I saw my Harry, his face bright with joy and excitement. He had performed his dangerous mission and returned without being seen or suspected. In going he had to wade the Shenandoah, and then to keep from freezing ran for seven miles with his clothes on him frozen. I never was so warm in my life, said he.

He did not stop till he was safe at Clover Hill. Returning he walked twenty six miles through deep snow, climbing fences, as his only safe way lay through fields and byways. At night he got to the edge of town and found a place of shelter in a black woman's cabin. He then got a piece of bread and lying before the fire slept till eleven o'clock this morning. The negro woman had him completely in her power if she had chosen to betray him; but most of them are loyal and faithful to the white people if they do love their freedom, and who can blame them if they do. Not many boys of fourteen could have planned and accomplished that feat. His carefulness and prudence are as remarkable as his intrepidity and endurance.

On his way yesterday he saw seven of our infantry capture eighteen of the enemy's cavalry. They were behind a stone fence, and as the Yankees rode up pointed their guns at them and summoned them to surrender, which they did with arms, horses and all, and without a word. One was a Major. Harry says a party of Yankees went into a store in Front Royal, and while they were robbing it, some boys belonging to the town despoiled every horse of its accoutrements, pistols and every thing, and some rode away the horses.

27th—Exciting rumours of an advance of our army. Spent the day in town, and had an interview with Gen. Milroy. Found him polite (for him) and disposed to grant what I asked, which was permission to buy necessaries for my family. He said his orders were to withhold permission from every one who would not declare himself or herself loyal to the United States government. I told him it was impossible for me to do it, as it would be entirely false; and added that it could not be a matter of importance what women thought or wished on the subject.

He said it was a matter of great importance and rather fiercely observed that if it had not been for the women the men would have long ago given up, he firmly believed, that their pride and obstinacy prevailed over the good sense and sober judgment of the men, who knew they were fighting in vain. I said nothing in answer to his passion, knowing well how our men hated them and knowing also that they would fight to the very last rather than yield to their unjust and unreasonable pretense of authority over us.

After a time he calmed down and began to talk of the right of secession, and the part Virginia had taken in it, saying that she never had a fair opportunity of letting her voice be heard.

That the delegates to the Convention that passed the ordinance of secession were all Union men. I could no longer refrain from words, as "the fire had kindled," so I spoke, and told him that there were many men in that convention who were opposed to secession, but that when Lincoln issued his proclamation demanding troops from Virginia wherewith to conquer the cotton states they took another view of the matter, and remembering that the State of Virginia was free to choose her own course, they, or her representatives concluded that her honour required them to take her out of the company of those who could make so base a proposition to her, as to furnish troops to conquer the Southern states or even to propose to her to stand quietly by and permit their enemies to cross her territory to do it, or allow it to be done while she was capable of an effort to prevent it. He turned red, and moved restlessly in his seat as if he had something to say and did not know how to say it.

At last he handed me a paper which he said was a permit and instructed me to take it into the next room to be signed by the adjutant. When I turned in, a trim-looking pert little

126

man in uniform, turned from a desk at which he was seated looking over some papers, and asked my business. I handed him the paper; he looked at it and then at me very inquisitively and said "Are you loyal?" I could not bring myself to answer that little creature's impertinence which I knew would follow the only answer I had to make, so I turned and walked out of the room without a word to him.

28th—There is a report that the Yankees are in Vicksburg, but as they allow no papers to come to the town or camps, it would seem that they have met with a disaster. It is also reported that our forces have captured the gunboat "Queen of the West" on the Mississippi. Their papers did not exult as much as might have been expected over our worse than blunder in blowing up and destroying the captured gunboat "Indianola" from a fit of pure fright. It is said, and is true, I believe, that the Yankees had put an immense tank on board an old barge, after boring the tank or hogshead which was circular in shape to make it appear as if a Columbiad lurked within, and only waited a mark to send forth its deadly projectile. In fact it was made to represent a Monitor, and the soldiers and sailors on the Indianola, as soon as they saw what they afterwards described as a "turretted monster" slipping by them, and on, by the defenses at and near Vicksburg, they, to prevent her from falling into the hands of the enemy applied the torch and the "Indianola" was a thing of the past.

The "turreted monster" went on through the misty dawn, and as she glided by, all the forts and defenses gave her a volley before the daylight enabled them to discover her real character.

The Northern papers could not have refrained from a good deal of ridicule of our folly, had not the Richmond Examiner seized the occasion to make so much fun over it as to disarm them.

30th—This afternoon I was in town and saw a regiment of cavalry that had gone out in the morning on a scouting expedition, return in hot haste with less than a hundred men. Many believed the Confederates were advancing, and there certainly was fighting at Newtown. Coming home I met my old quarter master at the door who told me he was packing to go. I assisted his panic by telling him how dreadfully defeated the cavalry were; how mud-bespattered they looked, and that they had come in town in such haste that I had thought the Confederates were close behind them. He was terribly agitated, and disappeared in his room, whence proceeded the sounds of hammering and nailing of boxes, etc., for some time. Mean time his wagons were backed up at the front door to receive his goods. I sat down and complacently ate my supper, not at all moved by his fears.

He is a funny old creature; I permitted him to occupy a room in the house because I considered him more inoffensive than the gay cavaliers who often applied for quarters, or sick men of whom I had a very just dread, for I know that if my door was once opened to them a train of ills would follow; so I let him come, and he is as kind as he knows how to be.

30—He comes in sometimes to pay me a visit in the evening, and I entertain him with stories of Ashby's exploits. How he would dart into a town and seize and carry off unsuspecting gentlemen attached to his army (the Federal) and pack them off to Richmond, to the Libby;[152] and how Ashby's men were given to exploits of the same kind; and while relating my anecdotes I would pause and listen as if I heard unusual sounds. The poor old man would get terribly nervous. I flatter myself he has not enjoyed an undisturbed slumber since he has been under my roof. Sometime ago he asked me if I had any objection to his wife's coming and paying him a visit. I pictured to myself the horrors of having a Western Virginia, Ohio Yankee female in the house; so collected myself and replied that it would give me a great pleasure to oblige him, as I knew it must be a great comfort to him to have a visit from his wife, but that it would be too great a risk as no one knew at what moment a dash might be made by the Confederates and the army driven off or captured and that would be so very unpleasant for her.

He was one day last week telling me of the fine opportunity to make money that now offered, of bringing goods from the North to sell to the inhabitants; and asked me how I thought it would "pay" to bring a lot of hoop skirts to Winchester.

I told him that though we were lamentably in need of hoops we could not buy without taking the oath, and I thought the ladies would prefer going hoopless to such an alternative.

He tries to be kind, poor old fellow, and knowing our straits invites us secretly to avail ourselves of opportunities to abstract his supplies. He leaves boxes of crackers invitingly open in the hall, and actually proposed to Harry to cut me a supply of wood from his pile in front of my door. It would seem but just to make reprisals, but my poor children seem each day to lose a portion of their respect for the rights of property. They think it no harm to steal or take from those who took all from us, and I often have to interfere and make them carry back things they have appropriated, but we must have wood, so I allow Harry to act on the old man's hint and cut wood for me from the United States woodpile, side by side with a Yankee soldier who does not trouble himself about who gets it.

March 2—Reports of another battle and our troops advancing. Cavalry dashed in in great haste this evening. The whipping the 13th Pennsylvania cavalry received last week was too much for them. This evening, I understood they fled without firing a gun. Those were the gallant fellows I saw racing in town covered with mud. Report says Fitzhugh Lee has a large force of cavalry in the valley.[153]

March 7th—According to the Baltimore American the loyal people in the North are awakening to a sense of duty, and are making a great effort to uphold the government in its efforts to "suppress the rebellion" as well as assisting it to take all the power into its own hands. The last Congress clothed Lincoln with the military power of the whole nation; allowed him to suspend the writ of habeas corpus, and placed all the finances of the country in his hands; obliterated the state lines, and abolished the state militias.

I read today an account of the departure of the paroled prisoners from New Orleans, and was deeply affected with the story of how those long-suffering men and women thronged the levee, "a countless multitude" the papers had it, loaded with gifts of all kinds for the prisoners, and with excited looks and tearful eyes pushed through the crowd to see and touch them. Their long suppressed feelings burst forth when they looked into each other's faces after being so long parted and about to part again maybe forever, for in those faces they saw the same endurance and determination to fight to the end that they themselves felt. Presently a long loud shout for the Confederacy went up from the crowd, and a shower of Confederate flags were flung forth and waved in the very faces of their enemies. Their enthusiasm was beyond control, and their oppressors seemed for the time dumb and confounded either with surprise or sympathy with the tremendous emotion which agitated the immense multitude, but in time an order was given, and the gunboats were brought into convenient position, the artillery was pointed at the sobbing, heaving multitude of men, women and children and "then," they said, "the crowd sullenly gave way." They take great credit to themselves for not firing into them.[154]

One announcement is to the effect that Fort McAllister has been captured; another is that it "will be."[155] One piece of intelligence is that we have blown up the Nashville. She ran aground and we were compelled to do it.

March 10th—The Nashville has really been destroyed, but not by us; the enemy fired her with shells while aground. As a compensation, however, we have captured another gunboat and they now think we may do them serious mischief.

12th—They are working hard to get Vicksburg, cutting canals, cutting levees, turning rivers, and they say, sacrificing men by the thousand. There are reports of a great battle and victory for us at Vicksburg, but they allow no such news to pass through the line to us. We do hear, however, that there have been illuminations and great rejoicings in Southern towns over something. The Federals themselves saw Fredericksburg illuminated.

The papers are very severe on the Peace Democrats. The speeches of John Van Buren and Wright are much lauded, as being purely patriotic by the "Copperheads."[156] They, the "Copperheads," are as much esteemed as the "rebels." They say that the vigorous prosecution of the war ought to engage the attention of the whole people to the exclusion of every other thought "till the wicked rebellion is crushed." Mr. Everett, too, is lending his influence and energies to stir up their hatred to the South.[157]

Will his reward be the same as that meted out to their former idol, poor old Scott, who they contemptuously put aside to make way for their bombastic "Young Napoleon," as they call McClellan, and at last now accuse of treason? Pronounced by no less a critic than the Duke of Wellington to be "The first Captain of the age," and honoured by all the world as such, he finds himself cast aside and made infamous by the unprincipled people to whose base purpose he lent himself and to please whom he betrayed his own state and people. They would willingly send him to his grave covered with infamy instead of glory. It is a pity he did not die ten years ago, or just after the Mexican War.[158]

March 14th—A direct and prolonged attack on Fort McAllister, and failing in the attempt they all withdraw and declare the place impregnable, that it is simply impossible to reduce it. At the same time they disavow any desire or intention to take the fort, but only wished to test their iron clads. The performance was pronounced a splendid triumph, as they all got off uninjured.

They are easily satisfied with their own exploits if they escape annihilation or any occasion or contact with us, they think they achieved a grand success.

If they built their great iron clads merely to see into what dangerous places they could throw them and get them out again uninjured they have succeeded to admiration. The Richmond Examiner remarks that such is the contempt entertained in the Confederacy for their naval abilities, that they have entrusted all their naval operations to Wheeler's Cavalry, which cavalry did actually capture some gunboats on one of the Western rivers.[159] If they fail in their attempt on Charleston, I shall believe we are to conquer by the help of God.

March 17th—Today Nelly pointed out to me a new regiment of soldiers filing into our grounds with a train of wagons. Soon they had all marched in and were making their way to the orchard. I had a misgiving that something unpleasant was at hand, so was in measure prepared. Before many minutes two surgeons called, and asked to be furnished with rooms. I told them there were no rooms that they could have.

In quite an authoritative tone, one of them requested me to show him the bedrooms. I declined to do it, and he deliberately walked to the staircase and put his foot on the lower step as if to ascend. I requested him to show me his written authority for searching my rooms. As he could not do it I requested him to forbear till I could see the commanding officer. I lost no time in going to town to Milroy's headquarters, and to my surprise going up stairs saw in the adjutant's room the selfsame man waiting to see Gen. Milroy. I had been told that the General was at dinner, so thinking my best plan to get a hearing before my enemy did was to waylay him on the landing. I did so, planting myself at the head of the stairs, and waiting unweariedly till the General had finished all his courses. I was at last rewarded by the sound of his voice approaching, and as he came bounding up the stairs in a manner neither befitting his position or his grey hairs (for he came up three steps at a time), I seized him "by the button" as it were. At any rate I seized his ear and his attention, and as soon as I told my tale, and showed him my persecutor in the next room, he told me to go in peace, or to that effect, and invited the gentleman to find quarters elsewhere.

A Federal officer was struck in the street by a snowball today, as he was passing a group of boys, among whom was Harry. As Harry had one in his hand the officer concluded he had thrown it, and walking up to him peremptorily ordered him to throw it down. This Harry refused to do at his order, and he was immediately arrested, hurried off to the Provost Marshall's and thence to the guard house. He had been in there long enough for his wrath to cool, a little, and to begin to feel very homesick and downhearted, when the officer put his head in the door to ask him if he would do what he told him another time. "No," shouted Harry, "I will not for you had no right to make me put it down." Maj. Quinn came about bed time and effected his release.[160]

I have to be constantly on the watch for fear of my boys doing something to provoke the persecution of the Yankees. Not long since I heard an explosion in the yard loud enough to create some alarm, and on hurrying out saw a squad of soldiers approaching the scene of action, thinking it was an alarm. The noise proceeded from a battery the boys had erected on the top of the cistern and had supplied it with guns they had manufactured out of musket barrels cut into lengths of eight or nine inches, and bored for a touch hole, then mounted on carriages of their own make. I had noticed them very busily engaged about the yard for some time but never dreamed what they were after.

April 3—Nothing written since March 17th, and a letter from my husband reminded me of the delinquency. It was sent through Mr. Buck and directed to Harry, the first since November. How hard it is to be shut out from hearing even of those we love. No intelligence from any quarter is reliable. The Yankees give very confused accounts of affairs at Vicksburg, but every day something transpires to let us know that their affairs are not altogether brilliant. One or two of their vessels have been destroyed.

They say they are ready for another attack on Charleston and this time they are sure to succeed as Capt. Ericcson has invented an obstruction remover to go before their gunboats.[161] I wonder what excuse they will give to their dupes when that fails. Notwithstanding the cry about "Copperheads" and the efforts of Union Leaguers,[162] etc., there seems to be a peace party steadily increasing in the North that is making itself heard. Rumours come that the Western States are resisting the draft, and some towns are said to be fortifying. No lead, powder or caps are permitted to be sold in Indiana or Ohio. So much for liberty and free government. The Yankee papers report that the negro forces under the wretch Montgomery have captured Jacksonville, Florida.[163]

On Saturday last a letter was published in the Baltimore American from a Mrs. Pairo to a friend in the North. The letter had been intercepted and the writer was sentenced by the valiant Gen. Schenk to be taken from home, husband and children and sent South.[164] She accordingly made her appearance yesterday with her daughter under a strong guard. Mary says she is a person of great refinement and intelligence and certainly her letter indicates so much.

3a—Came home from town tired and worn out and went through the task of washing all the children and getting their clothes ready for Sunday.

After that I was refreshed by a letter from my dear sister, Lizzy, and a roll of money from my husband, both brought by some unknown hand. Heard that the enemy had been again beaten back from Charleston.

To day Gen. Milroy had a sword presented him. A grand review of dirty Yankees took place and I am told the cheers from the soldiers were faint and few. Some of them are to be pitied, they are forced into the army, so they say, and hate the service. They, the privates, are generally disposed to be kind. I often ask those I daily see to buy me things I cannot get myself because of the oath, and they do it readily and seem glad to oblige me. Mary has got rid of her Yankees, but not before one of them behaved very badly. We have all liked Maj. Quinn. He is very kind, but is a rough Irishman.

4th—Easter Sunday, and the Yankees held their service in our own dear church—that church hallowed by so many precious memories of undisturbed worship, and communion with our Father and Saviour, when His sacred praises were so solemnly chanted, the sweet voices of choir and congregation with the deep roll of the organ.

There are other memories, too, hallowing the sacred place, of those who used to meet us there and will do so no more forever. I can see Frank Jones' tall form moving up the aisle with his pretty young wife and little child, and others also who with him were among the first to lay down their good and useful lives. We can vividly realize the description given in the Bible of the desolation of war.

"How doth the city sit solitary that was full of people!" "The ways of Zion do mourn because none come to her solemn feasts." "Jerusalem remembered in the days of her affliction all

134

the pleasant things she had in the days of old when her people fell into the hands of the enemy." It seems to me the description of our own desolation as the prophet pours out his sad soul in a wail for the voice of gladness and the voice of mirth, "for the voice of the bridegroom and of the bride that are no longer heard."[165] The fruits not gathered, the fields wasted, the old men and young children hunger-stricken; but the saddest of all is the moan he utters for "The precious sons of Zion," how they are esteemed but as earthern pitchers, the work of the hands of the Potter. Alas! now as then our precious sons, the pride and flower of our land must be daily given to the devouring sword, and the wasting pestilence. Their flesh to be meat for the fowls of the air. But the prophet also says "Woe unto thee that spoilest and thou wast not spoiled."

5th—Last night a terrible snow storm, and today drifts as high as my head; bitter cold and general discomfort; but I am thankful for a quiet day at home with my Bible.

With what different feelings I look forward to the spring from those with which I anticipated its approach last year. Though war was around us, and death dealt out its horrors, though the enemy had possession of our home and was doing his best to make it a desolation, still no shadow of death had fallen on our household. I planned and worked and hoped without wearying, and lived as if there were no life but this, so absorbed was I in the business of life and its remaining pleasures. Though thoughts of another life would come, they did not remain, for my heart was here, in the midst of my circle of rosy children, providing for their comfort, and defending them from all ills as far as I could, and when not oppressed with care, enjoying their mirth and cleverness. I could not realize that at any time the summons might come. "Arise! depart ye, for this is not your rest." Though it came not for me it came for my youngest and sweetest flower, and she arose and followed to that world of which I did not take time to think. But now my plans are more for a residence there than here; and I trust my greatest care is to have ready my wedding garment against the time when "He comes that shall come and will not tarry."[166]

That world now seems the reality and this the shadow; I look upon the children now as only travelers to another country, and on her who is gone as one who waits for us.

May I no more forget Him even for the precious gifts that come from His hands. I must weep now to see the flowers blooming while mine, the sweetest of all, lies hidden under the sod.

7th—The whole town has been shocked and outraged by Milroy's treatment of Mrs. Logan.[167] He wanted her elegant house for his own headquarters, and coolly gave her orders to vacate it with her family. They demurred, as was natural and Mrs. Logan and her daughters were ordered to a room in the house where they were kept close prisoners all day, without even a morsel of food of their own abundant stores; and at evening a rude wagon was sent to the door, the ladies put in and driven six miles out of town, where they were set down by the roadside, destitute of every thing. Her son was imprisoned in the guardhouse. As Mrs. Logan left her house Mrs. Milroy entered smilingly, and as she did so Mrs. Logan's keys were handed her with the information that in future they were hers.

It has been my lot to have many encounters with Yankee men, but one like that with a Yankee woman, it would have taken divine grace to enable me to sustain creditably. They say that our cavalry captured a force of eighty yesterday near Strasburg, and we have beaten them everywhere, at Charleston, Vicksburg, and also that Rosencrantz had been captured.

8th—Passed Mrs. Logan's house today, and saw Federal soldiers loading wagons with the furniture. The books from the library were being packed in one wagon; a basin and pitcher were sitting in one of the windows of the carefully kept drawing room. We have reports of great defeats for our enemies at Charleston and Vicksburg, but their papers only say that "all intelligence from these points is uncertain and conflicting, but that the siege is in all probability abandoned," an unlooked for result of all their preparations and glorifications over victories yet to be achieved.

9th—No letters yet from my husband. It seems as if impassable oceans divide us. The Yankees have been amusing themselves searching the houses for the hundredth time. They heard yesterday that Mrs. Conrad had made a coat, a great coat for one of her sons. They sent immediately to search the house in hopes of finding it. They did, of course, and today a Jesse Scout wears it on the street.[168]

Their meanness and littleness is evident in many things, but in none more than in dressing their scouts and spies in Confederate uniforms to insult and to deceive the people. Many poor simple country people are led to believe them friends, and fall into the snares laid for their destruction. Mrs. Conrad's daughter told me that the copy of the valentine I had made for Milroy was in the wardrobe where the coat was found, and was lying face down on a shelf that was, as the man thought, thoroughly searched. I had made a copy, an improved one, to show our men when they came again, as the girls were very anxious to have it done, and it had been handed about among our friends, and had remained with the Conrads. They searched Mrs. Tidball's house for the Mason's books and papers, which Mr. Dooley had told them were there.[169] They found and took possession of them.

To day Sue and Flora got by some means a letter from Will and Ed. They were well and expected to be in Winchester shortly, so it said.

10th—Went in town this afternoon and saw an ambulance drawn up in front of Milroy's headquarters, filled with ladies and children and one gentleman. They looked sad and wearied. I passed on and returning, found them getting out at Mrs. Sherrard's door, five ladies, three children and one gentleman. They were Mrs. Stuart, Mrs. James and another lady sent out of Baltimore for disloyalty. Ladies are daily dragged from their homes and the protection of their male relatives, and hurried off to a strange land without even clothes to wear. One party availed themselves of a short stay in Washington at the Old Capitol prison and got a servant or some one to purchase for them a few handkerchiefs and stockings, combs and brushes, etc., which they put in small satchels procured for the purpose. But on leaving Washington, the valiant defenders of the Stars and Stripes took all from them and left them without the means of washing or combing; for the purpose no doubt of making treason odious in their persons.

Some say there was an alarm last night, and I certainly heard cannon late in the night as I went to the door. A fight took place at Berryville, rumour says, and many troops left here during the night. I hope we will soon see our men and breathe freely once more.

To day a young girl, a teacher in Mrs. Eichelberger's school,[170] wrote a note to a friend in town, which was intercepted on its way and read by a detective. It contained some comment on Milroy's doings and was reported to him. This evening the young lady was sent out of their lines, six or eight miles out of town, and there left by the roadside to find friends and shelter as she may. This evening an order closed Mrs. Eichelberger's school, and now I have no where to send Kenneth.

11th—The week's work over, and all the children in bed and asleep, quiet of course, so the diary comes out. Went in town this morning with Mrs. Dailey. Heard a confirmation of the reported defeat of the enemy at Charleston and the loss of five of their gunboats.

A dreadful story has been circulating that when the negroes under Montgomery and Higginson got to Jacksonville, Florida, the town was given up to their will, and was sacked and burned.[171] We can readily picture to our minds the scenes that transpired, having so recently read and been shocked at the accounts of sackings and burnings in India during the Sepoy revolt.[172] That such can and do take place here in our country, and our people the victims is beyond belief, or would be, if we did not know how savage really good people can become when they are abolitionists and fanatics. But it seems hardly possible that the self righteous Yankees could have so far forgotten their regard for the World's good opinion as to inaugurate such a state of things.

I see with sorrow that the much abused Poles are again in revolt, and that dreadful measures are resorted to, to quell them.[173] I could grieve over them, but have not a tear or a sigh to spare for our own distressed people.

I sent a short letter to my husband today; dared say no more than that we were well, and would not distress him by saying we were otherwise than comfortable. I dreamed last night I saw him, and so vivid was the impression that all day long I have had the feeling of having really seen him.

14th—To day Milroy sent Miss Mary McGill out of the lines. Thinking it perfectly right and safe to write a letter to a Northern lady, an officer's wife who had been nursing her sick husband in Mrs. McGill's house, and who she liked very much, she descanted rather imprudently on Milroy's treatment of the citizens. At five o'clock in the afternoon a detective drove up and demanded Miss Mary, put her in a buggy and driving five miles out of town set her down by the road side, without a house or a human being in sight, and then turned and drove back to town.

The Baltimore American speaks very despondingly [sic] of affairs at Charleston, wishes they may have good news from there; also that Foster is surrounded in North Carolina and will have to surrender.[174] If they admit that much their affairs must be even in a worse condition. A very quiet announcement is made that their land and naval forces have abondoned the attempt to take Vicksburg. That is truly a grand result of all their bluster. The most unblushing assertion one would suppose even Yankees capable of making, is contained in the report of the grand attack made on Charleston, in which having been in contemplation for two years, and preparations going on for one year, and blustering and threatening enough to have demolished several cities, they failed gracefully. Their long string of iron clads, the Weehawken in front, advanced to the attack, preceded by the "Devil" with which they no doubt expected to carry dismay to the hearts of all "rebeldom" (as they facetiously style the South), determined on reducing the forts and destroying the city as they had announced so often.

But instead of so happy a result they find their great two turretted Keokuk unable to resist at all; riddled with shots she sank, and all the rest being unable to continue the combat "retired"; not, however, before the "Devil" who seems to have been their great reliance, became disgusted with his associates

139

and abandoned them.[175] Old Mr. Steele remarked that having lost him they had lost their only friend.[176]

To day the Baltimore American announces that it was a "reconnoisance in force to ascertain the strength of the rebel batteries and the position of their obstructions, as well as to test the strength of their iron clads and decide on their ability to resist any fire." The result they say is perfectly satisfactory, as it demonstrated perfectly the defensive qualities of their vessels; but they add very significantly that their offensive qualities have not been so well established.

16th—Well, the American for the first time has told the truth: today it comes out with the information that the whole nation is humbled and disgraced at the failure to take Charleston; but as usual the sacrifice of a great man must be made to appease the angry gods. Admiral Dupont is the victim this time selected, because he did not set aside all the experience in naval affairs that he had acquired in a life of service, and put his faith implicitly in the novelties of the Yankee Ericcson, and risk the lives of his crews, and the safety of his fleet by hurling it against unknown dangers and obstacles, because Mr. Ericcson had deputed the Devil to lead them through. Admiral Dupont exercised his own common sense and for that he is set aside.[177]

Poor old Aunt Winnie gets weaker every day. I fear she cannot last long, and what shall I do without her. This evening the Yankee pickets have been driven in.

18th—This morning cannonading near town; I thought surely there would be another battle, but it proved to be only artillery practicing. We have intelligence that Johnston has taken three brigades of Rozencrantz in the west.[178] The American of yesterday said nothing more than that Grant had "changed his base," which means that he has been defeated. Nothing is said of Foster, though it was thought he must surrender. Wise was marching on Suffolk.[179] Norfolk was threatened, and there was general alarm. We are triumphant everywhere, thanks to our Heavenly Father who giveth us the victory. The Confederate loan is well received in Europe, and every thing looks promising for us, but there is sadness with our rejoicing. We that are in the hands of the enemy, drink the bitter cup of humiliation and oppression every day.

Yesterday I saw a wagon full of Baltimore gentlemen drive up to Milroy's headquarters, and wait to be sent out of the lines. They had no baggage, were seized and sent off without a change of clothes.

They were guarded by a score of bayonets; every variety of persecution is now resorted to, to subdue our people, even sending negroes into the houses to search. Yesterday Jane Allen came up from her home in the country in pursuit of a negro woman who had been her servant, and who had gone off with nearly all of her's and her children's clothes, as well as a valuable diamond ring that had belonged to her mother. She appealed to the authorities, but as usual, when a pretended search was made nothing was found. Today Rumley was ordered out of his store, and it and its contents taken possession of.[180]

A hospital steward and his wife are quartered on Mrs. Hugh Lee. As the homes of the citizens begin to look attractive in the spring time, they will be driven from them to accommodate the officers and their families.

19th—Communion to day in Mr. Graham's church. I felt grateful for the privilege of once more joining in the commemoration of the death of our dear Lord. How touching are those words of His, "Do this in remembrance of me." He knew us so well that He gave us the command lest we should forget Him; Him who had done so much for us; who had broken the chains that had bound us in "misery and iron," and opened the gate of mercy to the lost and ruined. Four Yankee officers joined the communicants, the oppressors and the oppressed at the table of the Lord together. He who searchest the hearts knows who are His. Met Mr. Williams who told me of the death of my dear Annette.[181] Beautiful and amiable, she has gone, and left a little babe and a broken up household.

Went to my Bessie's grave. The white violets were blooming at her feet. I gathered some, and their sweet odour made me almost think it was her pure baby breath that floated around.

"Fit emblems they are of the pure and the bright,
Who faded and fell with so early a blight."[182]

My heart has been so full all day that I have scarcely thought of the news of the capture of Rozencrantz's army, but whatever happens, nothing seems to give us rest and peace. I feel as if I must give out, for I cannot see how such a strain of anxiety and struggle can be borne much longer.

26th—Nothing written for a week; to day a letter from Lizzy telling the particulars of Annette's death, also giving news of poor Monroe.[183] He was among that mass of suffering humanity left on the bloody battlefield of Corinth, or Pittsburg Landing, last summer, and has been suffering till released by death a short time ago. We are being more severely dealt with by our tyrants every day. Today every shop and place of business was closed to those who would not take the Federal oath. Not even a place to get a shoe mended; we have long ceased to expect to buy.

Nothing further from Rozencrantz. Tonight comes the news that New Creek has been captured with several million dollars worth of stores by Imboden and Jones.[184] If that is true we must soon be relieved. Our prayer meeting tonight was so sweet and comforting. What a dark place this world would be but for the light that shines on it from the One beyond.

3rd—Lincoln's fast day. We heard that all the churches were to be opened for service, and that the much dreaded tribe of womankind was to be marched there at the point of the bayonet. No order, however, was issued to that effect. We concluded that Milroy had too much to do to keep the "rebel" men at bay, to waste his strength in compelling their women to pray.

Many think our army is steadily approaching down the valley. There was a fight yesterday at Stasburg. Some of our men were brought in prisoners, and six dead ones of their own, who they say had died of wounds on the way in. "The advices from the War Department," says the Baltimore American, "seem to justify the apprehension that a movement is about to be made down the valley to Western Virginia and towards the Rappahanock at the same time."

If that is true we must soon be free, but if they do not come shortly, I fear we will be all ordered out of the lines unless we take that oath. The American says that Charleston is to be again attacked, sometime this week, and that this is a bonafide attack, not a "reconnoisance"; that the Nation demands that the "rebellion" be reduced either to submission or to ashes. They now allow no papers to come to the soldiers from their homes; they are all opened and detained at the postoffice. Many of them find their way out in the shape of wrapping paper, and those I have seen have a decidedly rebellious flavor.

May 4th—The lovely first of May has come and gone and no leaves as yet on the trees. The weather is warm and delightful, and the May moon looks sadly down through the bare branches of the trees. The spring seems reluctant to put on her beautiful robes when there is so much sorrow and desolation everywhere. Saturday's papers gave an account of a rebel raid into Western Virginia. One of the statements is that the cavalry were under the command of Col. E. H. MacDonald; another that there were two thousand under Jenkins.[185] A gentleman who saw them as they passed through Moorefield says there were twenty-one hundred of them. The papers acknowledge that they have destroyed a great deal of the Baltimore and Ohio Railroad and thrown Pennsylvania into a panic. Hooker has crossed the Rappahanock and invited an attack from Lee in the open field. The American fears it will be a terrible reverse if not a great victory. It says very wisely that there was so little opposition to his crossing, that there was danger of a repetition of the poor fly's disaster when it ventured to accept the spider's invitation to "walk into the parlour." His burning the bridges behind him seems not an act of daring, but one of uncommon stupidity. Two regiments of cavalry went out today towards Western Virginia.

6th—The rain is pouring and the night dismal enough. I cannot quiet my excitement, or rid myself of a dreadful depression of spirit. "For a field of the dead rushes red on my sight,"[186] and though I do not fear that our clans have been scattered, for I have faith that it is not so; but I cannot shut out from my inner sight the sorrowful picture that may this night be seen on the banks of that river. The poor wounded and dying ones; and in such a storm! with no eye to pity or arm to save. I dread to hear the result of that contest, but whatever it may be, there is none the less of anguish and death to those we love.

7th—Went in town to hear the news, and to my surprise and distress learned that Angus [IV] had been captured by a troop of cavalry that went out under Maj. Quinn, and brought him into town. He was escorted to Mary's house by a Mr. Graham, who by Maj. Quinn's politeness had been deputed to guard him instead of a bayonet.

He is to remain there while in town. He had been on a visit to his wife, who is at her mother's in Hampshire, and when on his way back was overtaken and captured. Maj. Quinn assured us that Gen. Milroy had heard such good news that he was in excellent humour, and would be likely to extend any privilege to Angus. The news he alluded to was a paragraph in the Baltimore American pretending to give an account of a great victory over Lee. No one believes it, on the contrary, it is evident to my mind from a careful reading of the paragraph that it was anything but a victory. Nevertheless the Yankees are satisfied, which they generally are with very small achievements; and are very jubilant. They seem to take it for granted that Stoneman's cavalry raid was successful,[187] but one proof that it was not so, is, that according to their own confession it has not been heard from. The most significant fact of all is though, that there are no telegraphic dispatches, and no communication from the victorious army with the War Department. The American goes so far as to say that the Germans were panic stricken and behaved very badly; they turned and fled; that Sedgewick's corps had been obliged to retreat across the Rappahanock,[188] and that it was rumoured that the "enemy" had retaken the Heights of Fredericksburg, but that Gen. Hooker had said that all that "was of no consequence." It concluded with a wise caution to its readers not to consider the matter as decided.

Friday. 8th—Felt so anxious about Angus that I went in town this morning to learn what had been done with him. Heard that they had sent him to the guardhouse but would allow him to go about the town, if some one would be his security; that he would not run away. Set out with Flora to try and find some one who would act that friendly part.

He was gone from the guard house, and we went to Milroy's headquarters where we found him. Mr. Philip Williams went security for him. The greatest proof of Milroy's brutality that I have yet heard of was his asking Angus during his examination of him when he was first arrested if he desired the "rebellion" to succeed, and believed it would.

Angus replied that he did desire it to succeed and believed it would; whereupon Milroy in a great rage declared it never would, but that they would send all the rebel's d_____d souls to h_____l. Such treatment of a gentleman so moderate and dignified as Angus, and a prisoner in his hands, could only have been inflicted by General Milroy.

As we passed about the streets, the private Yankee soldiers would turn around when walking before us, or come up by our side and sneeringly tell us how well we were beaten. Five o'clock came and we saw throngs of soldiers running to get the papers. Soon they came up the street reading them, their faces grave and manner quiet and subdued. Our hearts beat high, and countenances brighter in proportion. Dr. Boyd comes solemnly up the street with a paper in his hand. He goes into Mr. Williams' house; it is nearer than his own. Soon Mr. Williams follows with a paper in his hand and goes in too. We have sent Harry for one, and are waiting in Mary's parlour for it, Angus, Mary, the girls and I.

Now he comes with the paper in his hand and exultation in his eyes. I meet him at the door and seizing the paper read aloud, "General Hooker recrosses the Rappahanock." "That is enough!" they all shouted, "they are beaten." Angus had all the time declared his belief that they would be severely defeated.

Then came the sickening distortions, and endeavors to conceal the fact that they had been totally and severely defeated; had lost frightful numbers. Of course it was all attributed to overwhelming superiority of numbers on our part, and also to the heavy rains that threatened Gen. Hooker's communications.

In refreshing contrast to their disingenuous and falsified accounts were the extracts from the Richmond Examiner. First came a dispatch from Gen. Lee:

"General Jackson penetrated to the rear of the enemy
and severely defeated him. We have to thank Almighty God
for another great victory."

But there was another announcement—that Gen. Jackson
had been severely wounded. Of course our grief is almost as
great as our joy, for no man was ever better loved by a people
than Jackson; the inhabitants of the valley love and venerate
him ardently, and almost regard him as peculiarly their own.
So much skill and such daring bravery, and such energy were
scarcely ever before united in one man; and then his deep and
sincere piety gives him a place in the respect and affection of
all. We do thank God for our victory, but we exult all the same
that our vain-glorious enemy has met his just deserts, and we
triumph in our great leaders.

9th—Papers today are trying to make the matter better, but
tell much the same story. The soldiers revenge their defeat by
mockingly calling out to the ladies as they pass, "We've killed
Old Jack; Old Jack is dead."

Two regiments left to-day; some think they are about to
evacuate. They went to Washington I was told. There is a great
deal of sickness in town. Sue has typhoid fever, Mary's children
are sick, and my poor little feeble Hunter, too.

A regiment of cavalry have established themselves in the
yard; close to the house are their stacks of hay, and wagons
of food for their horses.

When they first came they stabled some of their horses
in the basement dining room, but after a while turned the
horses out and took up their own quarters there. So at all
hours of the day and night men's feet are trampling in and
out, and oaths and drinking songs float out of the windows
and penetrate the walls and floors till they reach my reluctant ears.

13th—Was distressed beyond measure today to see from the
papers the certainty of Gen. Jackson's death accounts copied
from Richmond papers. We can only hope they are not true.

This evening I heard from a source not to be doubted that
his arm had been amputated.

The extract from the Richmond paper saying he was doing well could not have been later than the message I heard. I can hope, however, that it is an exaggeration of the enemy. The Yankee papers say that Hooker is ready for another advance, and even that he has again crossed the Rappahanock. That, however, is contradicted by other accounts given by themselves. Some statements of their losses put them at 40,000 men.

News from Western Virginia is that we have Wheeling, and that Gen. Joe Johnston has defeated Rozencrantz. Mary Maguire is dying of consumption, and languishing in the close air of the town; but all requests to have her removed to the country have been refused. I heard today that Milroy had said that every house was to be burned, the owners of which had sent their slaves into the Confederate lines for safekeeping. Mrs. Taylor's was one that was to be burned.

15th—The shadows are darkening around us in the devoted town. Jackson is certainly dead. There is no longer room to doubt it. To say that it is a personal calamity to each and every individual is to say little. "The Mighty has fallen," but he carries to his grave the hopes, and is followed by the bitter tears of the people in whose defense he lost his life, and who loved him with grateful devotion. No loss could be felt as his will be. In every great battle fought in Virginia he has been a leader, and has never known defeat. Success crowned his every effort. Especially was Winchester the object of his care and solicitude. Last spring when he was driving Banks out, as he rode through the town, the people poured out of their houses giving vent to their joy and exultation, he was heard to say, "A noble old town. It and its people are worth fighting for."

Even the Yankee papers accord to him the praise that was justly his. One, the New York Tribune, the greatest enemy the South has, speaks of him as "A great General, a brave soldier, a pure man, and a true Christian," but adds that they are glad to be rid in any way of so terrible a foe. He needs not their praise to add to the lustre of his great name. His place will be forever in the hearts of the Southern people. Not only the Hero's laurels bind his brow, but a crown incorruptible has been placed on it by the great Captain whose he was and whom he served.

The people in town feel very despondent about being relieved from their bondage now that the Champion of the Valley is no more.

Well may they sigh for relief, for the tyrant's hand becomes every day heavier; besides there are indications, it is said, of a dreadful disease breaking out in the camps. Eight hundred of the soldiers are sick in the town, besides many dying, and in town there is scarcely a house where there is not sickness, mostly of young persons. Notice was given Dr. Boyd that he must vacate his house and give it up for a hospital, and tomorrow he and his family must go, and become wanderers like so many others. Of course, they will be sent out of the lines.

Mine will be taken also I am sure, the ill is only delayed; it will come. One satisfaction I have though in all this distress, and that is, that the children are comparatively well and enjoy life; not as they once did, but still they do enjoy it, and they are good children, all of them.

Nelly, little thing as she is, is companionable, and almost too sympathizing. Her feeling for me makes her poor little face often look sad and dejected. Roy with his unceasing busy energy, and Donald quite melts me when he comes in with a lilac, or a tulip or snowdrop, and his blue eyes look so confiding as he offers them. Harry and Allan are always engaged in making seizures of arms on the sly, and I am constantly afraid they will be detected in it. They have a repository in the garret where no searcher has ever penetrated and where they have quite a store.

Kenneth looks envyingly at them when they speak of stores of swords and pistols they will have to hand over to the Confederates when they come. Only once have I been made uneasy by the boys breaking through the restraints I have thrown around them to keep them out of harm's way. It was last spring, when we were all so anxious about the fate of our army while McClellan's attack was preparing. We had heard that there had been a battle but nothing definite; when one morning I missed Allan, and after waiting a day and night, sent Harry mounted on Kit to try and find him. He had become footsore and very weary of wandering and was taking a good cry when, he said, he spied Harry at the top of a distant hill, and recognized him

148

and Kit. When they met he mounted behind and they jogged on towards home, stopping to eat cherries whenever they saw any. On the way home, they said, they saw a cavalry officer capture several Yankees. Allan said he wanted to get news of the family, and that was his reason for going.

Last night I left this book in which I am writing lying on a table and went down stairs. Nell spied two officers approaching the house, and supposing they were coming for a search, first concealed the book and then went to see what they wanted. Great prudence on the part of a maiden of seven years. I might not have taken such a precaution myself. I asked her why she did it, and she said she thought there might be something in it the Yankees ought not to see. I had not thought of her knowing the character of the book.

Last night Harry informed me that he had discovered a number of fine sabres concealed under the Presbyterian Church on Kent Street, and announced his determination to possess himself of them. I had not think of it again, but last night he and Jim Dailey made their appearance, Allan also, just as the drums beat for taps, with delighted faces and sparkling eyes, and each threw down a large bundle on the floor. Soon Harry began to draw out sabre after sabre, each wrapped by itself in an old bag to keep from clashing; they laughed merrily to think how they had passed all the guards with the bundle under Harry's arm. One, he says, he actually bumped with the bundle, and when he saw the ubiquitous and all-seeing Purdy, he became quite excited; but even his Argus eyes disconcerned nothing wrong in the bundle, and after he was fairly out of reach he laughed back, "You don't know everything Mr. Purdy."[189]

17th—Just came from prayer meeting; heard that Ben White had been killed in the battle of Fredericksburg, his mother's only son and he a mere boy. Young Lyle and two others named Lighter, sons of a plasterer and his only ones, are among the killed.[190]

Heard that Gen. Jackson was shot by his own men while reconnoitering, expecting a night attack. We ought to feel willing to give him back to Him who gave him, and who has taken him to Himself. His mission was no doubt accomplished, but it was a bitter day for the South when he left us. Went to my darling's grave at sunset.

Spent a long time there trying to realize that she still lives in a better life. The grass grows on her innocent breast, and lilies of the valley and sweet violets bloom where she lies. While cares thicken and troubles perplex, and the sorrows of all around me make my heart sad, I can almost feel glad that she is away from it all.

22nd—Moore, the Captain of the Jessee Scouts, was yesterday captured by our men.[191] Today they sent and took George Ward and his little brother prisoners to be held as hostages for Moore's safety; him who they know deserves hanging.[192] George is the age of Harry, and his little brother about ten. They are now shut up in prison with all sorts of evil men.

To day I received another intimation that my house would be wanted for a regimental hospital. I feel a sickening despair when I think of what will be my condition if they do take it. Where can I go, what can I do without home or shelter, and no means to buy it if it could be had? The children, some of them are sick, and how can I leave poor old Aunt Winnie?

I have had so many startling visits, and been so often summoned to surrender the house, and so often intruded upon by rude men, that if I hear a step on the porch my heart palpitates and flutters in a way to frighten me. It is often long before I can quiet its beatings. I am growing thin and emaciated from anxiety and deprivation of proper food and am weak; and now have become faint-hearted. So I fear if they make many more demands I must give up and leave all, for I do not think I can much longer continue the struggle. The last vestige of beauty, and the last remains of anything green have been destroyed on the place.

The lilacs and syringas, and many beautiful things bloomed out in the early spring in the midst of the desolation, but they were soon destroyed; long branches of bloom would be broken off to decorate their horses' heads; thus adorned they would gallop around the house, to attract attention to their depredations. Every day, and twice a day two or three hundred artillery horses are driven by the house immediately under the windows on their way to get water. The noise and cursing with the dust of their trampling feet is intolerable.

To day there was cannonading, directed, it is said, against some of our men who are near town.

Some days ago an old woman came to me offering to sell vegetables, or something I could not buy. She insisted on coming in the house and penetrated up stairs to a private room. When she reached it she mysteriously dived down into her stocking, and drew thence a crumpled paper. It was a short note from my husband saying he would be with us soon. She would not tell me how she got it, or in fact any thing about her ostensible errand, but made signs so as to convey the idea of something approaching in such multitudes as to cover the earth. She had taken the oath, and with her tongue could utter nothing, but her eyes and hands were expressive enough to make me know that the Confederate army was on its march. I was so happy and so thankful that her conscience did not hinder her communication by pantomime.

They are again making demonstrations against Vicksburg, attacking now in the rear. They have taken possession of Jackson, the Capital of the state, and have burned it. If they succeed in cutting the railroad Vicksburg must give up for she can get no more supplies.

June 4th—Nothing written for many days; troubles without number. One day last week we were all about to sit down to dinner when a step was heard in the hall. I went out and there stood a gentleman in citizen's clothes, but with military gauntlets on. He introduced himself as Major Butterworth.[193] I knew what he had come for, so said nothing but stood waiting for him to tell his errand. He told me that he was a quarter master, and that he had been sent to inform me that I must give up the house, as they must have it for a hospital, that orders had been given for it to be taken immediately; that I could if I chose retain one room in it, but that Gen. Milroy thought I had better go out of the lines, that if I would consent to do so he would furnish wagons to take away all the household articles I might wish to remove, and also conveyances for myself and family as far as Edinburg. I heard him, but did not realize what he said, and could only cover my face with my hand and burst into tears. My feelings were beyond control; it was the first time I had given way before any of them, but I had lost the power of resistance, and all my self command.

The little children came running out of the dining room and clustered around me, crying violently without knowing why. He said nothing more, but got up and stood for a while by the door. At last he said, "Perhaps if you see Gen. Milroy yourself you may induce him to alter his arrangements with regard to your house." So taking leave he vanished. I lost no time in seeking Milroy's presence. It was a hot afternoon, the doors of Mrs. Logan's house all standing open, and the sentinel lazily walking back and forth before the front door.

I went in. Other guards were in the hall and an orderly waiting at the parlour door. I was directed to go in the front parlour and told to wait; sat down and for some time listened to voices in the next room. Milroy's voice in coarse harsh tones, and a delicate lady's voice replying in an apologetic manner, and entreating for something to be granted, something to be restored of which she had been robbed.

A final refusal, and the door opened. Mrs. Harrison came out flushed and excited, with angry eyes and resentful manner. She had driven alone twenty-five miles on that hot day to beg the return of her lost horse that she depended upon for every thing. She had been Matty Page, had all her life had whatever she fancied, and had never known an ungratified desire. Their estate was a large and fine one in Clarke County, but had been desolated. My time came. I went in with my heart in my mouth, for I knew he was angry, and felt some terror at encountering him. He was sitting by a table before a window, with his elbow resting on the table and his head leaning on his hand. I went straight up to his side. "Gen. Milroy," said I. He looked around impatiently. "They have come to take my house from me," as if it would be a surprise to him. He turned around and looked full at me. "Well you ought to go to your husband. I cannot suffer you to remain in that house any longer, besides," he said turning around in his chair, "you had better go before the exodus begins, for I expect orders to send out all rebel sympathizers, and by G____ I will do it," he said fiercely, striking his hand on the table. "Why should you expect me to shelter you and your family, you who are a rebel, and whose husband and family are in arms against the best government the world ever saw." I said not a word, and presently he spoke more quietly. "The authorities in Washington are informed of my allowing you to keep that house, and I have had orders to take it." "But Gen. Milroy, you are commandant here, and no one surely can interfere with your commands; you can take which houses you choose, and you can suffer me to remain in mine, where at least I can have a shelter for my sick children, or you can send me off to wander about with no house or food to eat, and no means to procure any. It is as you please; for you to say whether I go or stay. You were very kind to offer me conveyances, and I appreciate your kindness, but I do not know where to go." He looked out at the window and remained silent. I waited for some time and at last spoke. "What shall I do, Gen. Milroy, must I go, or may I stay. I will do as you say."

I waited again. At last he raised his head and looked in my face. "You can stay but I allow it at the risk of my commission. I have been threatened already with the loss of it for my indulgence to such as you." I thanked him; indeed I could almost have kissed his hand, and hurried home surprised at my success. I could not help pitying him for he seemed to be troubled, and his face looked very dejected when I first went in I thought. He has been good to me, but others have felt the weight of his hand.

June 5th—We have glorious news: Grant has been compelled to raise the siege. The papers say Gen. Lee's army is in motion, and the Yankees here are certainly in a commotion. They expect to leave evidently—some say there is a Confederate force as near as Kernstown, and a battle is shortly expected. Only exciting rumours, but no certain intelligence. The roses, all torn and scattered as the bushes are, are in full bloom in the place where the garden was. A large bouquet is blooming on my work stand that Nelly has placed there. The odour of one brings to my mind the image of one who, as pure and perfect as itself, I last saw holding in her pale hand its counterpart.

Its fragrance brings the picture of the little still form, and the fair face with its rapt look lying in all its serene loveliness in the little white coffin. Often does memory bring back that last look which she gave to earthly things, and often does it recall me from thoughts of sorrow and sadness to visions of that happy world where she has found her home.

9th—To day Dr. Baldwin was ordered to pay wages to a negro whom he had hired from his master. He refused to do it, saying the money was due the master and not the man, when Milroy had him seized and sent out of the lines with his wife at an hour's notice. His house and furniture have been seized.

10th—Reports that our troops are near the town. I have had another summons to vacate the house; but I may not after all be obliged to go. The orders were to be ready by the 11th; that wagons would be here to take me to Edinburgh. I had taken heart to have the house all cleaned and the matting put down, so if I have to leave some of them will enjoy it.

11th—No washerwoman and soiled clothes to carry away; so today I tried to have a few of the children's clothes washed. Harry and Allan brought up a long forgotten old washing machine from the cellar, and we all attempted the washing. The boys turned the machine and rubbed alternately, while I inspected the work. Aunt Winnie looked sorrowfully on at the usurpation of her prerogative. While we were busy at the clothes we were startled at the report of a cannon, another, and another. The boys leave all and run. Notwithstanding the cannon, I made an effort to hang out the clothes, but failed. I left them, too, and went in to sit down till my heart stopped beating as if it would thump its way out. My hand has a hole in it from the soap and the rubbing; on every knuckle. I tried to wash the dirt out of the wristbands. Heard this evening that the Confederates were certainly near town. Report for once said the truth. Heard that there has been fighting, and that many Yankees were captured. Went in town with Mrs. Dailey and saw no signs of their leaving, but the fighting continues.

12th—The battle raged all day in sight of town, shells screaming through the air so constantly that for some time we dared not go out. I sent the servant girl, Nannie, to town on an errand and as she came near the gate a shell burst in front of her. She was terribly frightened, and quickened her steps; when she reached the house, panting, she remarked that it was the last time she was going to town; and I do not wonder, for it was no holiday spectacle. The hardest fighting was on the old battlefield of Kernstown where Jackson fought them a little more than a year ago, and by his strategy changed their entire plans.

The Yankee soldiers say that Milroy will certainly destroy the town if he is hard pressed. A man told me that Lee has driven Hooker into Alexandria and from another source I hear that Trimble is in Front Royal and that Berryville is in our possession.[194] We have a large force near here and tomorrow there will be a severe fight. There will be a struggle for possession of the town and fort. The town may be destroyed as they threaten, but we can only hope and pray for the best. I shall sleep tonight, that is I shall try, to be ready for what tomorrow may bring. I can scarcely hope to see our men so soon.

14th—Victory! thanks to our Father in Heaven; our enemies are at last powerless to harm us. Musketry and cannon firing began early in the morning, but not very near us. Mrs. Dailey came over to stay with me as her house was so unprotected, and was within range of the shells. We sat together in the dining room before the windows looking to the West; and it seemed so strange to sit quietly in a rocking chair and watch the progress of a battle. We were yet on the outskirts, and could see the troops deploying, skirmish lines thrown forward and mounted men galloping from one point to another, batteries wheeling into position, and every now and then the thunder of cannon and the shriek of shell. Still they were at a distance, and there we sat, all that sweet June morning, and watched and listened, and occasionally shrank a little when a shell from a battery on the same hill opposite to the house, that one year ago our troops stormed and took, and sent its defenders panic-stricken down the hillside or rolled them in the dust; when a shell came crashing through the trees near the house, and reminded us that we were in danger. Thick and fast they presently came, one after another. A Confederate battery has possession of the hill, and the answering shots are from the fort. We are just in their path. Our battery is south of us, and the fort slightly east of north. So they go, whizzing screaming, and coming down with a dreadful thud or crash and then burst. We hold our breath and cover our eyes till they pass. I gather all the children in till the firing ceases.

About noon there is comparative quiet, and Mrs. Dailey goes home with her children. I begin to feel that the effort has failed and the Confederates are retiring; but it is only the lull before another greater storm. About three o'clock I went out into the front porch to see what was going on. The children were playing in the yard. High on the hill opposite the same battery spouted flame and smoke, and the fort slowly responded. Men were passing and repassing, and many looking pale and anxious. Some wearily dropped down and went to sleep under the trees. The two little boys, Donald and Roy, seemed to forget the shells and were playing in the yard, running and catching the men as they passed, saying, "I take you prisoner." Though there was a cessation of the firing in a great measure, the faces of the passing groups of men, or stragglers, as they were, did not look less anxious. I heard one officer telling another that Mulligan was coming from Cumberland to relieve them.[195] Then I felt comfortable to know that they needed relief.

I was, up to that time ignorant of the state of affairs, and of all except what was to be seen from my own point of observation. At five o'clock I again went and stood on the porch, dejectedly fancying that the attempt had failed, and we were again left to our fate. Two officers stood within hearing leaning against a tree, a linden tree that grew close to the house door, and filled the air with its perfume. They were pale and looked disturbed as they talked to each other in a low tone. Suddenly a blaze of fire from those western hills from which Mulligan was to issue for their relief. "That is Mulligan," said one; "Mulligan has come," echoed all around. But the shout was suddenly silenced when they saw the direction in which the balls were sent. Straight into their works they plunged, and soon a dusky line was seen making its way toward their outer works. Crashing of cannon and rattling of musketry till those were taken, and then the guns were turned on the fort. Then it seemed as if shells and cannon balls poured from every direction at once. One battery from the hill opposite our house rushed down and through our yard, their horses wounded and bleeding, and men wounded also, and pale with fright. More artillery and more horses and pale flying men rush by where I stood. Hurrying groups of stragglers, and officers without swords, and some bareheaded. They were all hastening up to the fort which they had imagined was a place of safety. Gen. Milroy with a few of his body guard galloped by; I saw his pale agitated face as he passed within ten feet of me, and felt sorry for him; so following my impulse of being kind I bowed to him; from pure sympathy; for I really did at the time feel for his misfortunes, though I would not have averted them. He may have thought it a piece of mock respect, but whatever he thought or felt, he bowed low, till his plume almost touched his horse's mane. The fort all the time was sending its huge shot and shell over and through the town to where our troops were, and from the west proceeded a blaze of fire and a cloud of smoke that carried death into their stronghold into which they were crowding by hundreds.

Until now they seemed to be flying to the fort for safety, and it was pitiable to see them as they were hurrying by, turn their eyes to the west, pause and look bewildered, then look around for a place of safety, and finally avail themselves of the only spot the shells did not reach, the angle of our house. I had retreated there with my children when the shots and shells began to fly so fast, and burst all around the house; and then as I sat on the porch bench men came crowding in. Now a surgeon bringing a wounded man; he, the surgeon, looks so humbled and frightened that I did not at first recognize in him the same one who had behaved so insultingly last winter when he demanded my house. He goes away, but soon comes back more frightened and agitated than ever. They talk openly of being surrounded. The soldiers say they will stay and be captured.

I tried to comfort the wounded man who sat on the bench by me, but he was past comfort; a ball was lodged in his throat and he sat with his poor wretched face distorted with pain through all those weary hours; close to me he was and the hard breathing as he struggled to keep the blood from choking him was dreadful to hear. Crowd after crowd of men continued to pour into the porch till it was packed full; then they crowded as close as they could get, to be sheltered by the angle of the house. Ambulances were backed up to let out their loads of wounded, and horses reared frantic with pain from their bleeding wounds. Some were streaming with blood, and looking wild, with their poor eyes stretched wide with pain and fright. All made an effort to crowd in there and the close atmosphere was almost suffocating. I could not move, or hide the dreadful sights from my eyes.

All the while the batteries thundered, and booming of cannon, the screaming of shells (who that has ever heard that scream can ever forget it?), and the balls of light go shooting over our heads, followed by that fearful explosion. All the weary while the children were leaning on my lap; I was holding my poor little Hunter. Roy and Nelly were perfectly composed, looking up at the shells as they flew over and came crashing down.

Donald, poor little four year old baby, hid his face on my knee and sobbed. Old Aunt Winnie sat not far off, crying and wringing her hands. "Oh Miss Cornelia," she said, "you will all be killed." I did not know whether we would be or not; it really seemed impossible that we could come out of that chaos alive. One object my eyes were so fascinated with that I could scarcely withdraw them; it was the face of Tuss; a more abject looking wretch it would be difficult to conceive of. The expression of woe on his ugly old face was ludicrous; his eyes were fixed on me with a beseeching look as if I could help him if I would. He remembered, no doubt, his past misconduct and that must have given an additional sting to his distress; he was the impersonation of grief and fright.

At last the sun goes down, and the firing is less constant; soon it ceases altogether. Some of the men get up and make a move as if to go away, but only saunter off a few steps, and stop in the yard. Some get to laughing and talking, the reaction from anxiety and dread. These same men had been fighting for two days. Some looked really happy, and I doubt not felt greatly relieved. I got up and went to the kitchen and had some milk boiled for the wounded man that sat near me. He tried to take it but could not. I had him taken in and laid on the hall lounge; others followed, and before I knew it there were at least fifty men in the house. They asked permission to come in, it is true, but it was useless I knew, to withhold it, as they were many and I was one; and I did not then know the result of the contest. After dark I left the children with Aunt Winnie and walked out in the back yard to see what was going on. Most of the men and all the officers had dispersed, and gone I do not know where. Some of the ambulances with wounded, and all of the horses had gone. I met Mr. Wood and Mr. Steel near the house.

They say our forces have captured nearly all of Milroy's command. While that lull was taking place in the middle of the day Early was silently making his way around to the rear of the enemy, and suddenly burst on them with his batteries from the hills at the west, in the manner I have described.[196] When I went into the house the floors were all covered with men, some asleep and others preparing for it by stacking their muskets in a corner and stretching themselves on the floor. It was vain to try to get anything to eat for myself and children, so I took the little ones and preceded by Harry and Allan who had arrived a few minutes before, with Kenneth who had followed them, all full of news, I came up stairs and sent the children to bed without even shutting a house door.

What is the use, have I not a strong guard down stairs? I do not feel the least fear, but will quietly lie down and take my rest.

15th—I did not lock my chamber door and then went to bed and slept as soundly as I ever did in my life. The scenes of the day floated through my brain all night, the maneuvering troops scudding over the hills, shells flying, men rushing back and forth, artillery, infantry and ambulances confusedly hurrying by, and amidst it all my little ones playing in the yard in the bright summer sunshine, as happy and unconcerned as if all was peace around them. Poor little things, they have long been used to scenes of strife and confusion, and I suppose it now seems to them the natural course of things.

I was wakened at dawn by cannon, dressed and went down; the floor was still covered with sleeping men. Their sleep was deep for they were very weary I suppose. At any rate I had to push one with my foot to arouse him and told him to awake the others. I waited for them to go, and invited them to depart, but still they lingered. The cannon had ceased. I went to the front door and there filing into the yard was a column of grey coats! I could not help it, but waved my handkerchief high over my head. They came up and halted before the door. I told an officer the Yankees were in the house; he asked me to send them out. I told them to go, and each one laid his musket down and marched sadly out.

They marched them off, and I ran through the wet grass up to the top of the hill where the fort was. I went to it. The United States flag was waving in the morning breeze, but not a soldier was to be seen. They had all gone and destroyed nothing. I stood looking with amazement at the immense work they had constructed so near me and I had never seen it before; never dared to go in that direction. Some one came galloping up the hill. It was Capt. Richardson.[197] He told me of Early's flank movement; he was with him. The Louisiana brigade charged the first outwork and took it, then turned the guns on the fort. That was the time when the firing was heaviest, and the terror so great. General Gordon and his staff soon come riding up, and I turn and go down the hill.[198]

Went in town this afternoon; the girls told me that in the early morning, long before light, many ladies expecting our men to come in had assembled in the streets to greet them; and as the marching column drew near they with one accord burst into singing "The Bonnie Blue Flag." The bands all stopped, and the troops stood still till they had finished, and then their shouts rent the air, caps were waved, and hurrahs resounded. Some Yankee prisoners were standing on the Hotel porch, and one was heard to say the men could fight when they knew such a welcome awaited them.

Lieut. Richardson came to tea; he gave me a description of their approach to the town. Milroy evacuated the fort during the night and stole away leaving the flag flying. All his force was captured about seven miles from town. We captured all their baggage, even their officers' trunks and mess chests. Milroy escaped alone by a byroad. Our men threaten to hang him if they can catch him on account of his treatment of the people of the town. Today I saw forty-five hundred prisoners marched by. Many faces I recognized as those I have had to look at all the winter.

15th—This afternoon a squad of Confederates marched up to the door with a woe begone looking surgeon in the midst of them. When they got him to the door they sent for me to ask if he was the one who behaved so badly to me last winter. I recognized in him the one who had been kind and serviceable in helping me to take care of Aunt Winnie when she was ill, and was glad to testify in his favour. He had asked them to bring him to me that I might convince them that he had not been offensive in his behavior. Every surgeon they had taken was ironed and sent to Richmond to the Libby prison. Dr. Patton was my man, and I think they got him, but for fear of missing him they took all.[199]

16—Went to town to help make a Confederate flag out of two captured ones. Made it by the new pattern. White flag with the battle flag for the Union. We had to work hard for Gen. Ewell waited to see it float before he left for Pennsylvania.[200] I stood on Mrs. Hopkins' porch holding it up to see how it looked, when Mr. Williams passed. Men were going by, Yankees and all. "It is imprudent," said Mr. Williams, "to let them see you with it." I laughed at his fears, feeling so triumphant, and so secure that our army was there for good.

Saw Gen. Early and staff on our way from the fort where we had gone to see the flag raised. We call it "Fort Jackson." Saw Hunter Maguire, who told us Jenkins was in Pennsylvania.

17th—Have been hoping all day to see Mr. MacDonald, but have not even heard from him. We hear the army is all passing towards Maryland, some think to take Washington.

18th—No Mr. MacDonald yet. I am filled with anxiety, but he must be on the way or he would have written. Gen. Lee is to be in town this evening. Major Snodgrass of Gen. Early's staff sent me the contents of Gen. Elliot's mess chest today.[201] A good rain, but it prevents me from going to see Gen. Lee enter the town.

Heard that Milroy reported that he had cut his way out with five thousand men and had taken many prisoners.

September, 1875—The diary ends here; as anxieties and trials increase it is forgotten. As a narrative of the events that followed may be interesting to my family, I will try to give it as nearly as I can recollect.

Narrative of our refugee life

I waited vainly to see my husband, for he never came. Never again saw his home. He was lying ill in Richmond while I was waiting and expecting. The triumph recorded in the last pages was shortlived, for soon the dreadful echoes from the field of Gettysburg sounded in our ears, and put an end to our joy. Once more the streets were filled with wounded and bleeding men, not to find rest and relief, but to be hurried on to a place of greater security, all at least who could be moved, and all who could walk, however severe the wound might be. Uncertainty and dread of the evil to come seemed to fill every heart; preparations were going forward to evacuate the town again, and all was confusion and distress.

It had been decided that we must go if the army retreated, and so I sadly went about preparing to take my flight. I sent from the house such things as I could get away, the Confederate soldiers carrying for me. A sick Lieutenant was staying in the house, a sad looking man with a scarcely healed bullet wound in his left cheek, a deep, angry wound that disfigured him dreadfully. He told me one day that he had not seen his wife and children for two years; his children were two little things. He said he feared they had suffered in his absence for the necessaries of life, but that he never expected to see them again; he said that such was his distress on their account, that he often wished that death would come speedily and end his suffering, for he knew it would come before he ever reached home, and he could not endure the prolonged misery. I remember now the piteous look of his sad eyes; he had been sick a long time and perhaps that had deprived him of his hope and courage. He superintended all my arrangements, and did all he could for me.

I got a chest packed with the house linen and winter clothes and the silver, rolled up a few carpets and waited.

July 1863

Once morning, the 17th of July, Edward rode up and told me that he would send a wagon that evening and that I must get it packed

163

and sent off under Harry's care, and try to get away with the children as I best could. He was on the march and could stay only a few minutes. He left, and I tried to collect my energies to devise a way to go the next day. Edward had said I must positively go then, but how to go, or what to go in I could not imagine.

After some consideration of the subject I concluded to apply to a man living near me who had a spring wagon. He agreed for me to take it as it would probably fall into the hands of the Yankees, and I promised to have it sold for him when I reached Staunton. Edward had left me a horse to work in it. After these arrangements I went in town to see what Mary and the girls would do. Susan and Flora were to leave that evening in a carriage with Dr. Wilmer[1] and Julia Clarke.[2] Mary was to wait for a lucky chance.

The whole town seemed to be trying to get away; every thing that had wheels was in demand, and even a cart was deemed a prize. Few were willing to risk another Federal occupation, for the next might be a prolonged one, as Gen. Lee had been obliged to retreat, and if they did not go when they had the opportunity to take some of their belongings, they would in all probability be thrust out helpless.

Harry departed the same evening sitting on the top of the wagon, a man driving. The beds had been mostly packed up and sent off so I made pallets for the children and put them to bed for the last time in their home. I went into a room alone and tried to sleep, but not till the dawn of the morning did I fall into a moment's forgetfulness.

I was wakened by a flutter of wings in the room, and saw a bird frantically trying to get out.

One of the sweet singers perhaps that I used to rejoice so to hear in early morning, pouring forth their sweet music. Breakfast soon after daylight and we were ready to go. I took a last look at all the familiar objects in the rooms, and knelt and prayed to be guided in my journeyings, and in whatever place I might be. There was no time for regrets. I had wept all my tears away the night before I thought, but my heart was breaking at the prospect of leaving my happy, happy home, for I felt it would be forever.

Old Aunt Winnie stood in the doorway crying, and as each child took leave of her she cut a lock of its hair. She held in her hand a little brown shoe of Nell's that she said she would keep for her sake. Some provisions were put in the wagon and a few changes of clothes. Nell, Roy, Donald and Hunter seated themselves on little crickets in the back part of the wagon, while I, with Allan to drive, took my place in front. Kenneth, poor child, was mounted on an old horse that had been by some chance overlooked by the marauders. After taking leave of Aunt Winnie, and Tuss (who wept abundantly), and Mrs. Anderson, the blacksmith's wife who had come to tell us good bye, we drove down the avenue and turned out into the road, for the long, long journey. And thus I left my pleasant home, to see it never again. Heavy-hearted I was, for I knew nothing of what was before me, and I felt that I had let go the only hold I had on anything.

The sun was just rising, and few of the houses were opened as we drove through the town. Mrs. Dandridge was standing on her doorstep and came out to say "good bye." She wept, and I gave way for the first time that morning. This was only the beginning of our sorrows.

By eight o'clock we had left the old town far behind, and the fresh morning air, and the green fields, sweet with the fragrance of early day, had in some measure banished my sadness and my spirits rose. I began to see something of the bright side of my situation. I should see my husband soon, and would at any rate be surrounded by friends instead of enemies. The children had forgotten their grief, and chatted gaily, so I tried to forget mine and for the time succeeded.

A hot, hot day that 18th of July, and I expected to suffer dreadfully in the broiling sun with no cover to the wagon, but the road was smooth, and we drove rapidly along creating a breeze as we went, which with a parasol to keep off the sun, kept me quite comfortable.

All the morning we drove pleasantly along and stopped at noon to eat our luncheon and rest the horse.

We were close to the bank of the Shenandoah and seated ourselves under the trees to enjoy the cool shade and eat our luncheon. The shining river lay smooth and placid under the hot bright beams of the sun. While I spread out the repast, Allan, my fourteen year old protector, undertook to water the horse. He accordingly divested her of her encumbrances, or most of them, and led her to the brink of the river, whence she slid down into deep water, to his consternation and my distress and terror, for I thought our only

165

dependence was gone. He held on by the rein, however, and in a little while she, splashing and struggling, reached the bank and climbed up, to our great joy and relief. Part of the army were in front of us, and more followed, and from this time we were constantly in sight of, and often jostled by moving crowds of people and vehicles. Many wounded men were among them making their way to a place of safety, while fugitives of every grade and degree of misery were toiling on, on foot, or in any kind of broken-down vehicle. Sick men, hungry men, and women with crowds of children, all hurrying on. I despised myself for thinking of any privations I had to bear while all those helpless ones were around me.

One man I saw lying dead by the road side. He had lain down to rest, and never rose again, but died there while the people were hurrying by; and no one took time to stop and look at his poor dead face. We got to Woodstock about sunset, and I enquired for the plainest and most out of the way tavern in the place. I was shown a long, low wooden house with a porch in front, and there I found a room with one bed and several pallets on the floor that was disengaged. For this I was thankful, and taking my tribe up to it washed and combed them and freshened them up for supper. I was sitting in the parlour when the landlady made her appearance, and I was startled at her gorgeous array; had not seen so much finery for two years. She informed me that she was a bride; had married the hotel keeper two weeks before. She told me all about the wedding and how many bridal presents she had received. I could not help being amused and entertained, in spite of anxious cares. She proposed to me to go to her room and see her new dresses, but concluded that we had better wait till after supper. It was soon announced by the lady herself, who had a few minutes before gone out to make some final arrangements.

She led me to the upper end of the table and seated me and all the children as near to herself as she could get us. A silver butter dish was before me and a silver teapot and cream jug on the tray with the cups and saucers. She explained to me that they were her bridal presents. A good supper was given me and the children, hot waffles, beef steak, light rolls and good coffee. I noticed that no one else fared as well, for the rest of the guests had before them cold bread and fried bacon. I was glad that none of the few good looking carriages had stopped at our poor hostelry, for in case they had we would not have fared so well.

I deposited the children on their pallets and had just betaken myself to my couch when I heard a carriage drive up and an inquiry made if some ladies could sleep there. Presently a knock at my door, and when I opened it saw Julia Waring.[3] She begged to come in and lie on part of a pallet; her mother and sisters were, some in a little room with one small bed and the rest in the parlour on pallets. Of course I took her in, and made Nell give her her place in my bed.

At noon the next day we reached New Market, passing over so many of the scenes of Jackson's battles and defeats of the enemy.

My poor little tired Kenneth had ridden all that weary way in the hot sun on a saddle large enough for a man, and was nearly worn out. We soon caught up with the carriage containing Dr. Wilmer and the girls, but they soon left us behind as our horse had lost some of his speed and spirit in her long journey.

At Staunton we met again, and besides Dr. Wilmer and the girls, saw a great many people we knew.

The hotel parlours were crowded with refugees, officers, and all sorts and kinds of roving people.

The next day Mary drove up with a crowd of people in an old stage coach. She had at the last moment heard of its projected departure, and that there was in it a vacant place; so to avail herself of the opportunity she had to get ready in great haste. Not taking time to change her calico morning dress, she hastily got the children ready, and at the last moment seeing some forgotten articles, hastily took a sheet from the crib, tied them in it, and was ready when the old stage coach drove up for her, with a child on one arm and the white bundle on the other, while another child held to her dress. In this unbecoming plight she began her journey, and except when she met some one who knew her or her family, all the way missed the attention she had a right to expect, "all on account of the white bundle," she said.

After a day's rest at Staunton we went to Charlottesville, I to go to Amherst Court House, where I had been advised to go, both on account of its abundance of provision, and because it was out of the way of armies. At Charlottesville I parted with every one I knew, and set out, with Flora and the children for Amherst Court House. All the way I had traveled, whenever I saw by the roadside or in the distance, a neat white house with green blinds, and a grove of trees about it, I would wonder if I was to have one like it, quiet and shady; or if I saw a white or red brick house in a little town or by the road side, staring in the bright sunshine, without a tree or bit of shade, and no window blinds, my heart would sink with a fear that such a one would fall to my lot. Only the shade did I care for, and the quiet. It was very pleasant at Amherst, the hotel was an old fashioned place full of comfort and with no pretention.

There I established myself and sent for Mr. Richardson to whom I had been directed to apply for aid in getting a house, and settling the family. Two days after seeing him I spent in the effort to secure a house or a few rooms. He could be of no use as he was not well and could not go about to inquire. So Flora and I undertook to do it. We took several long walks in the neighborhood and asked at many places for rooms but none were for rent. At last after seeking at many places, Mr. Daniel, the hotel keeper, told me that if I would inquire at the old Powhattan House he thought there were some vacant rooms there that could be had rent free, as the place was in bad order and the owners did not rent it at all, but that one or two families were living in it. When we reached the front door of the Powhattan Hotel we found quite an imposing entrance, carved wooden pillars and some other traces of old time elegance. A long hall at least twenty feet wide ran through the house and several passages branched off from that. In the first room we entered all the windows were out and the frames broken to pieces. In the next the floor had sunk nearly a foot and a half, and the walls streamed with water from rain the day before. Another had a large hole in the ceiling and the hearth fallen in. It was such a place of desolation that I did not wonder that no rent was asked. We went to the head of the stairs on our way to explore the upper floor, and were met by a pleasant looking lady-like woman, very carefully dressed in bright green, the dress cut after a fashion some time gone by. A pink neck ribbon and a good deal of lace about her neck. It was a pleasant sight after all that sombre decay, so at her invitation we followed her into her room. All was bright and cheerful, and as neat as tireless work could make it. She told us she had made her temporary home there, but was well satisfied, and would be glad to have us for neighbors. Some rooms on the same floor were comparatively good, and we could get three adjoining.

I went to inspect them, and though they looked rather doleful, with the paper streaming down off the walls, the hearths sunk, and rat holes all around, I thought that what she could do I could to make it habitable, and so concluded to settle there at once, as my great anxiety was to get a place for my husband to come to, as he had said in his letter that as soon as we were settled he would join us.

That evening a dispatch came from my husband asking me to join him in Richmond as he was unable to travel. I was to leave the boys except Hunter, and with him and Nelly to join him in Richmond immediately. The next day I set out leaving the little boys in Harry's charge as Flora wanted to return to Charlottesville, and Harry promising never to let the little ones go out of his sight, I left them without many misgivings. Mrs. Daniel also promised to have an eye over them and I knew she would do it. So I started off lighthearted at the prospect of seeing my husband. Left Flora at her destination, and at four arrived at Richmond with the two children.

When I entered the room where he was, what a sight met my eyes! I at first could not believe that wreck was my husband. Worn and emaciated, and with hair snow-white, he was unable to move from his chair. "I have listened all day," he said, "for the sound of wheels stopping at the door and whenever a vehicle did stop expected to hear your voice." I remembered how in my heart I had blamed him for not meeting me at Staunton, but I had not the last idea that he was too ill for a journey by rail. He would not let me leave him for a moment, and his poor sad eyes followed me wherever I went.

I had been there for nearly ten days, and we had laid many plans for our future; one was to get a house and some reliable person to stay with the children, while I went with him to the Hot Springs where he would have a chance to recover. We thought of many places, but it struck me that Lexington would be the best, as I knew the Daileys had gone there, and I would have friends, besides it was just on the way to the Hot Springs.

As there was no present prospect of his being able to travel, we thought it best for me to take the children from Amherst and go to Lexington, when after settling them there in the care of some one, I could return for him and take him to the Springs. I was to set out the next morning; and while I was out on some business he sent to the Department to get 700 dollars back pay due him, and which he had been saving up for an emergency like the present. When I had returned, and had packed our baggage ready for the journey, I went in to sit with him in the twilight for the last time. I found him sitting with his face buried in his hands in an attitude of the deepest dejection. I put my arms around him and begged him to tell me what troubled him. He raised his head and looked at me with a face full of distress. "I can get no money for you," he said. "They have refused my pay because I am unable to go on duty. What will you do?" he sobbed out in the deepest grief. I wept, too, for him and me and the poor children, for I did not know what I could do. We were homeless as well as penniless.

We sat for a long time silent, and I thought it all over. I had $65 Confederate money in my purse, worth about fifteen. I tried to comfort him, telling him I was not afraid, that I could manage till something could be done, and that my only apprehension was for him, that he would be anxious and troubled about us. How thankful I was that he was where he could have the comforts of life, and some one to care for him. In the early dawn of the next morning I took leave of him and left him sad and lonely, sitting in his chair.

I went along the silent streets with the two little ones, and Mr. Green[4] to take us to the train. No sadder or heavier heart ever beat than mine was that morning. The sorrow at leaving him, the forlorn feeling of being homeless and with no money or friends that could help, almost deprived me of the power to think or act. I did think the matter over, however, while on the train, and devised a sort of plan. I had some dresses and jewelry I could sell if I could find a way to do it. No new or handsome goods were to be had now, and some people there were who had the heart to think of and buy finery.

We got to Amherst late in the afternoon and the children were at the train to meet me. They had a great deal to tell of what had transpired in my absence. Harry had taken good care of them, and Mrs. Daniel had done everything for their comfort. She had cut their hair and seen that they were neat. She laughed and told me of how Harry had obeyed my directions not to let the little boys be out of his sight by taking them with him on all his expeditions. He had kept them in the water swimming till the sun had blistered their skin and Mrs. Daniel had to remedy it at night by the application of cream. I had to remain several days at Amherst while I got the children's clothes ready to go to Lexington, and the day before I set out Harry left to go to Richmond to take care of his father. He had asked me to send him, and Harry wanted to go. When I went to the Hotel table I noticed a very genteel looking man in black clothes (which was an unusual sight in those days when nothing but homespun was respectable), and I asked Mr. Daniel who he was. He said no one knew anything about him, that his appearance at an out-of-the-way place like that, and with no ostensible business had created a good deal of comment. "Indeed," said he, "most people say he is a Yankee spy." He sat opposite our party at the table and I noticed him playing with the little ones when they left the dining room, but I did not notice that any one spoke to him, though he was polite to all at the table.

On the afternoon of my departure I had gathered my forces to go to the train. A cart had gone on with the trunks, and Mr. Daniel had my small valise while I led Hunter by one hand and Donald by the other. To my surprise when we issued forth I saw the "Yankee spy" waiting to accompany us. He came up with a bow, and took Hunter in his arms and Donald by the hand, and in the most natural manner walked on by my side. I was dumb with astonishment, and expected Mr. Daniel to rush to the rescue, which he did not, and I was fain to walk on, deeply mortified at the disgrace of being attended by any thing with the suspicion of Yankee attached to him. Mr. Daniel looked quite unconcerned when I stole a glance at him, and took leave of me at the train without any apparent uneasiness at my being so disreputably accompanied.

The man found us all seats, and took one himself with Hunter on his lap, and so we rolled along in the summer evening, I full of heaviness, and the children as merry and talkative as they could be.

I had time to think of my desperate circumstances. I had given Harry ten of the $65, and a small sum to Allan to take him to Staunton to get our furniture, and after taking enough to pay our way to Lynchburg, gave the rest to Mr. Daniel for our board, promising to pay the remainder when I could. What to do at Lynchburg, or how to go from there I knew not.

I only hoped, and I prayed fervently that we might meet some one who would assist us. It was nearly dark when we drew up at the Lynchburg station, and my Yankee without a word took Hunter in his arms, and Donald by the hand, motioned me to follow with the other children. I did so of course, and felt glad for the first time that I had even him for a protector. We pushed our way through the crowd and reached the hotel where I got a good room.

While I was brushing my hair, a knock at the door, and my guardian appeared for me to go to supper. I took all the children and followed him and was annoyed to find when we reached the dining room that we had a table to ourselves; that is I, and the children and the Yankee. He said very little and I tried to be polite but did not succeed very well. While we were at supper I noticed a gentleman come in, look at and speak to my escort, closely survey our party and walk on. Presently he walked back the same way and scanned us again. I left the table as soon as I had finished, with Nelly, and told the children to follow when they had done. Standing on the porch for a moment by the parlour window, I spied my bête noir coming up to me smiling. He told me that the gentleman who had passed through the supper room was an acquaintance that he had not seen for a long time; and that he had expressed surprise at seeing him with a large family, not knowing that he was a married man. I bowed stiffly and left him and went into the parlour, but presently he appeared bringing in Hunter.

In a few minutes I heard a sweet familiar voice and my dear Charley Tyler came in at the door.[5] His face was like the face of an angel to me then, for it was the promise of relief from my pressing trouble. I told him of my need, and he lent me money enough to pay my hotel bill and take me to Lexington. Oh! what a relief was that, for a constant vision of facing the Hotel keeper the next morning and telling him I had no money was before my eyes. I went up and put the little ones to bed and returned to him, when he proposed to go and see his wife and his aunt, Cousin E. Tyler.[6]

We went and in a few minutes after I had seen Lizzy and she and I had arranged for the disposal of the finery. They returned with me to the Hotel and I gave them into her charge, not, however, without a pang, for among them was the beautiful brocade shot with gold that my husband had brought me from Paris, and which I had had made to wear to a dinner party he was to give to Gen. Jackson and his staff.

The morning the dinner was to have taken place, the 1st of January Gen. Jackson marched away to Hancock with his army, and I gave the good things I had prepared to the passing soldiers, folded the dress up and put it away.

172

Aug.

Just before leaving Lynchburg I started Allan to Staunton for the things, so I, with Kenneth, Nelly, Donald, Roy, and Hunter, set out on the canal boat for Lexington.[7] The next day, August 17, we reached there, and in looking for my baggage I discovered that one piece was missing. That contained all the clean clothes of the three little boys. I could have wept, such a loss it was! No clothes were to be bought even if I had money to buy them, and I had been so many months gathering materials and making clothes for them in anticipation of our flight, and residence among strangers. The only answer I got to my inquiries for it was that some negroes had left the boat some miles down the river, and had probably taken it. There was no time for repining, for every one was hurrying off the boat, and my distress about the clothes was presently made to assume quite a different aspect in comparison with a greater trouble. Here I was landed in a strange town with only one dollar in Confederate money in my purse; that was to take us all to town, a mile distant, and our baggage also. To my surprise, the omnibus driver agreed to take all for one dollar, and though it was my last, I cheerfully gave it, and felt relieved that I could lean back and close my eyes, and try to gather courage for what was coming.

When we reached the Hotel,[8] I was glad to observe one familiar face among the crowd of strangers, that of Dr. Dailey.[9] It was a comfort indeed to see some one who knew us. He insisted on my going with the children to his house to stay, but I thought of his own eight mouths to feed, and of his delicate, pretty wife who looked worn and old from care and rough work, and declined.

We were shown to a room in the third story of the hotel with poor furniture and altogether uncomfortable, but the place was crowded and we could get no better accommodations. I was glad to get into it, however, where I could be at least free from people coming and going and chattering and laughing, and when night came was glad of the darkness and stillness, for I must think, think it all over and try to see something bright in the gloomy prospect; try to see something that could be done; that I could do, for who else was there to do it.

All the anxiety, perplexity, and distress though, did not and could not hide from my mental sight the melancholy figure sitting in the

173

chair at Richmond; of the weary eyes, the thin form and the white, white hair, that had grown white so suddenly. All night long my eyes were open gazing at the half-lighted window, or at the ceiling, for I could not sleep, and images of distress crowded before my eyes whenever I closed them. My thought was, what must I do when morning came; I had no money to pay even one day's board there.

I made up my mind to try and get a house or a room if a house could not be had, and go to it, for I expected the wagon with the things that day. Dr. Dailey kindly assisted me to get settled. He walked with me nearly a whole day in search of a house; all the next day and the next, with no success. One man had good rooms over some shop, but would not rent them to me because I had children.

In the mean time the wagon had arrived and was standing with its load in the middle of the street, and there was nowhere to store the things. Allan looked very much elated, and very important at having performed his mission so creditably, and indeed it was a remarkable undertaking for a boy of his years. He had to hire a wagon, horses, and driver, and see the things loaded and take care of them to their destination. He borrowed money also to pay expenses. Failing in our efforts to get a house, Dr. Dailey succeeded in finding a place to store the things, and alone I resumed my search for a house. After a week so spent, and large board bill at the Hotel as I knew, Dr. Dailey came one evening and told me that if I would walk out the Mr. McElwee's,[10] a short distance out of town, he thought they might take us in to board, at least for a short time. That was better than the hotel with its crowd of people and the hot, uncomfortable room, where my poor little Donald was already sick with fever, and could not get a breath of fresh air. So I not very hopefully set out to go with him.

The sweet air of the summer night was all around, heavy with perfume, and the stars were so bright that I enjoyed the walk greatly. As we approached the large pleasant house with its pretty porch and bay windows, looking so peaceful and cool as we went up the smooth walk, I feared that it was too good for me, that I could not hope for such a resting place as that.

The shadow of the porch concealed the faces of those who were sitting on the benches, but when the Doctor introduced me to Mrs. McElwee I straightway made my request, expecting almost certainly to be refused; but when in her sweet kind voice she said she would take us for ten days, not longer, as she had promised her rooms to other persons at the end of that time, I could not thank her for the choking sense in my throat. I could have wept, and was so near it that for some time I could not force myself to speak. I can never forget the sound of her voice when she said she could not refuse a stranger and a refugee; that all had a claim on her. She read her Bible too faithfully not to know what is said there of being kind to the stranger, and to sympathize with the "heart of the stranger." I went back to the Hotel elated at the thought of even ten days abode in that lovely place, ten days of rest. How I blessed her and loved her for her kindness, and I learned to love her better when I knew all her worth, and in all these years have relied on her unvarying friendship.

Just as I was leaving the Hotel a coach drove up, and Marshall got out, so haggard and thin that at first I did not know him. His eyes were sunken and cheeks hollow and even his voice so altered that it was strange to me. He had been paroled at the capitulation of Vicksburg, and had just succeeded in making his way to Virginia. He came to Lexington because the Virginia Military Institute had been so long his home, and was now the only one he had to go to. Sick and broken down he was, with sleepless nights, anxious days, with danger threatening every moment, with starvation as well as disease to contend with. I saw him leave for the Institute, and was thankful he had a place to go to.

We were soon all settled in a large airy room with a wide pleasant hall adjoining, where the little boys could sleep on pallets. We made the change not any too soon, for Donald was by that time quite ill, moaning constantly to be taken back to our "sweet grassy house." "Mama," he said, "did the Yankees drive us away?"

Mr. Logan was at the hotel when I left, and though I did not know him at all, I presumed on his being from Winchester, and asked him to see the Hotel keeper for me, and tell him that I had no money, and to assure him that he would be paid, as I expected some in a short time. This I promised, hoping soon to get the money from Lizzy Tyler for the dresses.

Mr. Logan went and paid the bill for me, which kindness I had not the least right to expect, as I had had no acquaintance with him or his family though we had lived in the same town for years.

A few days after I received $300 from the sale of my dresses, and joyfully repaid Mr. Logan.

My dreadful depression gradually wore off after I had been settled in my new habitation a day or two, and I again began to experience hope for the future. In proportion as my spirits rose I began to enjoy my surroundings. My eyes could never weary of gazing at the mountains. Morning, noon and night they wore an aspect so charming to me that I never wearied of them. At sunset they appeared in all their glorious splendour. "The Golden City of my God," I could not help exclaiming when I would see the billows of cloud coloured deep with gold, crimson and purple, hanging over their summits like a glorious canopy, and as the shadows crept down their mighty sides, shrouding the deep green fields and pleasant homes in darkness, peace and thankfulness always filled my soul. I also had my anxieties relieved by the letters I got from Richmond telling of the improvement in health of my husband, as well as better prospects for the future regarding money, the government having examined his case, and restored him to his privileges. Moreover, he was soon to be assigned to such duty as he was able to perform, and that would insure a certain salary.

I felt relieved of care for the time, and was able to entertain my kind host and hostess with accounts of the scenes I had witnessed, and experiences I had had while in the enemy's lines. They laughed when I said it looked strange to me to see gardens and fences; I had not seen a fence for nearly two years, till I got to Amherst Court House.

One morning I was sitting on the porch near the windows of the dining room, and overheard Mrs. McElwee as she washed her breakfast things say to her husband, "Dear, don't you wish I was as handsome and clever as Mrs. MacDonald." He being a slow man, answered slowly, "I like you as you are, Annie; you are handsome and clever enough for me." Kind and true, simple-hearted and loving they both are. Well he might think her lovely and clever, for the purity and earnestness of her soul shone in her clear grey eyes, and her soft voice and gentle ways made her presence a real pleasure. Besides that she was clever in planning, and energetic in executing, so that her household arrangements were perfect, and her husband was content to let her have her own way, for it was a wise and good way, and he could go on with his preaching without a care.

After their talk, all of which I did not hear as I moved from the window, she came out on the porch singing a hymn tune, and with a happy look on her face that her husband's kind words had left there. He is a Presbyterian of a peculiar school. I believe the thing in which they differ from others is that they persist in adhering to the old version of the Psalms that was used in the days of the Covenant. They sang them in the family worship night and morning, and the quaintness of the verse was sometimes ludicrous; utterly guiltless of poetry it was, for in the effort to adhere to the original they had lost sight of the beauty and the poetry also, only seeming to think it important to make the verses fit the tune. I was near losing my gravity one morning at prayers when they were singing that Psalm where David likens himself to the sparrow sitting alone on the house top. It seemed to me like a caricature and I found myself looking at them to see if they were not struck with the oddity of it, and I wondered how they could sing it with grave faces. I sang, too, but dwelt very lightly on the words.

The people did not come and I stayed a month and was happy. The children also began to look as they used to do. I could sit all day and watch the children rolling on the grass, and playing with Mrs. McElwee's children, and felt so glad that they could revive from the weary life they had had. I had made every exertion to get a house, as my husband had said that as soon as one could be had he would come, and at last heard of one that was vacant some miles in the country.

Mr. McElwee told me that the person who owned it was very anxious to let it to some one who could teach a school, as he had several daughters, and there were many others in the neighborhood who wished to go to school. What a prospect that was! Not only a house but the opportunity of making an addition to our very insufficient income. I joyfully mounted a horse and rode with Mr. McElwee to the place, seven miles up the bank of a creek, and when we reached it I was pleased with the place. The scenery around was lovely; the principal building was large mill, and around that had clustered many others, a store, a blacksmith shop, and most important of all the residence of the mill owner who was to be my landlord and employer.

I was shown the house we were to occupy, a small brick one, too small entirely, but I stood and surveyed the rooms and mentally arranged every article of furniture I had; fixed a place at one window for my husband's chair, and at another for mine, and concluded that cramped as it would be it would be home, and I should have husband and children all together. We were to go up there in a week. But a letter came that filled me with disappointment and distress; it said that my husband would not come to Lexington, that he, being able to attend to duty, had been assigned to it on a court martial, which might sit for months. He requested me not to go to the country but to get a house in town.

At last I heard of one and went to see it. It was a realization of my dreary imaginings when on my journey up the valley. I would picture to myself the place of rest I might find. A staring white house without a shutter, without anything pleasant near, not a tree or a bush, but a woodpile in front, and a dreary garden (with cabbage in it) that climbed the hill behind it. A seamstress with several children clothed in butternut jeans inhabited the other side, for there were two tenements.

I tried to be thankful and cheerful and would have been so if only my husband could have come; but after I had busied myself in arranging it, and making it as pleasant looking as my means permitted, it would seem so desolate when I remembered that I could not even expect him. I had beds and carpets and some table furniture, but no tables or chairs, so we ate off a chest, and sat on boxes. I had only a small skillet and a tea kettle for cooking untensils, but got a negro woman near to bake our bread, and if we had meat, to cook it for me.

Sept. 1863

I had many visitors, and made many friends, friends who were afterwards kind and serviceable; and for a while we did not want for anything, for many people sent me things, vegetables, milk, and butter, but that of course could not last, and we soon began to feel that it took more money than we could command to buy comfortable food and provide fuel.

Great as the inconveniences and privations seemed then to be, I would not have regarded them if I could have had my husband there. It seemed so hard that after so long a separation, I had come south to be with him, and at last had to be separated from him.

The sleepless nights and anxious days I spent in that house I always remembered whenever I used to pass it afterwards; a sense of pain I had always when I saw it; for there I made acquaintance with disappointment such as I had never known before and did not, or could not bear it patiently.

Marshall often came to see us, and we would laugh at our subterfuges, the cookery, the table and all. The little parlour was pleasant in the early autumn nights, and he would sit and tell us of the siege of Vicksburg, of the closeness of the enemy's lines, so close they were that they could talk to each other, the sentinels on either side, and exchange tobacco for sugar, etc. He told me of his being at Gen. Kirby Smith's headquarters, waiting for an order (he was aid to Gen. Smith then), that as the General was writing the order, a shell broke through the wall and exploded in the room.

He said the General went on writing after looking up for a moment, but that nothing kept him from beating a retreat but the presence of his commanding officer. He said he fairly shook with fear, as he looked at the dreadful thing and waited for it to explode. He said that at night in walking on the parapet and looking over into the valley where the dead were buried the whole surface of the ground would be lighted up with phosphorescent lights.

He bore the flag of truce and the terms of capitulation from Pemberton to Grant. He said that after a truce to bury the dead, or for any other purpose, when the batteries began to fire again on the besiegers, he would feel dreadfully to see the hand grenades thrown down on the very men with whom they had been but a few moments before talking and exchanging commodities.

Then I heard of the sad and mysterious disappearance of Commodore Maury's youngest son.[11] A gunboat was reported in a position that made it a probably easy capture, and men left the city and rode some distance down the river to try and take it, and many went to see it. Among the rest rode gaily away the boy just nineteen, a fair delicate golden haired boy, but full of spirit. His horse came back without its rider, and never was he seen again; his fate was never known. Every Federal prison was searched after the war but he was not found.

Nov. 1863

Soon Sue came to pay me a visit, and while she was there much company came, persons she or I knew, who were on their way to the springs, or to some resorts in the mountains. When the rainy weather began I found my house scarcely habitable. So hearing of one farther up in town I secured it and left my disagreeable quarters very willingly, for whenever it rained the water poured from the hill side and made a pool all around the house, which with the rain coming in at the door made it unbearable.

I succeeded in getting a comfortable house and after arranging it as well as my means would allow was quite well satisfied. I had a pine table made for the centre of the room which I covered with a red cloth I had brought from home, and with a gay carpet and some red curtains also brought from home, it assumed quite a cozy look. It was in November when I moved and bitter cold. Sue had gone to Richmond where she and Flora helped out their support by copying. The sum of Confederate money I received each month was not enough for the barest necessities, and many were the sleepless nights and anxious days I passed not knowing where or how to get the means to live. My husband sent me nearly all he had, but how insufficient! The little boys were without shoes, and the winter close upon us. So I made up my mind to ask Deaver, the shoemaker, to trust me for the payment and to make the shoes.[12] He was a Union man, but one who had never been unfriendly to the Southern people, and was truly kind and good. When I made my request, he never even asked me upon what my expectation of paying him was based, but merely said he would wait to be paid till the close of the war, and only asked me to agree to pay him in whatever money might be good at the time. So he took the measures of five pairs of feet, and made the shoes. Allan went to Richmond to take Harry's place as companion to his father, and all my dependence was on Harry. He rode about the country to try and find supplies at prices that I could command, and was in everything as useful and efficient as he could be.

Dr. Dailey told me that he thought the position of Commandant of the Post could be gotten for my husband, and that he would try to get it for him. He did, and succeeded. So it was decided that in December he was to join us at Lexington. Now came the care to have things comfortable, and to keep anxiety away from him. So I made every effort to get supplies of wood, vegetables, etc., before he came. One morning Mr. Tutwiler[13] sent me word that he had twelve cords of wood that I might have for five dollars a cord (the usual price in peace times), instead of thirty dollars, the present price. But other supplies we had none, and had nothing in the house but some flour and a very little sugar. I was told also that if I did not get my vegetables before the winter set in, they could not be had, so I determined to let my friend, Mrs. Powell,[14] know that I had a set of jewelry for sale, a beautiful set of onyx and pearls set in Etruscan gold. In a few days she came and told me that her brother, Capt. Charles Lee, had been very anxious to get something of the kind for a present to his bride. He was to be married the next week. I joyfully gave them to her, and she brought me that evening two hundred and fifty dollars for them, about twenty-five dollars in gold, but it was a fortune to me then, for I was enabled to buy a number of things which contributed to our comfort, as well as to pay for the wood.

Dec. 1863

I had many kind friends in Lexington who would have sent me anything they knew I stood in need of, indeed had done it a great deal when I first went there, but that could not be kept up, nor did I wish it, kind as they were, and as much as I valued them. A week before Christmas my husband came and Allan with him. Poor little fellow, how glad he was to be at home once more with his brothers and sisters. My husband was able to go all about, but such a change was wrought in him, not only physically but mentally, that he was no longer like the same person, his form was withered and shrunken, his face pale and anxious, his spirit grieved and disappointed, partly from not being able to take an active part in the war, and partly from having been, as he thought, unjustly dealt by, and his zealous and consciencious service not appreciated. He seldom spoke of the bitterness he felt, but he was never the same man. "A wounded spirit who can bear?" Perhaps many of us know what a wounded spirit is, but few are so proud as to bear it in silence, and fewer still are

181

so high-minded and patriotic as not to speak a word of blame of the men who did him a deadly injury (as he thought was done when his military efficiency was called in question), because those men were bravely fighting his country's battles, and enduring till the end should come.

After he came things were little better as far as comforts were concerned, but I was satisfied because he was at home, and I could attend to his wants as no one else could, though in Richmond he had every attention from his daughters that they could give. His time was mostly spent in attending to the duties of his office, though he seldom left the house. A room in it served for his office. In the evening as he sat by the fire with the children clustered around, he would be amused at their sallies, but at other times he sat sad and silent in his arm chair, rarely smiling, but listening to what was said. More generally he would be lost in thought, often broken in upon by sighs.

A dreary winter it was. It seems as I look back at it, the grayest and dreariest I ever knew. The pinching to make a pound of meat serve to dine seven hungry children besides the servant; the coarse fare, the pinching in every thing, and that sad, hopeless figure always in the chair.

The children kept well, but they must have been half-starved, for all that was good and delicate I prepared for their sick father. The neighbors often sent nice things, but it was all used to tempt him to eat. Marshall remained at the Institute for a few weeks after he came, but he was shortly exchanged and left to join Gen. Joe Johnston's army.

We had many visitors, people whom we had known passing through the town would call, and I could almost laugh now to think of the dinner I used to have when a friend from the army or a fellow refugee would come.

I always tried to make things appear as well as possible, for I shrank from seeming so very poor, and above everything else I tried to keep unpleasant things from the eyes and ears of the weary one whose life seemed threatened with heartbreaking anxiety, as well as disease. So when a friend came and the talk would restore something of the old fire to his weary eyes, there should be no unlucky exposure of want or trouble to mar the passing gleam of pale sunshine.

182

Feb. 1863[15]

I did my best to keep the children neat and comfortable, but soon there was nothing more to do but mend and patch, for there were no materials to work on. So having much time at my disposal I spent it in drawing, so as to learn well what I might afterwards be able to teach. I took long walks to sketch, and used to be greatly revived by the exercise as well as the influence of the beautiful scenery around the little town. Variety enough there was, rocks, mountains and river furnished good subjects for my pencil, but how often I would lay it down in despair because I could not put on my paper the purple peaks the gloomy gorges clad in their veil of gold as they used to be at sunset, with the smooth and placid river at their feet, reflecting on its shining surface all the grandeur and loveliness of the scene. At any rate I learned a great deal I did not know how to do before. I could take time to the task, for I had more of that than I wanted. How gladly I would, as in the times gone by, have seen in my possession rolls of cloth and linen, and how busy would my fingers have been night and day cutting and making comfortable clothes for my darlings. I always had something neat for them to wear to church, and did not grieve over their patches, but ever anxious and taking thought for the morrow, I could see the day not far distant when there would be no clothes to patch.

All this while we had ill news of our army. It was not beaten, at least not signally, but it was retiring; steadily our lines were drawing in. At least they did not maintain their position after driving back the enemy. All this was disheartening, for it seemed to portend a more prolonged struggle.

With all the gloom of our surroundings there was still some brightness. At night when the children would gather in and chat and laugh, the gaiety would be contagious, and I would for a time be merry with them. Later in the winter came Rosser's brigade, and encamped near the town.[16] Will and Ed were with it, Ed commanding the 11th Virginia Cavalry, and Will on the staff. They often came, bringing news of the army and its successes and reverses, and of persons and things; and they would succeed in amusing their father with tales of their camp life, and anecdotes of their friends and acquaintances.

Others also came, and the evenings would be often quite gay with the pleasant little circle of friends gathered in the parlour, which though it had a carpet, boasted no furniture but a pine table, an old sofa and a few chairs. The pine table, however, was covered with a jaunty red cloth, and the windows were draped with red curtains brought from home; the sofa was covered with flowered calico, and all looked quite bright and comfortable. In this salon we received many distinguished visitors, from military as well as from civil life. If they stayed all the evening, as often they did, tea would be brought up, dreadful tea; I shudder now to think of it, sweetened with brown sugar.

This the poor soldiers thought the greatest of luxuries; bread without butter, and that was all. And I, I actually used to find myself forgetting everything but that I was pouring out tea for, and entertaining agreeable people, and never felt once humiliated because I had nothing better to offer.

The Spring came, and Rosser departed, taking with him most of our brightness and pleasure. He could not tarry there though the soldiers and the young ladies of the town were happy together, dancing and merrymaking; for the grass in the valley had grown and he must hasten to open the spring campaign, to gallop after that insolent enemy who now ventured further into that valley than they had ever before dared. They could march at any season for they had food for their horses; ours had only the grass, and they had to wait for it to grow.

Flora came up from Richmond, and as the spring had opened things began to look more bright and cheerful. She was so gayhearted that the house seemed sunnier. The children were delighted at her coming, and she had a reviving influence on us all. She was young, and her spirits never flagged. The time for gardening had come, and my husband could interest and occupy himself with it, teaching the little boys how to work it, and watching them do it, as well as listening to their remarks. It seemed so odd to me not to have any spring sewing to do, no garments to cut and make, and not to be busy with household affairs, but I spent my time with my drawing, and brought home from my walks, instead of lonely, dreary mountains grey and sombre, trees with bare branches, and colorless skies; bright landscapes, masses of trees with thick foliage, and the shining water reflecting it all. This I saw, but pencil of mine could never portray the color and beauty of that scenery, even if it had been better skilled than it was, but I could always see something new and beautiful, and my whole being would be lifted up and taken out of the troubles and anxieties that surrounded me.

June 1864

With June came news of dreadful battles, that of the Wilderness and Spottsylvania.[17] Will received a dreadful wound in the side at the last named battle and was brought to Lexington where we could attend to him. Our army seemed to be in retreat, though the battles were victories for us. I had failed to keep up a knowledge of current events, and in my absorbing anxieties the news of reverses did not afflict me as they formerly would have done. I believe that I was growing hopeless, for the prospect of peace was still so far off, even though we had lost so much and struggled so hard.

Though I never for one moment dreamed of the failure of the South to establish her independence, I often felt my heart sink when I heard of the scarcity of food for our armies and people; and I knew that our men who were in the field were in want of everything.

Will had been with us for a short time when we were startled by the intelligence that Hunter[18] was advancing up the valley with no one to oppose him, and our army was nearly all over the Blue Ridge, that he was destroying all as he went, and would undoubtedly reach Lexington. As many troops as could be collected were sent to meet them, among them the cadets of the V. M. Institute. A fierce battle at New Market in which the cadets took part, beat back their advance guard for a time, but there was not sufficient force to hold their host long in check. The cadets, many of them old enough to be in the army, behaved very gallantly, considering they had never before been under fire, but I was told by an actor in the scene, Charles Anderson of Richmond, that the little fellows, mere children in size and years, behaved as well as the rest, and were even more eager to join the fray. He said that after the battle when they were collecting the dead, that he had picked up the body of a little fellow who he knew, and who looked not more than ten years old, so small and childish he was. He said he found him lying in a fence corner as if asleep, his musket at his side, and he picked him up as easily as he would have done an infant.

June 12th, the approach of the enemy was announced. Everybody connected with the army prepared to fly. Gen. Smith[19] departed with the corps of cadets, and Gen. McCausland[20] after burning the bridge that led to the town, made good his retreat, leaving the terror-stricken people to their fears, and to the tender mercies of the enemy. My husband determined to go a few miles into the country, and remain till they had passed on their way. So he prepared to leave with Harry in an ambulance. As he stood on the porch giving orders for his journey, he looked so little able to undertake even a short journey, that it filled me with misgivings. He spoke cheerfully of coming back, but in the morning he had told me that if he never saw me again, that I must bring up the children as he would like to have them brought up, his boys to be true and brave, and his little girl modest and gentle. He also said that if his property should be confiscated, as he was sure it would be, that I had a right to one-third which could not be taken from me; that if I could struggle on till the close of the war, I would have abundance.

I scarcely heard what he said, for I felt that the future was nothing if only the terrible present was not here, portentous and dreadful, and I thought only of his going, and that he might not ever come back.

Will had gone off in another direction, on horseback, and when the ambulance had driven off with my husband and Harry we all felt lonely enough, and filled with apprehension.

Early the next morning the enemy began the bombardment of the town, imagining McCausland still there. Some shells went through the houses, frightening the inhabitants terribly. They were posted on the opposite bank of the river, and bombarded quite vigorously. Our house was struck in several places but no harm done. Indeed I was past being frightened by shot and shell. Nevertheless, I, the children and Flora retreated to the basement and waited there till the storm should be over. After a while there was a lull, and Flora, wishing to see what was going on, raised the window and put her head out.

Just as she did so, a piece of shell struck the window sill, knocking off a large piece.

No one looked out any more. At high noon the bombardment ceased, and soon through the deserted streets of the little town poured the enemy, coming in at every point. A troop rode by our house, Averill's cavalry.[21] Two negro women rode at the head of the column by the side of the officer. We had shut all the doors and pulled down every blind, but peeped, to see without being seen. Looking down, Flora espied Hunter sitting on the front steps earnestly gazing at the passing soldiers. She immediately raised the window and called to him, "Hunter, are you not ashamed to be looking at those Yankees? Go under that porch, and don't you look at them again." Poor little fellow, perhaps he thought they were old friends. He retired under the porch, and did not emerge till they were all gone by.

We have been engaged all the morning in hiding the things we thought might be taken from us, among the rest a few hens and chickens that I had been trying to raise. The children quickly caught and transported them to a garret where we also put a few other things that might tempt them, the silver, etc. I was passing by the stairs and saw Hunter sitting on the lowest step crying bitterly. I stopped to kiss and comfort my poor little three year old baby,[22] and asked him what the matter was, when amid his sobs, he said "The Yankees are coming to our house and they will take all our breakfast, and will capture me and Fanny."

Fanny was Nelly's doll which was nearly as large as he was, and who he had been taught by her to consider quite as important a member of the household.

We remained as quiet as possible all the afternoon while the town was alive with soldiers plundering and robbing the inhabitants. Some came into our yard, robbed the milk house of its contents and passed on their way, picking up everything they could use or destroy. About four o'clock I heard a knock at the front door, and cautiously looking out before opening it I saw Maj. Quinn. He came in, and I must plead guilty to having been glad to see at least one Yankee. He offered to remain at the house to prevent any annoyance to us or injury to property, and seated himself in the porch. Of course no marauding parties came near while he was there. I declined his offer to stay during the night, as I thought the sight they had had of him in the porch would serve to warn them off. The next morning a squad of men with an officer came to search for provisions and arms. They laughed when on examining the pantry they found only a half barrel of flour and a little tea, all the supplies we had; but their laughter was immense when on ascending to the garret they saw the hens and chickens running over the floor.

The next day, Sunday, we were constantly hearing of outrages inflicted on the towns people; breaking into houses and robbing them. I was too well used to those little affairs to think them very severe, but was intensely amused when I heard of their entry into Dr. Madison's neatly kept and well furnished house, carrying off molasses and preserves in pieces of old china, and wrapping up flour in Mrs. Madison's purple velvet cloak.[23]

At sunset we saw a man led by with a file of soldiers. The children came in and told me that it was Capt. Matt White; that they were taking him out to shoot him.[24] I thought they knew nothing about it and gave the matter no attention. Sunday began a fearful work. The Virginia Military Institute with all the professors' houses was set on fire, and the distracted families amid the flames were rushing about trying to save some of their things, when they were forced to leave them officers standing by for the purpose. Not even their books and papers could they save, and scarcely any clothes. Col. Williamson,[25] the only officer of the Institute who remained in the village, and he had to keep quiet and say nothing when his daughters were driven from their house and all its contents burned, even the old black mahogany desk where hidden away was a yellow lock of his wife's hair, and her letters tied up with a blue ribbon.

This, one of his daughters told me, as if it was the greatest loss of all. One officer, Captain Prendergast,[26] knew Mrs. Gilham's[27] brother, Col. Haydon, of the U. S. Army, and for his sake granted her the particular favor of removing some of her household goods, which after she had succeeded in removing, she was compelled to stay by with her little boys to guard. There she sat through the afternoon by her household goods, to keep them from being stolen by negroes and soldiers, and through the long night she remained at her post, and not a man dared to help her or offered to take her place. All the warehouses at the river, all the mills and buildings near were burned, all in flames at the same hour, and it really seemed as if the Evil One was let loose to work his will that day. The town people were so frightened that few dared to show themselves on the streets, and Yankees and exultant negroes had their full satisfaction. Negroes were seen scudding away in all directions bearing away the spoils of the burning barracks—books, furniture, trunks full of the clothes of the absent cadets were among the spoils. The new and beautiful carpets and curtains of the Society Hall were appropriated by the thieves. My cook brought home a beautiful brocade curtain among her spoils, which she used as a counterpane and which she was glad enough to hide a few weeks after when the legitimate reign was restored.

They all held high Carnival. Gen. Crook had his headquarters on a hill near me, in a large handsome house belonging to Mr. Fuller[28] and as it was brilliantly lighted at night and the band playing it was quite a place of resort for the coloured population. They must have been treated with great civility by the Yankees, for in the afternoon I was sitting on the porch, and there passed by a very fat and very black negro woman who I knew well as she often worked for me. She was arrayed in a low-necked short-sleeved brown silk dress, with a large pink rose pinned on her breast, and several others fastened in her wooly hair. In her hand she held another red rose which she smelled vigorously, fanning herself slowly at the same time. She did not look towards me, but stopped before the gate and called the cook who put her head out of the basement window. "Are you going to the camp Susan?" she asked. "I am. I went up there yesterday and the white gentlemen treated me like a queen and invited me to come and spend the evening. You had better come." Susan, with an expression of contempt drew her head in without replying, and the lady continued her walk.

We were told that they would leave on Tuesday, which we rejoiced at; and when the time arrived the signal was given to depart. Some had already gone, when on looking down the street in the direction of Gov. Letcher's house I saw it on fire. I instantly put on my bonnet and ran down there to help Mrs. Letcher as I was able, for though many persons were in town who knew her better than I did, none dared to leave their houses. I was too used to their ways to be afraid of them, and so in breathless haste got there in time to see the house enveloped in flames. Mrs. Letcher had consented to entertain two officers at her house, that she had been civilly asked to do. They had spent the night, and eaten breakfast with the family, sociably chatting all the while.

When they rose from breakfast, one of them, Capt. Berry, informed Mrs. Letcher that he should immediately set fire to her house.[29] He took a bottle of benzine, or some inflammable fluid, and pouring it on the sofas and curtains in the lower rooms, applied a match, and then proceeded up stairs. Mrs. Letcher as soon as she became aware of his purpose, ran up stairs, and snatching her sleeping baby from the cradle, rushed from the house with it, leaving everything she had to the flames.

Lizzy[30] ran up stairs and went into her father's room to secure some of his clothes, and had hung over her arm some of his linen, when Capt. Berry came near her with a lighted match, and set fire to the clothes as they hung on her arm. He then gathered all the family clothes and bedding into a pile in the middle of the room and set fire to them.

When I reached the scene, Mrs. Letcher was sitting on a stone in the street with her baby on her lap sleeping, and her other little children gathered around. She sat tearless and calm, but it was a pitiable group, sitting there with their burning house for a background to the picture.

Some officers who had stayed all night at Mr. Matthew White's and breakfasted there, had in reply to the anxious inquiries of the poor old mother about her son who had been arrested some days before, assured her that he was in the jail just opposite her house; that he was temporarily detained, but would be immediately released.

That afternoon as I sat by the window I saw a wagon pass on its way up the street, and in it a stiff, straight form covered with a sheet. It was poor Matt White on his way to his mother. He had been taken out to the woods and shot as the children had said, and had been left where he fell. Mrs. Cameron's[31] daughters hearing the firing, went down to the place when the party had left, and finding the poor body, stayed there by it all night to keep it from being mangled by animals.

No men were near to do it, and they kept their watch till word could be sent to his parents where to find him; and that was not done till Tuesday evening, for no one could pass to the town till the troops had left.

The next day, Wednesday, was his funeral. Everybody who knew the family was there, I among the rest. We went to the cemetery and saw the poor fellow buried, and I turned and walked sadly away with some ladies; we parted at a corner and I went on alone. Soon I met Mrs. Powell, my dearest and most intimate friend. She looked very pale, and turned to me as if she would speak, but passed on. I thought it strange that she should pass me in that way, but went on home without following to know what the matter was, as was my first impulse. I sat on the porch in the twilight, and one of the neighbor's little boys came and climbed up on the porch till he reached my ear. Holding to the balustrade he leaned over and whispered, "Did you know that Col. MacDonald and Harry were killed and were lying in the woods fifteen miles from here?"

I got up and called Allan and sent him up town to ascertain if there was any truth in what the child had said. I hardly dared to hope it was not true, for had I not just had before my eyes an example of their relentless and wanton cruelty?

While Allan was gone the father of the child, the drummer of the Institute, came and told me that it was true that they had been attacked, but that there was no certainty that they had been killed; that it was thought they were prisoners. The next day Mr. McDowell and some other gentlemen came and told me that the place where they had encamped had been visited, and that the body of Mr. Wilson,[32] an old gentleman at whose house they had been staying, and who had accompanied them, had been found; but that my husband and Harry had been certainly carried off, as no trace of them had been found. Their trunks and all their property except horses, wagons and arms had been burned. Mr. Wilson was not quite dead when found; a sabre cut across the head had struck him down, and after he fell a pistol had been fired at his temple, so near that his eye was shot out, and his face filled with powder.

June 1864

Dark days of misery and uncertainty followed, and one day a young lady from the country drove up and asked to see me. She brought a bundle of half-burned papers which I recognized as some of those belonging to my husband. She was the niece of Mr. Wilson and had gathered them up at the scene of the capture. Many, many days passed by, it seemed months, when one afternoon I was sitting hopelessly in my room, I heard a noise of shouting on the street, and voices as if in exultation over something. I had scarcely time to think what it was, when a step on the stairs, coming up three at a time, announced my Harry. There he was, covered with rags and patches, an old hat on his head, and pair of the roughest shoes on his feet, but his eyes were bright, and his smile the same sweet one. His first question was, "Where is Papa? I thought he had been sent home." When told No, a shade of sorrow and anxiety clouded his face, and he told us when he had parted with him, three days after the capture. "I brought in two Yankee prisoners, and that is what the shouting was about."

He and his father had gone to the house of Mr. Wilson, reaching there the same day on which they left home, a distance of about fifteen miles. Almost as soon as they reached there they received information that there was danger of a raiding party visiting the house.

After consultation my husband and Mr. Wilson concluded to leave the house and go to a secluded spot on the mountain where no enemy was at all likely to go. Mr. Wilson took some of his valuables, plate, etc., and some of his negro men with him, while my husband and Harry had their ambulance laden with some of the articles they had carried from home. And so they set out on the day after their arrival at Mr. Wilson's for the mountain.

They had quietly waited at their retreat for a day or two, when on the third day they noticed near them as they were at breakfast, a horse feeding, which seemed to have strayed from its owner.

Soon after a man appeared, looking for the horse, which having secured he led away. He had seen the party, and closely scrutinized their situation and surroundings. Mr. Wilson expressed some uneasiness, as, he said, the man was an avowed Union man, and not by any means an honest and reliable one. He regretted that they had not crossed the river and pitched their tents, and so made their safety certain.

In the afternoon of the same day they were all in camp, my husband asleep in his ambulance, and Mr. Wilson sitting near. A young man named Greenlee who with Harry and the negroes helped to make up the party, was with Harry lying on the grass.[33]

Suddenly they heard the sound of horses' feet, and a voice calling on them to surrender. On looking up Harry espied three horsemen rapidly advancing toward them. He instantly raised his gun which was close at hand and fired, emptying one of the saddles. The others wheeled about and rode off, taking the wounded man with them.

Of course all was confusion and alarm in the camp, and they hastily gathered their effects together, having determined to cross the river as soon as it should be dark.[34]

Their position was in the edge of the wood on a hillside, with a fence separating their camp from an open field which had been cleared of woods but in which the stumps remained. About sunset they saw advancing through this field, and not sixty yards from them, a party of fifty men. They called on them to surrender, but were answered by shots from Harry, my husband and Mr. Wilson. Young Greenlee had fled as soon as he became aware of their approach. The party then charged the camp, but were again met by shots from the three defenders of the position. They halted and poured in a volley of musketry which did not much damage except to wound my husband in the hand. Harry and Mr. Wilson, as well as my husband, continued to load and fire, succeeding in keeping them at a distance till all their powder was spent, and the fence was carried and they surrounded.

Even then they would not have surrendered, Mr. Wilson being disposed to continue the fight, but for the thought of the sacrifice of Harry's life as they must certainly all have been killed in so unequal a contest. At last with oaths and curses they took possession of their prey. One officer, infuriated at having been kept at bay so long by two old men and a boy, struck a blow at Mr. Wilson with his sabre, and he fell to the ground with what was to all appearance his death wound.

Not satisfied with that, he came near, and stooping, fired his pistol into his temple, so near did he place it, that the ball glancing slightly, took his eye out, and his whole face was filled with the powder. He laid in the woods after the party had left, all night, and in the morning one of his negro men who had fled from the fray came to his family and informed them where he was, and that he had been killed. They, the enemy, had burned his house, and his family had taken refugee in an outhouse.

A year after I visited the spot where the fight took place. There were the piles of ashes still where the trunks had been burned, with leaves of books and scraps of paper lying about. The prints of their footsteps were still there, and marks of the bullets on the fences and trees. The seats they had improvised, pieces of boards resting on logs. I went to Mr. Wilson's house and saw him. He had recovered from his wound, but his eye was gone, and the whole side of his face black with the powder that the wretch had blown into it. He was still living with his family crowded into the cabin to which his family had retreated when the house was burned, and seemed to have little heart to try for better things.

In the meantime the others turned their attention to Harry and his father. My husband's cap was seized from his head, his pockets searched and all things taken. He had about eight dollars in silver in his pocket which he took out when they went to search him, and secretly gave to Harry, who held it tight in his clenched hand while he was undergoing the search. When the commanding officer came up, Harry recognized Major Quinn. He of course did not know my husband and did not see the indignities offered him, as he was not among the foremost who came up. Their beds and all their property were burned, as well as their trunks; all except Mr. Wilson's plate which they took, as well as the horses.

Maj. Quinn was as civil and merciful as he dared to be. He had my husband put into his ambulance with Harry, and did what he could for him. Just at dark they began their painful descent from the mountain, leaving Mr. Wilson lying alone in the woods. That night they reached the Federal camp at the river bank, where they remained all night. A small village was near and they were ordered to go to a rough board house to spend the night. Many soldiers were there, and one lay on a pallet dying, the same, Harry thought, that he had wounded when the three charged on them. Harry found a board, and went and pulled up grass with which he made a sort of bed for his father, and covered him with a blanket he had brought on his shoulders. As they left the place the next day they were burying the man who was wounded, he having died in the night.

They crossed the river that morning where Gen. Hunter had his headquarters, and my husband was immediately taken to him. He was met at the tent door by David Strother who was aid to Hunter.[35] He looked insolently at him turned around without any greeting, and shut the door in his face.

When the journey was resumed in the morning it was not in his own ambulance, but in a wagon loaded with boxes of nails, and on the bottom of which, loose pieces of iron, horse shoes, etc., rolled about with the motion of the vehicle. In the uncomfortable conveyance, seated on a box, for three days they pursued their toilsome journey; up tremendous heights, with only a narrow shelf cut out of the mountain side for a road, and down steep declivities, dangerous even when not crowded in between heavily laden wagons and toiling teams that often from sheer exhaustion would give out and slip backwards, pressing on the vehicle behind, and rolling it off the road and down the precipice. This occurred more than once, and they did their best to keep their wagon as far behind every other as possible, but if they were seen to lag, they were hurried on.

Poor faithful Harry drove; and with one arm supported his father who was obliged to lean on him, there being no support for his weak frame and nothing to prevent his being jostled off the seat at every lurch of the wagon. They were crossing the mountain between the Peaks of Otter, and every hour there was danger of their being backed down and pushed off the edge of the road over the frightful precipice. At night when they stopped they had some fat meat and crackers given them but a sick man could scarcely eat such food, and as they were not allowed to make coffee, and no one permitted to give them any, they would have been completely exhausted if Harry had not discovered in the wagon a bag or package of ground coffee. This he gave his father from time to time and it had the effect of strengthening him.

The people on the route had been exasperated at the treatment some of their number had undergone at the hands of Crook and Averill, who the week before had passed that way on their march to join Hunter.[36] Not a few shots were fired at the passing columns, and not a few saddles emptied.

Fearful vengeance was visited on every man who was seen with a gun in his hands; and one day a shot was fired from a tree near the roadside, and the next moment half a dozen muskets were pointed at the place from whence it proceeded; a wounded man fell to the ground, and in an instant he was stripped and left lying by the roadside dead, as they passed on their way. Every night the wagon my husband and Harry were in, was dragged up close to Hunter's headquarters. No one spoke to him, no courtesy or kindness was extended him, and only the coarsest food furnished him. They had passed Liberty[37] and were on their way to Lynchburg when they came up with the main body. Then it was told my husband that he was to accompany Gen. Hunter alone, and that Harry was to return and recross the mountain with the other prisoners. The poor boy heard with bitter grief that they were to be separated, for he knew that only his care and kindness could keep his father from severe suffering.

At parting, his father told him to make his escape at the earliest possible opportunity, as being no soldier he would be accused of being a bushwhacker. "He told me," said Harry, "never to let them see that I was afraid of them, but to bear all they would inflict like a soldier. I knew afterwards what that meant. It was that when they took me out to be shot not to let them see any fear." While Harry stood waiting for the order to march with the prisoners, he heard Capt. Berry order his father to march off after the party with Gen. Hunter which was then moving; he to go on foot in the rear of the detachment. This he refused to do, being unable to walk; whereupon Capt. Berry ordered a rope to be brought with which he was to be dragged by the neck at the rear of one of the wagons.

Harry watched to see what would be done, and poor fellow, burning with indignation at the insult to his father, no doubt would have defended him at the risk of his own life, but for some reason the design was relinquished, and he was placed in the wagon. Harry did not tell me of this then; not till long afterwards, and I was thankful that I did not know it at the time.

He told me of the silver money his father had handed him when he was being searched; that he had held it tightly clasped in his hand and it had escaped notice while he was undergoing the search. Though after his escape he suffered for everything, shoeless, hatless, ragged and hungry, not a cent of it did he spend to purchase for himself any alleviation from hardship, but kept and brought it home where he knew it was needed. When he was marched off with the prisoners they retraced their steps and again passed through Liberty, and began to ascend the Big Sewell mountain he thinks,[38] but has never been certain where they were, as the country was strange to him. He was with a large company of prisoners, many civilians who had been taken as hostages, or from mere wantonness. Mr. Philips, an old gentleman, principal of the Staunton Female Institute, and an Episcopal Clergyman, was among them, and some others that he knew. All were fatigued and wretched, but that did not prevent their captors from urging them on to their utmost speed, for they were even then pursued, and flying before Early's army, who were close on their steps.

Files of soldiers were in front and rear, and on each side of the column of prisoners, a line of soldiers marched. They climbed mountains by steep and difficult roads, marching night and day, such was their haste, only stopping to rest two hours and prepare their food. A half pint of meal or flour was given each one, with a piece of fat bacon an inch square. This they could not cook, at least not so as to be eatable, so the poor child had to march on hungry and sleepy and nearly dead with fatigue.

The second night they stopped for a few hours sleep, and Harry was determined if possible to effect his escape. They had been allowed to go into a dilapidated barn to sleep, and at dawn in the morning Harry moved a loose board in the floor and slipped through and clung with both hands and feet to the rafter so that he could not be seen. In this painful position he remained, clinging with desperate effort, till the preparations for the march were completed, and they all moved away. After the column was in motion it was stopped and the prisoners counted, as some one was suspected of having remained behind. A Lieutenant and squad of men rode back to the barn, and after a diligent search found him. The officer had him dragged out, and cocking his pistol, held it cocked to his eye with a buckskin glove on the hand that held it. The slightest movement would have sent the ball through his brains; he knew it, and expected him to shoot, but remembering his father's admonition to show no fear, he looked steadily in the face of the brute, and answered not his cursings. He abandoned his purpose of shooting, if he had such a purpose, and ordered his soldiers to make him run at the point of the bayonet, which they held close enough to pierce him if he slackened his speed. Thus he ran a mile before he reached the party of prisoners who had been sometime on the march. Poor boy, in that race his shoes were lost, and his feet torn with the thorns and briers through which they made him run.

For ten days they pursued that dreadful march; by night and by day the weary prisoners were urged on. They could not stop to rest more than a few hours, for the pursuer was on their track and they were afraid to tarry. Up the steep mountains my poor boy toiled, with them, so worn out and exhausted that he often fell asleep while walking along, and when a halt was made he threw himself down and slept instead of trying to cook his raw flour and meat as the others did. After a few days his feet were so sore, and he was so chafed and galled by the unceasing march in the hot weather that he became almost frantic. He said he was desperate enough to do something worthy of their wrath, so that they would put an end to him. He had spoken to a young man named Effinger[39] who marched next him in the column and proposed to escape; to this his companion agreed, and it was understood that they were to make the attempt together. One day they had halted about noon near some water. They were near the top of a great mountain, the Warm Spring

Mountain he thought, and though the others were allowed to go to the spring by twos, he was not allowed to go at all, as the officer had several times had occasion to threaten him for making a disturbance. Some of the prisoners brought water and handed it around to those who were not allowed leave the ranks. It was a long time getting to him, as he was near the last. His lips were parched and cracked with the heat and dust, and just as the order to march was given, a dipper of the precious water was handed him. As he put it to his eager lips, a great brute twice his size and weight and three times his age snatched it from him, although he had already had some. He did not drink it, however, for Harry flew at his throat, seized the dipper from him, bore him to the ground and pommelled him well. He was taken off the man, and told that whatever the cause, if he made any more disturbance he would be handcuffed. That night he determined to risk all and attempt to escape.

The column had stopped at dusk to cook their rations, and had been marching some hours when my boy began to think the time had come. It was a bright moonlight night, and broad strips of white light would now and then lay across the road between the dark shadows of the pines and hemlocks that darkened the mountain side.

They had begun the descent of the great mountain, and the road was steep and rocky with a towering height on one side, and a steep precipice on the other, down which nothing could be seen but black darkness. He said his heart beat so loud that he was afraid the soldier who walked by his side at the outside of the column would hear it, so excited and wrought up he was. He had arranged to touch Effinger when he was ready, as he marched just in front of him. This he did, and waited till another bright patch of moonlight had been passed. Effinger took no notice, and when he was again in the shadow he touched him again—still no response, so he resolved to go without him. He had held his blanket unrolled, and in a position to throw it from him and over the head of the soldier that flanked him, and as soon as the next strip of moonlight was passed, and the friendly shadow of the trees intervened, he threw it over the soldier's head, darted by him and swung himself down the steep precipice below. He fell, or slipped, for about twenty feet till stopped by the root of a tree. Here he lay perfectly still, while musket after musket was discharged down the dark mountain side after him, but they dared not pursue, for they were in a dangerous country, and it would take time, time which was of so much importance to get them and their prey out of the reach of their pursuers.

Harry lay still till he heard them moving on and not until the last footstep died away did he venture to move. He then left the slippery mountain side, climbing down holding by roots and bushes, till he came to more level ground, where he could in comparative safety lie down. Exhausted, he soon fell asleep, and if danger was near, he happily was oblivious to it. Not till the bright morning light woke him did he arouse from his deep sleep.

Stiff and sore, covered with the cold dew from the mountain mists, the poor boy rose and looked around to see if an enemy was near. He had no idea where he was, and no hope of finding a habitation. But he determined to get something to eat if possible, so he made his way over rocks and fallen trees, often stumbling from weakness and exhaustion, till he was at last rewarded by hearing a cock crow. Straight he made for the place whence proceeded the delightful sound, and soon came to a house, a poor one indeed, but still one in which he might find a breakfast.

Boldly he walked up to the door, when a number of dogs rushed out to greet him in so demonstrative a manner that he was forced to ascend a gate post till he could become better acquainted with their intentions towards him. After he had gained the place of safety he called loudly for some one to drive away the dogs. A woman looked out, but went quietly back to her business inside the house, not seeming inclined to encourage the entrance of so doubtful a looking figure.

And no wonder! without a hat, part of an old shoe on one foot and none on the other, ragged clothes, matted hair and soiled hands, he looked indeed forlorn. The woman, after a time came out and called off the dogs, but seemed disinclined to entertain him; would answer no questions as to his whereabouts or anything else. But after a while she did allow him to enter the house, and gave him some breakfast, which, coarse as it was, he devoured eagerly and thankfully. Soon two men came in, who in answer to his questions, told him he could learn all he wished at Col. Beard's, which was not far from the place where he was.[40] He went accordingly to Col. Beard's, who as soon as he learned who he was, kindly received and assisted him.

One of the persons he met there had belonged to his brother Edward's regiment, and as soon as he recognized him was kind, and of great assistance to him.

He found that the men who were in the house, and others in the neighborhood belonged to a guerrilla party who had organized themselves for the purpose of harrassing the retreating enemy, and making war on any parties who might be detached from the main body. He was furnished with a musket and allowed to join the party. Often while lurking in a hiding place did he embrace the opportunity of aiming his musket at, and shooting down any straggling blue coat who happened to show himself. Poor fellow, he felt that he had wrongs to avenge, both of his own and those of his father, and I cannot blame him for taking vengeance in the first way that offered itself.

One man of the party made it his chief business to hunt and destroy the stragglers. On one occasion a dashing sergeant rode by with a number of men, in reach of their rifles. A shot from the man sent him rolling in the dust, while those from others of the party brought down several more.

Harry learned that the man who was so vindictive in his pursuit had not long before escaped from a Yankee prison where he was loaded with sixty pounds of iron. The cruelties and atrocities committed by the part of that army who had passed through that country on its march to the upper valley were remembered, and swift vengeance was being meted out to them.

Mr. Creigh was hung by the neck in the garden of a near neighbor while the commander and his officers breakfasted quietly in the dining room after giving the order for his murder, and seeing him led out. His crime was beating a drunken soldier out of his daughter's apartment into which he had forced himself while they were asleep in bed.

The man in the fray, was struck on the head, the blow causing his death. For this act of parental duty he was taken from his own house to his neighbor's garden and there put to death. On one of his excursions Harry came upon a Yankee soldier fast asleep in the woods, his musket lying by his side. He possessed himself of the musket, and waking the Yankee informed him that he was a prisoner.

July 1864

That one, and one who was handed over to him by another man, he guarded and marched all the way to Lexington. Two wagon loads of handcuffs had been found by the mountaineers among Hunter's effects left behind him in his flight. They were intended for the Southern soldiers and people who were to be adorned with them to grave Gen. Hunter's triumphant entry into the cities. Harry put none on his prisoners, but brought home one or two pairs to let us see what had been intended for us had Gen. Hunter's flight been less hasty. Harry remained among the mountaineers nearly a week, going with them in all their adventurous searches after Yankees, sometimes coming upon a party rather more formidable than they cared to meet, and being obliged to seek safety in flight, or by strategy. He after being supplied with a pair of shoes, made by one of the mountaineers, set out for Lexington, a journey of ninety-five miles, where he arrived with his prisoners as I have related.

One act of grace on the part of the Yankee army that ought to be recorded as it was the only one, was that as the party that entered the town from the south, passed the cemetery where lay the remains of the august Jackson in quiet repose, they halted, and every man uncovered his head, and still uncovered, marched by slowly and solemnly. A beautiful silk flag had been sent from England by Mr. Beresford Hope to wave over his grave;[41] that, of course, had been removed to a place of safety.

One week later Gen. Early's pursuing army passed, the flag was there, and every officer and soldier saluted it, and went slowly by the grave of their Hero uncovered. The circumstances were remarkable, and so poetic that Mrs. Preston[42] in her volume of war songs had a lovely poem in which she describes how the two armies, though arrayed against each other in deadly strife, were united in their respect and admiration of the great soldier and Christian. Will had in the meantime returned, but could give us no news, and up to the time of Harry's arrival all was uncertainty concerning the fate of either him or his father, or indeed of any of them.

August 1864

After Harry came, and said that his father had without doubt been carried to some Northern prison, I wrote to every one of which I had heard the name. Flora also wrote to several and the letters were sent to our Government to be forwarded by flag of truce. Harry was persuaded that he was well treated, and his hopefulness imparted itself to us. After some time though, I saw a person who told me that he had talked with a gentleman who said he had seen him in Cumberland, Maryland. That he was well and had been paroled, and was well treated. I knowing that he had many acquaintances in Maryland, and some warm friends in Cumberland, dismissed my fears and though I was grieved at his absence, and his separation from us who could do more for his comfort than anyone else could, I felt easy, and tried to be reconciled to what I felt sure could only be a temporary detention. One evening in August (I took no account of time then), I was on my way to Col. Preston's to drink tea. Will, who had nearly recovered from his wound, had already gone with Flora. I stopped at the postoffice to see if there were any letters, and one was handed me directed in a child's hand, and in a yellow envelope. Supposing it was one of many letters I was constantly receiving relative to articles of furniture left in Winchester, I did not open it, but put in into my pocket intending to wait till I got home. Some time after tea I was sitting rather apart from the others; Phoebe Preston was at the piano playing, and the others standing around her. Being thus alone I thought I would open the letter. I did so, and found a few lines written in pencil in my husband's hand. It said that he was in Cumberland, but in jail; in a cell paved with stone, five feet by seven; that a straw pallet was his only bed; that his hands were manacled, and that he was not permitted to see or speak to anyone, or to communicate by letter to persons outside. That the jailer's little daughter sometimes brought his meals, and that he had got her to enclose, direct and mail that note for him. It had been enclosed to someone who knew him in their lines, and that person had found means to get it through to me.

I soon took leave, not wishing to disturb Col. Preston's family with my misery, but as I went I gave them my reason for leaving so suddenly. This was a sorrow greater than any sorrow. No letter could reach him, no word of love, and he might die there in that stone cell! The very thought was agony, and our very powerlessness to help added to our grief. We talked it all over, Will, Flora, the boys and I, and nothing could be suggested but to write to all persons in power, and entreat for his release or a mitigation of his sufferings.

We wrote to President Davis who was his friend; to the Secretary of War, Mr. Seddon, to try and effect his exchange, but to wait was then all we could do.[43]

One only ray of comfort could I see in all that darkness, and that was, in the pencil note he said that the jailer's daughter had brought him a Bible which he had asked for. Could it be that the Merciful Father had taken him from all he loved and leaned upon in the world, to compel him to seek Him and find Him, to prove that every other dependence is as a broken reed? That one thought I found comfort in, that he had sought "Him who sticketh closer than a brother, and would not be comfortless."

Awake, in the long nights, how often would my thoughts revert to the time when happiness and prosperity surrounded us; how I used to feel that we had too much happiness for our deserts, and how the dread always filled my mind that he should be taken from life, a stranger to his God, and he was, not a scoffer, not one who despised religion, for that he never was; and he always respected it and its true followers. But he sought it not for himself; and often when these apprehensions would arise in my mind, of his dying out of Christ, my prayers would go up that his eyes might be opened, more earnest and fervent than I ever prayed for myself or any other living being.

If my prayers had been answered, how could I complain if God had done it in His own way, not mine. Many, many days passed, and at last a letter came from Dr. Boyd of Winchester who had been taken from his home as a hostage, and after weeks of confinement had been released on parole, but detained in Wheeling, where he had been imprisoned.

He wrote that my husband was in Wheeling at the Atheneum prison, that a letter could reach him there.

He told all that was favorable, and nothing distressing. He had sent money to relieve his necessities and also articles to contribute to his comfort, but we afterwards learned that he was not allowed to receive them.

I wrote telling him of Harry's safe arrival at home and the letter being open for inspection reached him.

Soon one came from him full of rejoicing. "My heart is lifted up," it said, "to know of the safety of my intrepid boy." Not much of himself, except to say that he was well and had a good friend in the prison, Dr. Daugherty, who attended to his wants as a physician, and saw that he had everything necessary. Nothing more, but an exhortation to patience and hope that all would be well.

August had nearly passed, and my dear Sister Lizzy, knowing that we would be badly off for winter clothes, wrote me that she had a bag of wool for me if I could get it from her house in Warren County, a distance of more than a hundred miles. Directly Harry heard of it he offered to go, saying that he knew if he set out with it he could get many a lift from wagons passing, and was fully able to carry it part of the way. He set out, and after an absence of three weeks he arrived with the bag, which weighed about 50 pounds. This he had carried a greater part of the way on his shoulders. Bless his heart! He was a gallant boy, ready to undertake any task, however difficult or dangerous, if for the welfare of his family.

My time was now fully occupied in preparing the wool; utterly ignorant of the process, I made many mistakes, greasing when it ought not to be greased, and blundering with the black dyes till I was almost discouraged. At last it was ready for the carding machine, when a difficulty presented itself. It could be carded at no factory in the neighborhood except by consent of the authorities, as the government had all the factories in its employ. After many a long walk to petition the different great men who had the management of them I obtained consent, and started Kenneth on a horse with the huge package before him. He declared when he came back that he had seen nothing but the ears of the animal all the way he went. He was a very little fellow but he performed his task well. Though we have but little else in the way of food we always had bread, and I had a little coffee which kept me from the need of other things, for that sustained me as nothing else could have done.

Sept. 1864

There were two apple trees in the garden that supplied the children with roasted apples, and the cow Cousin John Pierce left me when he went south with his cattle, furnished them with milk.[44] That, with the little that my husband's pay could procure (I was fortunate enough to have had it paid to me) kept us from actual want, though it was often a difficult matter for me to make a meal on such food as we could get. For clothes for the children I had ripped up a cotton mattress and had it carded and spun, had dyed one half brown with walnut hulls, and left the other white. Out of this a very neat check was made which clothed Kenneth and the three little boys, while Nelly was dressed in some red Turkish cotton which had been used in former times for bed curtains, with aprons and white frocks of muslin that had also served as window and bed curtains.

The most remarkable device I ever remember to have seen, even in those times, was a "Confederate candle." No one but the most affluent used any other, and I felt myself fortunate in having one by which I could sit at night and read or sew. I often wonder now how my eyes stood the ordeal. It was made of a small cord, or candlewick, drawn through a pan of melted beeswax and tallow. The cord was about six yards long and was repeatedly drawn through till it was so thickly coated as to be as large as one's little finger.

A candlestick was made of an upright stick about a foot long, fixed in a block two inches thick and about four inches square. On this this candle was wound in close coils, till on reaching the top the end was put through a loop made in a narrow band of tin which was fastened on the top of the stick and served to hold the candle upright. Every minute it had to be snuffed and drawn farther through the loop, as it wasted rapidly away.

Not much of anything could be done by its light as constant attention had to be paid to the candle.

How to clothe the two large boys, Harry and Allan, was a serious question, but my friend, Mrs. Powell, had met the difficulty by offering two suits of her husband's clothes that were not military, for part of the red and white bed curtains to make frocks and aprons for her two little girls, Eleanor and Laura.

Flora had been with me all the summer, and in the early part of it, when our hearts were not too heavy, we had occupied ourselves in plaiting wheat straw and making hats. She made one for herself, and I one for Nelly and very pretty they were. Will was so far recovered from his wound as to be able to join his command, and in August he left us, and with him went all our brightness and cheerfulness, for his gentle humour and pleasant talk greatly alleviated our sadness; besides there was a feeling of being protected while he was near.

Meanwhile the Valley of Virginia was being fiercely contended for. While Gen. Lee was opposing his weakening lines to Grant, heavy bodies of cavalry and infantry were struggling to enter, with varying success. I kept no account of the battles; I only knew that however opposed, they constantly gained ground in that valley so dear to Jackson's heart, and so long and bravely defended by him. Gen. Early had command of Jackson's brigade, but the old spirit no longer seemed to animate them. Jackson's battlegrounds were fought over many times, and Winchester was in the hands of the enemy, after many fierce struggles.

About the last of August, a letter was handed me from my husband. It did not come through the regular channels, but was sent by some one to whom it had been secretly entrusted. It told me the true tale of suffering, tyranny, and malicious persecution.

Ill, he was not allowed to go to the Hospital, but was confined in a room with one hundred and forty deserters and pickpockets; no military prison, no courtesy due to a prisoner of war, but treated like a common criminal, handcuffed, and deprived of everything that could make existence endurable.

The money and bedding Dr. Boyd had sent him was not allowed to be received. The ordinary courtesy of addressing him by his military title was not observed; till when standing in the ranks of criminals and felons of every grade as his name was called as "MacDonald," he refused to answer till they gave him the title which belonged to his rank. He had learned that he was indebted for all his cruel treatment to a creature named David Strother, alias "Porte Crayon," a cowardly renegade, who after having offered his services to the Governor of Virginia to help her in her need, became alarmed over the prospect of losing his gains as writer and caricaturist in the Northern journals, as well as that of the hard fighting and privation he would have to undergo if he cast in his lot with his own people, fled, and with the Governor's commission in his pocket, beyond the lines of the Confederate states. The next time he appeared within those lines, it was with the advancing hosts of the enemy, who entered his native town, insulted his parents and friends and destroyed his neighbor's property, the very people with whom, and under whose protection he had left his wife. It was said that he went to the enemy because they offered him better pay and higher rank. To cover up this cowardly wickedness, he pretended that he did it to avenge the ill-treatment his father had received at the hands of the Confederates; and as my husband was the officer who had had charge of Col. Strother, upon him did he inflict all the indignities his evil nature could suggest.

In the matter of Col. Strother's detention, and of his arrest in the first instance, my husband was blameless; indeed did all he could to make his short captivity as light as possible, and exerted himself to have him released. Col. Strother, being a violent Union man, was arrested by a troop of my husband's regiment of cavalry, under command of Capt. Myers and brought to Winchester, where were the headquarters of the regiment.[45] He was greatly distressed at his arrest, and would have had him released instantly, but could not do so without orders from Richmond. These he sent for, at the same time recommending his release, which was accomplished in three days from the time he was brought to his camp, and while there he had every comfort, and every courtesy. Not long after his release he sickened from some cause, being quite old, and died during the summer. This David Strother pretended to attribute to the treatment he had received at my husband's hands.

So far from being unkind or severe to him, my husband could not be too kind and considerate, for he had a very tender regard for him.

Col. Strother had been his father's friend and companion in arms, and at his death, at Batavia, New York, during the War of 1812, he was with him, received his last sigh, and brought to his wife and children his dying messages, as well as his sword, sash, etc., which were all he could bring. He and his brother always cherished the kindest feelings for Col. Strother, and my husband would have defended him from an indignity, or shielded him from any distress.[46]

On that long and miserable journey after he had parted from Harry, he was allowed to speak to no one. The soldiers were given to understand that he was a criminal of the deepest dye, and must not be noticed, or the least kindness shown him.

At night the wagon he was in was drawn up close to Hunter's headquarters, guarded by soldiers, and for all those eighteen days of weary journeying he was never offered water to wash his face; nor was any covering given him for his head, his military cap having been taken from him, at the time of his capture, till the jailer at Cumberland gave him a hat. At Charleston in Western Virginia a kind lady was permitted to speak to him, and she sent him water and towels and a change of linen. His hand had been wounded by a bullet in the fight at the time of his capture, and in all that time the wound had not been dressed.

With my husband's letter came one from Dr. Boyd, saying that he had been released and sent home. It enclosed one from my husband, to him written from the prison on the occasion of Dr. Boyd's departure from Wheeling. "When you are gone," it said, "the last link will be broken that connects me with the world that is still lighted by the sun, and fanned by the breeze of Heaven." Ah! how the words of the Psalm came into my mind; they came with a force and reality they never had before. "Oh let the sorrowful sighing of the prisoners come before thee!" How I could feel it now, and how often I recalled to memory his love for Mrs. Hemans' song, "Bring flowers," and how he used to sing with Mary the words.

> "Bring flowers to the captive's lonely cell,
> They have tales of the joyous woods to tell,
> Of the free blue stream and the glowing sky,
> And the bright world shut from his languid eye."

Appeals had been constantly made by every member of the family to those in power for his exchange, or for efforts towards effecting his release. We learned that Col. Crook had been put in irons in a Southern prison in retaliation for his treatment. More private letters came to me urging us all to make every effort for his release or exchange. Alas! the influence of the persecutor was too powerful; a deaf ear was turned to every appeal. One letter said that he had heard that Col. Crook was subjected to cruel treatment in retaliation for that inflicted on him.[47] This, he said, only pained him; why should an innocent man suffer because he was cruelly treated? The knowledge of it could not mitigate one pang, but only added to his misery. All the older boys had sent word to David Strother, or written him, that whenever, or wherever any of them should meet him, they would kill him. Edward wrote a note to his wife, of which the following is a copy. His regiment was encamped near her mother's house.

Mrs. David Strother:
    My father, Col. Angus McDonald of Winchester, Virginia, was recently arrested by the forces under Gen. Hunter as a prisoner of war; and taking into consideration his feeble health, should have been at once paroled, but for the influence of your

husband, David Strother. His detention, and exposure with a moving army, will greatly endanger if it does not destroy his life.

I have therefore taken this means to give Col. Strother notice that the measure of pain which, to gratify his private malice, shall be visited on my father, shall be meted out to him even unto death, if death be the result of my father's confinement and this determination will survive, no matter when the war ends, or where he may be found. To this purpose I pledge the lives of nine sons.

E.H. McDonald,
Major 11th Virginia
Calvalry.

Rosser's brigade, June 22nd, 1864.

Early in August I had received a letter from Mrs. Goodwin[48] of Charleston, Western Virginia, telling me that she had seen my husband as he passed with Gen. Hunter, that he was the only prisoner with him; that he had said he was in his usual health, and would do very well, and not to be uneasy about him. Her letter came through the lines, and of course nothing could be written in it of the real state of the case. Before it, however, I had heard through the sources mentioned of his real condition. I mentioned above that Edward was encamped near Mrs. Strother's home[49] when the letter to her was written. When I saw him some time after, he told me that all night he struggled against a burning desire to capture her and carry her off to a remote place within our lines till his father should be released. He said that nothing but the knowledge that his father would consider it an unmanly act prevented his doing it. He therefore contented himself with sending her the note. She had been intimate with his sisters, and had acted as bridesmaid to one of them, and often stayed for weeks at our house.

Letters continued to come, some hopeful, but all urging every effort to be made to effect his release or exchange. Some of them spoke of weakening health and consuming anxiety to get home. Anxiety, impatience at the tediousness of arranging the exchange deprived me of all quiet; and sleepless nights and sorrowful days slowly passed without, as it seemed, bringing any nearer what was so earnestly wished for his release and return home. Steps had been taken for his exchange for Col. Crook, but there was no near prospect of its being effected. Meantime every effort had to be made to supply food for the family. We still had bread for which we were thankful, but there was little else except a very small allowance of army bacon, which I was allowed to buy at government prices, and which just sufficed to feed the servant. The two hundred dollars I received in Confederate money barely served to get a few of the most necessary articles, so valueless had it become that two hundred dollars was required to buy a calico dress, eighteen dollars a pound of Rio coffee, and forty dollars a pair of very coarse children's shoes. My friend, Mrs. Powell, often had necessaries and comforts which were beyond my reach, her husband being in the commissary department at Richmond, and he often sent her things, coffee, sugar, molasses, etc. She generally sent me some, a little sugar, or molasses for the children was a great treat.

Oct. 1864

One evening I remember well, and can scarcely help laughing now when I think of it. I was sitting sadly by the fire in the dusk of the evening; the door opened, and her pale, thin face appeared; her pretty black eyes bright with interest in something she carried under her shawl. It was a little coffee pot full of molasses for the children's supper, about a pint. Sometimes she brought a cup of coffee or sugar, and many a time it came when I had none, and was faint for want of my cup of coffee. We had many laughs at our privations, and especially at the increasing appetites of our boys, which concerned us much. She had six hungry mouths to supply, and I had seven. Our fellow sufferer, Mrs. Dailey, had eight. There being little else but bread for them, of course they had to consume a great deal of that. One of the Powells was expostulated with for eating six biscuits for his supper. He replied that that was nothing, for Allan MacDonald and Grif. Dailey each eat sixteen! Mrs. Powell had arrived in Lexington with no household effects, and was obliged to supply herself with such articles as other people did not want, and would sell, lend, or give her. She had no servant, and no convenience for cooking, which had to be done by herself and her children.

We were one day talking over our perplexities and smaller trials, and she was bemoaning her fate in being obliged to make her own bread, and especially being obliged to put it to rise in an immense coffee pot—some cast off of a hotel. With her thin hands clasped in her lap, and her eyes fixed on the floor, she said, "I would not mind it half so much if I did not have to clean that dreadful old coffee pot." I burst out laughing at her woe begone face as she recited such grief and she joined me.

A day school had been opened at the college, and I gladly accepted the invitation which was given me to send my three older boys, Harry, Allan and Kenneth, as I had lamented their waste of time for so many months. September had brought us dreadful news from the lower valley; our army had been defeated in three battles, or on three successive days; driven from Winchester and closely pursued in their retreat by the enemy. At Fisher's Hill a battle was fought in which Alexander Pendleton who was aid to Early, and Gen. Pendleton's only son, was mortally wounded.[50] I had to go with Mrs. Powell to tell them the dreadful news. A sad task it was, but the poor bereaved old mother seemed to smother her own grief to comfort the poor crushed wife. On the 19th he was shot, and in two days died in the lines of the enemy with no one he loved near him. One night early in October, I was fast asleep, and was awakened, as I thought, by a movement of men in the room. Asleep or awake I never knew which, I saw distinctly my husband's form lifted up by four men and laid on a bed or lounge. He was not dead, I could see that, for his face, though thin and emaciated, was very red.

I screamed out and waked Flora. She said of course it was a dream, and begged me to try and compose myself; but it seemed to be no dream; it had all the distinctness of reality, and even when the busy morning came, it would not be replaced by other interests and concerns, but remained to persuade me that something had happened to him. I felt as if I could no longer stay where I was, and endure the uncertainty, and so I determined to try and get to Wheeling, where I might at least hear how he was. I had a little Virginia money that had been sent me a few days before, the proceeds of the sale of a stove that had been left in Winchester, and that I thought would pay the expenses of the journey. I wrote to him that day that I was going, but my departure was delayed by unforeseen circumstances, for a few days, and then I had intelligence from Richmond that he might any day be exchanged and set out from Wheeling. So I delayed, and a letter came from him dated the 16th of October, saying that his health was failing fast; that he had had two epileptic fits in succession some days before; that he might be able to endure his captivity a month longer, or until cold weather, but if not released before winter he felt that he never should see home again. The letter was written at his dictation by Dr. Daugherty. He begged that I would not think of going to him as I would not be allowed to see him if I was there.

In the mean time Anne had written to Gen. Hitchcock who had been his classmate and friend at West Point, and the companion in arms he had loved in his youth and continued all his life to love.[51] She had heard of his appointment as Commandant at Fortress Monroe, and felt sure that a letter to him would bring about his exchange or release. Her letter elicited a favourable response, and an order for his release on parole was sent immediately. I received a letter from him dated Nov. 1st in which he joyfully announced that he should that day leave the prison for home.

With the cold weather came added anxieties about winter supplies. A large patch of potatoes had been planted in the summer by my boys, and had been gathered in and laid in the attic to dry. On the night of October 22 there was a severe freeze that destroyed them all, and so perished our only certain hope of food for the winter. The cloth for the boys' clothes was ready to be woven, but there were long delays about it, and I feared it would be badly needed before we got it. The red curtains having all been made up and worn out, I devised a plan for clothing Nelly which proved a good one.

I found among some things in a chest that had been brought from home, a quantity of red worsted fringe that had formerly trimmed some chamber curtains. It was all made of fine good threads, strong and well twisted. I showed it to Rose Pendleton and told her what I thought of doing with it. She thought the project a good one, and insisted on my taking it up to their house and letting them help me to ravel and wind it; this I was glad to do as it was a long piece of work.

I took it up to the Rectory, and evening after evening, her mother and sisters, and Mrs. Lee, her married sister, all helped till it was finished. It made a very pretty plaid for Nelly's frocks, with the addition of some white and black thread. I never can forget the kindness of that family; nothing that they could do for me was ever omitted, and they were always ready with sympathy in any trouble that assailed me.

212

My poor little boys were still barefooted, and it made me so sorry their little red feet as they went out in the frost of the November mornings. Night after night I laid awake, trying to devise plans for getting them shoes, and paying for the weaving of the cloth; how I should get wood, and above all, how I should keep the released prisoner from the distress of seeing us want, and how I should provide him with comforts when he came. I prayed then as I have never prayed before, for food and clothing for my children, and tried to believe and trust that they would be provided. I determined after much thought to go again to Deaver, and ask him to make the children's shoes. But oh! everything was more hopeful then, money was more valuable, and the end of the war did not seem so very far off, at least the prospect of paying him was better. I went to him, nevertheless, and told him just what my prospect was of paying him, and told him also that I felt that I was making a most unreasonable request, for him to wait an indefinite time for his money. He said he would make them, and I must not feel uneasy or anxious about it; that he knew I would pay when I could. I turned away and left the shop with tears I could not keep back. So the little ones got their shoes, and I found sale for a few remaining articles of jewelry that supplied wood and other necessaries for present use. I bought stockings for Harry and Allan, knit by the mountain women, knitted some for Nelly of cotton, and for Kenneth, Don, Roy and Hunter I cut up old knit undershirts and made them.

After the reception of the letter telling of my husband's illness, I felt persuaded that he must be too weak and exhausted to endure even the fatigues of a journey home; and I was full of anxiety, restless and uneasy, so that at all times my nerves were easily affected; if I slept it was to dream sad and uneasy dreams, and all my thoughts by day or night were of the released prisoner now traveling homewards. One night, I remember well, I had a dream that startled and distressed me greatly. Though in happier times, when my life was calm I paid no attention to dreams, only thinking them idle wanderings of the mind when the body slept; but Oh! I have since thought that they sometimes come as shadows of the event; as premonitions to prepare the anxious and expectant soul for grief and calamity. Well on that night I slept, but "my heart was awake," and I dreamed that he was to be married, that preparations were going on for the wedding; that I came into a room and saw him

213

sitting alone at a long table covered with a white cloth. On the table, just before him was laid a large green wreath; nothing else was on it.

On the 9th of November I received a short letter from him at Richmond. He had arrived there on the 7th; was too fatigued to write much; he would be at home as soon as he could be exchanged for Col. Crook. Col. Crook was in North Carolina, and some days must elapse before he could be taken to Old Point to effect the exchange. My disappointment was great when I found there was still to be delay, after all my watching and waiting. The truth was, however, that he was too weak to travel further and required rest. I was much provoked, not knowing all, that anything should keep him longer from home. On the 28th I had a letter from Flora, written at his dictation, telling me that he was not as well as he had been; that I must come immediately as he might not be able to travel for sometime. I was compelled to wait two days to arrange for the children during my absence.

After sending Nell and Hunter to Col. Williamson's and seeing the other boys comparatively comfortable, I left them under the charge of Susan, the cook, with Harry and Allan to take care of the little boys, and set out.

Dec. 1864

At dawn on the 1st of December I left the house with the little ones fast asleep, and everything quiet around. It was a bitter cold day, and I could scarcely keep from freezing on the way to the canal boat. It was comfortless on the boat, so cold that everybody had to sit close to the red hot stove. The boat was full, and I never remember to have seen so many people together who displayed so little merriment.

Every one was sad and anxious, at least from their talk I inferred so. One group talked of the conscription; a cruel thing they thought of it, and I did, too, when I heard what they had to tell of it. One man, a rough mountain man, was one of the conscribed. He was on his way to the army; was over forty-five, for in the country's extremity everybody had to go who could bear arms. He was telling of a neighbor of his on the mountain who had had two sons killed, and one a prisoner; that he, the father, had been taken as a conscript, and that the poor wife had been left alone in her hut to abide the winter's cold, with no one to provide for or take care of her.

Groups of murmuring men were all around, and I first began to realize that the patience of the people was worn out; that their long suffering and endurance was to be depended on no longer; that they were beginning to see that it was of no avail to deliver the country from her enemies. It is strange after so long a time how distinctly I remember every circumstance of that journey; how the boat looked; how dim and faded its once bright and smart decorations were; how dilapidated all its furniture was, and how gloomy everybody looked.

When meal time came each one opened his or her little package of provisions (some had only a crust of bread), for there were no meals served on the boats. At night there were two poor candles lighted and placed on a table, and by it two girls seated themselves, and seemed to be trying to extract a little amusement by speculating on the character, station and occupation of the other passengers. I was near enough to hear their remarks, and was a little amused at the manner in which they sketched the position and antecedents of the different persons. At last they came to me, as I knew by a glance my way. One said, "A poetess, a widow, been married twice."

I did not know why, but the last observation annoyed me. I wondered why they thought so, and kept wondering, till at last I got up and went and looked into the poor old looking glass to see if there was anything festive in my appearance. What I saw was a thin, anxious face and black garments; so I was reassured.

At Lynchburg we stopped, and I went on to Richmond next morning by rail. I met some friends on the cars, Mrs. Magill and others, and when we were in motion and fairly on the way, I felt light-hearted, even elated; not for months had I had so much lightness of spirit.

I sat all day happy, talking and laughing with friends, and joyfully anticipating my arrival at Richmond.

When we reached the depot, Mr. Ran. Tucker came to meet Mrs. Magill. He spoke to me very affectionately, and I remarked to myself how sad he looked, but did not think of it long, for I was occupied in wondering why some one was not there to meet me. Mr. Tucker got me a carriage, and I drove to Mr. Claiborne Green's where he was staying. Mr. Green met me at the door, and stood rubbing his hands and absently looking at me without saying a word. At last he went out to have the trunk brought in, and I stood in the hall rather at a loss to imagine why no one came to the door to meet me. Soon Mrs. Holliday came out of a room, and in her usual unthinking way pointed to an open door and asked me if I would go in there now.[52] I went, and the object I first saw was my husband's corpse, stretched on a white bed with a large green wreath around his head and shoulders, enclosing them as in a frame!

They had not intended that I should have had such a shock, had not expected me till nine o'clock by the south side train, and when I went in had just finished the wreath and laid it around him, that I might see him first with the horror of death a little softened. Ah! how familiar it looked, that wreath; I had seen it, weeks before; when my body slept, but my spirit was awake.

If I only had seen him to have spoken one word, I could have borne it better, but to have him go without one kind word or look, to be gone forever!

That same night I heard of the death of my dear sister Lizzy, of the shock and distress of seeing their home invaded and pillaged and everything burnt and destroyed.

Many friends came to sympathize with and try to comfort me. Mrs. Mason among the rest. "My dear," she said, "if he had lived his life would have been a burden to him, so enfeebled was his constitution by hardship, and you may yet be thankful that he was taken now, before greater calamities come upon the country, and greater suffering for him." The only thing that gave me comfort was the account they gave of the change in him. He who had always said that he loved his friends and hated his enemy, that he believed revenge was a duty, left word that his sons were not to avenge his death, that they were to let the wicked alone to the vengeance of the Almighty. He said he did not wish the children, the young ones, to remain in the country if it was conquered, that he did not suppose the older ones would survive our defeat, but that the younger ones must not remain in the country to suffer the humiliation. Mary, Anne and Flora were with him. Poor Anne had just that morning gone to her little baby's bed and found it dead.

The 1st of December, the day of his death, he had asked to have the Psalter for the day read. When Flora was reading, and came to the words, "Oh Lord my God if I have done any such thing, or if there is any wickedness in my hands, if I have rewarded evil unto him that dealt friendly with me, (Yea I have delivered him that without cause is mine enemy) then let mine enemy persecute my soul and take me, yea let him tread my life down upon the earth, and lay mine honour in the dust."[53]

He spoke of the resemblance to his own case, how he had been accused by David Strother of injuring and persecuting his father, and causing his death, when he would have protected him with his own life if it had been necessary.

On Thursday, the 1st of December, he died, and on Sunday he was buried. An immense crowd of people, I was told, was there. The President and all the state and high military officers were mourners. General Cooper[54] and others of his old West Point friends were his pallbearers, and wrapped in the folds of the stars and bars, with bands playing the dead march, they carried him to Hollywood, and there laid him to rest with all the honours of war. Nothing was omitted to do him honour, or to show how deeply his sufferings were regretted. I would have been comforted by the thought that such a burial was the one he would have desired, that his true soldierly spirit if it could have seen, would have been glad, but for the knowledge that he had been sent to his grave by inhuman treatment; it seemed to me then not so much the will of God, as the wickedness of man that had taken him from the world.

All comfort I had was in the account they gave of his resignation and gentleness, "The Lord had caught and tamed that fiery heart," as one of the greatest and best said of himself; had done it by terrible suffering, but had done it. I could feel the assurance that his redeemed spirit was with God, though it had come out of great tribulation. Anne said when she spoke to him of the love of the Saviour he said to her, "I know Him, and He knows me."

Some days passed and many discussions arose with regard to the future of myself and the children. Mr. Green thought I had better come to Richmond where I could find employment in one of the Departments. All thought that the children ought to be distributed among the older members of the family. Roy to Angus, Nelly to Anne, Mary wanted Donald, and Mr. Green said he would take Kenneth with him to the army; he could provide for him there as well as teach him, he being commissary and not in active service. Hunter I was to keep, and Harry and Allan were old enough to take care of themselves.

I listened, but was resolved no matter what happened not to part with my children; but often when pressed, and reminded how hopeless my condition was, and indeed how unreasonable, it was to persist in refusing to do what was the only thing that could be done, as far as any one could see, if my heart was inclined to yield for fear I would not be doing the best for the children, the thought of my poor little lonely ones, for they would have been lonely without me and each other, the thought of not being there to hear their prayers at night, to soothe them if they were worried, or comfort them if they were troubled, that thought would nerve me for resistance. I would try to picture to myself my little proud sensitive Donald, going to bed with grief in his heart that he would not tell to any one.

My little hot-headed Roy, who would understand him and have patience with him as I would?

My dear affectionate Kenneth, estranged from me and home by a life among strangers and soldiers.

Nelly, my little shadow and great comfort, absent from and grieving for me; and above all, my two manly boys, Harry and Allan, sent so young to live among strangers, and exposed to all the hazards of a city life without a home. I knew their brothers and sisters would be kind to them, but I knew also that my children were given to me to care for, and bring up, and I could not put the duty off on any one else and do right. Of my hands would they be required, and of those of no one else. "Where is thy flock, thy beautiful flock?"

Cousin John Maguire, the minister from Fredericksburg, came to see me one day, and began to press the subject of my giving up the children, saying that it was perfectly hopeless for me to attempt to keep them together with no means, not even my husband's pay; that it ought to be a source of satisfaction to me to have them so well provided for. I was not moved by his arguments but after he left the room was greatly relieved by a remark from Mrs. Daniel who had been present at the discussion;[55] for though my resolution was fixed, I still had doubts of my decision being the right one. She said, "You are right, do not give up your children." I could have embraced her for it. I received more encouragement from Edward who came that day. He advised me to keep the children with me.

I thanked all the family for their kindness in offering to help us, but told them I could not consent to part with the children, that they were all I had, and that I could not consent to part with them. They gave up kindly, without any prediction of misfortune, or failure, as many would have felt it their duty to make, and so I left them and went back to Lexington. The day before I left I went with Flora to Hollywood to see the place where he was laid. It was bitter cold, and a keen wind blew in our faces all the way. After a long walk we reached the hillside where he was, with Anne's poor little babe by his side.

How like his brother who laid in the cemetry at Winchester with my little angel close beside him.

The wind whistled through the leafless trees, and everything looked so bleak and desolate that I felt as if my heart was broken. The falls of the James River were just below and the melancholy sound and cold look of the icy water added to the dreariness. It was bright sunshine, but a grey and cloudy sky would have harmonized better with the scene and my desolation. We could not stay long with him, but were obliged to hurry away to keep from freezing in the bitter biting wind. So we turned and left him to his lonely sleep, with the bare branches waving over him, and the sound of the rushing water the only one to break the stillness. The hillsides were covered thickly with fresh graves; but we tried to find another, that of poor Wood. He was buried in Mr. Rutherford's lot; he and Frank Sherrard were buried there the same day; we saw the two new graves, but could not tell which was his. Poor Flora wept bitterly at not being able to identify him, but we left him, too, and went back.[56]

Two years afterwards I went to Richmond to see about having their graves marked. I had a small marble slab made for each, which was all my limited means admitted of, with names and dates, so that they could be identified at some future time. Mrs. Powell's little son, Simms, went with me and helped me to plant some white roses over their heads. The long grass was growing over them both, the trees thick with foliage, and the happy voices of birds singing their songs to their mates made the place a scene of beauty. The water poured on with its rapid rush at the foot of the hill, but the waves looked glad in the summer sunshine, and when I turned to go, it was with a feeling of thankfulness that he was at rest, and had escaped the misery and humiliation of that melancholy time which followed so soon after his death. One half of the privation and misery endured by the Southern people will never be known, the delicate ladies who went without shoes or necessary clothes, and with scarcely food enough to keep them alive, they and the poor famished children; it makes me sad now to recall it.

While I was in Richmond, I heard of a lady who was well connected and known in society, who had a place in the Treasury Department.

One morning on beginning her work, she fainted, and when taken up, her feet were found wrapped in long pieces of lint, as she had no shoes, and just clothes enough to cover her, not enough to keep her blood from freezing. She had had nothing to eat for two days. On my way to Lexington I stayed all night in Staunton, and occupied the room with a Miss Ball. She belonged to a wealthy and highly respectable family of Prince William, and had been employed in one of the Richmond Hospitals to take care of the linen. She had set out to try to get into the Federal lines to take care of her brother, Col. Ball of the 11th Virginia Cavalry, who had been wounded in one of the battles in the valley. She was to travel in an open wagon seated on a plank by the driver, had three days travel before her, and her only wrapping was a thin shawl, her clothing a calico gown with a cotton petticoat, and not a particle of flannel on her. She had a distressing cough, and I hated to see her drive off in the cold, dark morning, for I felt that she would not reach her journey's end.

When I got home, I found my boys all on the front steps watching for me. Nelly and Hunter were sent for, and soon came. Nelly was dressed in mourning the Pendletons had prepared for her, and all the boys had crepe on their hats.

Kind friends had seen that everything was done that could be done. Miss Anne Rose Page, the boys told me, had gone to the house every day to see that they were properly prepared for school, and on Sunday morning to hear the little fellows their Sunday school lessons. Miss Sally Grey had sent the skirts of some of her black dresses, and the Williamsons and Pendletons had made them up. The grief and disappointment of the children was great at not seeing their father.

Harry told me that on the night I had left, the 1st of December, he had suffered with the toothache, and had awakened Allan and induced him to go down to the basement with him where was a fire. The two little fellows, Donald and Roy, had been left up stairs in their room.

After a while Harry heard them screaming, and on going up they told him there was an "old thing" in the room, that had come in through a window pane. He brought a light, and there on the foot of their bed sat a huge owl.

220

Kind Mrs. Moore[57] had made Harry a suit of clothes out of a piece of cloth, the purchase of which Mr. Powell had negotiated for me in Lynchburg while I was absent; and indeed no act of thoughtful kindness was omitted by those kind, dear Lexington people. All that sympathy could do to express their feeling for me was done, and not only sympathy, but substantial benefits were given on every side. Col. Williamson had had to seek shelter in a wretched house after his was burned, and had scarcely furniture or comforts for his family, but he found room for my little Nell and Hunter, and they had a sweet home and kind care while I was away.

Col. Gilham also kindly came and offered to do anything in his power to contribute to our comfort; he had no house either, his having been burnt by Hunter, and he was living with his family in a few rooms. He sent me a quarter of beef, which was a great gift then, and kept me from the harrowing anxiety of what we were to eat, when my heart was too heavy with grief to think of it. The days slowly dragged on and Christmas came. Our friends took care that we should not be entirely without its pleasures and comforts; so one sent a turkey, another cakes and oysters, and all something, the best they could get. Of course that could not last, people could not give always, nor did I wish them to do so. I knew that I must make an effort of some kind to provide for the family, what it was to be I knew not. I had three hundred dollars in Confederate money, worth about fifteen in silver or paper of the Federal Government. How I tried to make it last, so that I would not have to go out among strangers to try to earn money when I only wanted to hide myself and my sorrow from the light of day.

Those dark days, can I ever forget them?

The money was soon all spent for wood and other things, and I had none now. My sad, hopeless hours were often interrupted by friends who came to cheer and comfort me. One lovely girl, now in her grave, whither she went in a year from the time of which I write, Lottie Myers was her name, a pure and lovely Christian, one whose "conversation was in heaven," came often, and was so sweet and good. I can see her innocent, kind eyes now, and hear her voice as she repeated the promises of God to the widow and the fatherless. "Your bread and your water shall be sure," she quoted one day, and her words carried the conviction that they would be sure. Often would my mother's voice sound in my ears in the still night, as I used to hear her sing one of her favorite Psalms:

221

"He helps the stranger in distress,
The widow and the fatherless,
And to the prisoner grants release."[58]

He had done the last, the prisoner was free! And would He not provide for us? How prophetic they seemed, the words she loved, and chose to sing. I used to wonder if the thought even crossed her mind that I, her youngest child, who used to sit in the twilight with her as she sang, would be the widow, and my husband the prisoner, and my children the fatherless.

Mrs. Preston came in one morning bringing some of the proof sheets of her poem, "Beechenbrook," for me to see.[59] "It is almost a history of your family," she said. I suppose she meant that there was a resemblance in the story of the death of her principal character. In January Miss Baxter came and told me she knew of some young ladies who wished to take drawing lessons, and I could also get a class in French if I wished it.[60] She said I should have no trouble in arranging the matter as she would do it all for me. The thought of being daily obliged to meet strangers, of not having the privilege of retirement in my present state of distress was dreadful to me; but the alternative was starvation. So the classes came, and I taught them in the morning for three or four hours, and in the afternoon two other young ladies came to read poetry and history. With this there was no time for grief, besides there was plenty of work to keep the children's knees and elbows covered. With all I could do we had barely enough food to keep from actual want; and that of a kind that was often sickening to me. I generally went all day with a cup of coffee and a roll. The children could eat the beans and the sorghum molasses, but I could not. We seldom saw butter, but some idea may be formed of the difficulty of getting food when I say that I sent one hundred dollars (the proceeds of two weeks teaching) up town, and got for it a pound of fat bacon, three candles, eighteen dollars for the three, and a pound of bad butter.

The quartermaster proposed to me to let my boys cut wood in the woods for the Government, and that they should have one cord out of every three they cut, and that the Government wagons would haul it for me. I joyfully agreed, and they were willing, but as I could not spare both boys, I sent Harry and kept Allan at home.

Harry took Roy for company, and if the snow was deep would carry him on his shoulders out to the place where he worked. So we were supplied with wood, indeed never wanted for it, and a bright cheerful fire was a great comfort and delight to us.

In the dusk of the evening when my boy would come home there was great joy. He would come in rosy and happy after his hard day's work, and little Roy full of delight at being of consequence enough to accompany him. One morning when about to set out, Harry discovered that Roy's toes were out of his shoes, and told him he must not go in the snow with his feet exposed, but Roy insisted, and away they went merrily, with Roy on Harry's back.

Feb. 1865

In every piece of intelligence from our lines before Richmond, there was now matter for discouragement and apprehension. It was plain that things were not going favourably; the enemy with ever increasing numbers pressed our thin lines, and worse than all, the men were becoming disheartened and many were deserting, as the dark and gloomy February days dragged along, everything seemed more discouraging, and though I did not permit myself for a single moment to apprehend a total defeat, I could not see or imagine how we were ever to hold out.

I felt when offering up my prayer for our deliverance from our enemies, that that prayer *must* be answered; it was almost a frantic cry to Heaven demanding help and success. Defeat seemed such a calamity as was never known, and as no people ever survived, it would be so for us; our enemies were implacable, and defeat would be utter ruin to us all. How hard it was to say "Thy will be done"; how hard to feel that God knew best.

The thought of all our tremendous sacrifices being in vain; of the blood of our people shed for nothing; of the probable seizure and death of our leaders; it all seemed too horrible to think of for a moment.

The prolonged struggle, dreadful as it was, was better than defeat, and the scorn of our insolent enemies.

It was bitter when we were victorious, how would it sting when we should be vanquished; how could we endure their taunts? I knew how they could insult and gibe and call us sneering names. How furious have I grown at hearing the word "rebel" applied to our great and good leaders, and the brave men who followed them. I had no spirit for that now, but I had a heart for sorrow, and it ached with a ceaseless pang for the country as well as for my own griefs.

Mar. 1865

March came in gloomy and melancholy, and brought with it a dreadful certainty of disaster and defeat. One thing that almost quenched the last hope in me, was seeing the men coming home; every day they passed, in squads, in couples, or singly, all leaving the army. What must have been the anguish of Lee's great heart when he saw himself being deserted by his men when pressed so sorely by the enemy. Many stopped at my house asking for food. I gave them a share of such as I had, though I felt a scorn for giving up when defeat was near, instead of remaining to the end. It is hard to call them deserters, but such they were, and they knew it, for each one would tell of how hard Lee was beset, and how impossible it was for him to hold out any longer, as if to excuse his own delinquency. After all though, when I thought of it afterwards, I could not wonder that they did desert. The conscription had forced many unwilling ones to go to the army, leaving unprotected wives and children in lonely mountain huts to abide their fate whatever it might be, freezing or starvation. Though the conscription was made necessary by the exigency of the times, it was nevertheless a dreadful tyranny; and though I have never said so, I have often thought that no greater despotism could be than that government was in the last months of its existence. To those whose education and habits of life made them enthusiastic, or whose pride acted as an incentive for them to endure and suffer, as was the case with the higher classes, it wore no such aspect, but to those who had but their poor homes and little pieces of ground by which they managed to provide very little more than bread for their families, who knew that they would be as well off under one government as another, it was oppression to be forced into the army, and not ever to be free from the apprehension that their families were suffering.

One man told me that he had remained in the trenches till a conscript who had lately arrived from his neighborhood told him that his family was starving. All the winter hordes of deserters had been gathering in the mountains, and entrenching themselves; had resisted all attempts to arrest them. Indeed they sometimes captured officers and soldiers of the Confederate army and detained them.

One night Col. Richard Henry Lee was retiring from a fight in which he had been separated from his command, and was captured by them and held for several days. Those men had resisted the conscription, though they would not desert to the enemy, and were ready if attacked or pursued to defend themselves.

They proved rather formidable neighbors to the dwellers near their mountain dens, for they often descended upon helpless people and took all their grain and cattle.

No one was to be blamed for such a state of things, but the cruel circumstances in which we were placed compelled it. If the brave, the well born and the chivalrous could have done all the fighting there would have been no shrinking, no desertion; but alas! their boys lay buried on every battlefield in Virginia; a whole generation nearly, of young men of good birth and breeding had been swept away, and as many others who, though of plainer people, had true soldierly hearts, and bore themselves bravely in the shock of battle, and patiently and unmurmuringly in the long march or the weary watch. There was no house, high or low in the length and breadth of Virginia, that had not to mourn some lost boy.

One evening I went to a house where I was having some weaving done, and saw there an old woman who talked a great deal about the war, but did not seem to understand very clearly what it all meant. She spoke of having lost her only son in some battle in the valley near Winchester. She did not know the name of the place. "I never knowed where it was," she said, "but they told me he was killed about there though I did not know he was killed for certain for more than a year after." I found out afterward that it was the battle of Kernstown.

One sad instance of the kind of tyranny that seemed a necessity in those hard times, made me feel very sorrowful. A butcher by the name of Hite lived in a nice little cottage at the lower end of the town. He had a wife and two small children. I often went there to get meat when he had it, which was not at all times now. He was conscribed and marched off. What became of him I never heard but in mid-winter (he was taken off in November), his wife finding it impossible to provide for her children where she was, sold her furniture and got a horse and wagon with which she set out with her children to try to make her way into the Federal lines to join her people who lived in Pennsylvania. When two days on her journey she was stopped by some lawless people who questioned her about where she was going, and when she said she was going to Pennsylvania, they said she was a traitor and enemy, and that her wagon and horse were confiscated. So they set her down by the roadside and took her property.

That was of course done by no authority, but it served to show how little law there was that was effectual in anything but filling up the ranks of the army. Now, however, it failed even in that, for men deserted faster than the conscripts were brought in.

Rainy, gloomy, muddy and sad was that month of March. Appeals began to be made to the townspeople for food for Lee's starving army, fighting as they were day and night in the trenches, they must be fed, so the citizens were called on to supply them. All responded who had anything to give, and I particularly remember Deaver, who Union man though he was, sent a barrel of flour and bacon, which I doubt not he could ill spare, as he was a poor man. Sometime in March Edward wrote me that in one of his raids he had made in the enemy's country, he had taken some beeves, some of which he was allowed to keep for himself after turning the others over to the government. One was to be sent to me, and we built our hopes on it, watched long and anxiously for its arrival. At last the news came that it was in Staunton, and Harry must go for it. He went, and on the third day it was reported that the beef was on the other side of the river, but could not be got across, as it was very wild. I thought if it had so much spirit left after so long a march it must be in good condition, so I made my plans. I would send the Williamsons and Mrs. Powell a roast, and would corn all we did not want for present use. That would furnish us for a long time with meat.

The skin Shirley might have for killing it, as well as some of the meat.[61] And the tallow, oh what a treasure the tallow would be. If there were even six pounds, that would make thirty-six candles, and that would give us light for seventy-two nights. No more Confederate candles, and no more giving eighteen dollars for three miserable dips. I went into the cellar and searched and found an old set of candlemoulds, which some occupant of the house had used in former times, had them rubbed up, and even prepared the wicks as I had seen my mother's servants do years before.

All the children went down to the river to welcome the beef, Shirley going with them. They were gone six hours, and when they appeared with the beef I did not know whether to laugh or cry. It was so thin that the sides were transparent between the ribs, not a particle of fat on any part of it, and a teaspoon would have held all the tallow. Harry, hot and tired, declared that for two days he had done nothing but chase "that thing." He believed it had an evil spirit, for go along the road it would not, but galloped off in wide circuits on each side, and though he had a man to help him, it was as much as both could do to get it to the other side of the river. It was young though, and tender, and we were not very particular. I sent the Williamsons a roast, but had no candles.

Edward was always thoughtful of the wants of the members of the family when he had an opportunity of procuring anything on his raids in the enemy's country. Once during the past summer, that of 1864, I received the welcome intelligence that he had procured a parcel of goods, and had a set of hoops and a toothbrush for each female member of the family. They were great prizes, for money could not buy them in the Confederacy as they were not to be had.

My own boys had zeal enough, if not judgment in selecting, to supply us from the tempting wares they often saw abandoned after a battle or on the occasion of a panic, when the sutlers would effect a stampede. Their zeal, I say was sufficient, and perfectly equal to the occasion, but the diversity of good things would distract them to such a degree that it was difficult to settle on any one thing. Once I remember, when the Yankees made one of their hasty retreats from Winchester, Harry and Allan went up to the deserted camp, and after helping themselves to a number of good and useful things, were about to bring them home, when they espied a family of young puppies. These were too great a temptation; they dropped the articles they had taken and after a severe contest with the mother of the puppies, came home, each with a dog under his arm.

When Milroy had fled and all the depots and storehouses were on fire, Allan, who was always on hand if there was any agitation, saw many desirable things which he knew would be useful at home, and by turns he appropriated many different articles. After taking possession of one he would see another that he thought better so would throw down the first and appropriate the second. He threw down a whole piece of bleached cotton to pick up a roll of flannel; then threw that away for something else. At last a large cheese attracted his attention and its charms eclipsed those of all else. So

227

he abandoned all for the new prize. He took it up, and finding it too heavy to carry on his arm put it on his head. The cheese was thoroughly warmed by the heat of the burning buildings, and after he had got it on his head it gradually sunk to his neck, where it finally seated, with only his eyes above it.

The 20th of March had come, and Harry was within three weeks of being seventeen years old. He said he was old enough to go into the army, and seemed so anxious to go, that I felt it would be wrong to refuse him. To get him equipped was the great consideration. He said if he could get the clothes that his brother Edward had promised to furnish him with a horse, and equipments. So I determined to let him go, and bethought myself of a remaining piece of finery, a crepe shawl. I took it up to a shop and exchanged it for a piece of grey cloth, such as before the war had been worn only by negroes, but which now was the only material used for soldiers' clothes. Coarse and rough as it was, it was worn by the best of the land, and no gentleman himself above wearing it. Some were fortunate enough to get a finer quality of grey cloth, but grey it must be.

Broadcloth would have been considered disreputable on any but old men, and even they preferred the grey. White shirt fronts were seldom seen. It was perfectly en régle to visit in coloured flannel ones; these, however, were very fine and nice; some neatly ornamented by mothers, wives or sisters.

A white collar was indispensable, as it was then and must always be the distinguishing badge of a gentleman. Some ladies helped me to make the clothes for Harry; stockings were knitted by a neighbor, and he was soon equipped, and my boy was gone.

His brother's regiment was over the mountains, and part of the enemy's cavalry was between him and the blue ridge, but he said he could get through, and I had to trust him to Providence. Some time in February, as nearly as I can recollect, the attempt to take Richmond by Col. Dahlgren was made.[62] He was after his death lauded as one of the noblest and bravest; was the son of the Federal Commodore Dahlgren, and is, or was considered a gallant officer and brave man, but the papers found on him at his defeat and death, showed him to be the meanest of cowards, as well as the blackest hearted of men. The papers revealed a plan which had been submitted to the Federal Government, and won their approval. The plan was for Dahlgren and his command, of one or more companies,

228

supported by others at a short distance, to make a dash in the rear of Richmond, take the outworks by surprise, rush into the city, and hurl balls soaked in explosive or inflammable fluid in and over the houses and in the confusion, and amid the fire, they were to go to the prisons and liberate all the prisoners and instruct them to sack the city. The men being all in the trenches in front of the town, there would be no one inside to resist, so the women and children, and helpless and old were to be a prey to the fury of the long imprisoned soldiers. He thought to win for himself unfading renown if he succeeded in capturing the long sought and long struggled for prize, even by a stratagem so unworthy, for he knew his employers were not particular as to means. Happily he was found out and circumvented in his stealthy approach to the doomed city, and his mean and unworthy life paid the forfeit.

Great efforts were made to capture our forts at Drury's Bluff, to secure a passage by water to Richmond, for they had little hope of taking it by land, having been kept at bay for nearly four years.

They had no idea how thin Lee's line was, and how near to its end the Confederacy was drawing.

It became necessary to have another gunboat built to defend the approach to the city, and the authorities had called on the people for means to build it.

Even the ladies responded, but with offers of their hair. A friend of mine a year or two after all was over, told me that she had determined to give her beautiful and luxuriant suit, and had taken the scissors to cut it off, when a relative sitting by suggested that she wait a few days. She did so, and those few days decided that the sacrifice would be in vain. Each day our wants become more difficult to supply. I was easy about the house rent, for I had managed to pay it by the sale of half a fine set of china I had brought from home.

Getting food was the great difficulty. What I earned by teaching supplied little more than bread, beans and a little fat bacon, which last was nearly all consumed by the servant. The breakfast was bread and water, except the cup of coffee for me, which I believe I would have died without. The dinner was bean soup and bread, of which I never ate a particle, but got up as I sat down. The children ate it, and if they did not enjoy it, did not complain. Supper we had none, for there was not bread to spare for a third meal.

I grew so thin and emaciated, and was so weak that I scarcely had strength to take my usual evening walk. When I did go out, as I passed by the houses, and by a glance within would see the pleasant tea tables set ready for the family, the nice hot rolls, and tempting fare, for many still had those comforts, I would feel almost rebellious at the thought that I had no pleasant tea table to return to. My servant would cook our poor dinner and then go away to visit her friends, for I could not afford her light and fuel to sit by. As March drew to a close the news from the besieged city was more alarming. The condition of the army was such that no one believed or hoped it could be kept together long, and one terrible circumstance was that the enemy had forced his way down the Valley, had crossed the Blue Ridge, and appeared in a quarter that threatened Richmond in the rear, and there was no force to repel them. Stragglers and deserters now came in in parties of ten or twenty, and we could no longer doubt that the end was at hand.

Apr. 1865

At last the crash came. Richmond was evacuated, and Lee retreating before Grant, who threatened to surround him. The horrors of that evacuation I have often heard recounted by eye witnesses; the flaming buildings fired by thoughtless hands, as if it could do any good to burn our poor stores to keep them from an enemy who could command, and the world would lay its resources at his feet. The lawless bands of prisoners and negroes, the frantic ladies and children deserted by their protectors and left to take care of themselves in all that dreadful confusion.

I could imagine all the dreadful scene, and was thankful I was spared participation in it. Flora related to me a part of her experience at the time. Mary had with her family, Susan and Flora, occupied a house rented from Dr. Cullen, an old Englishman, and when the evacuation began, he insisted on their leaving his house, as they being rebels, might cause the fury of the victors to destroy his property. Mary warded off the blow till the Federals came in, and then Flora went out to try to find quarters.

This she did in the course of the day, and they determined to move their effects on the following morning. A wagon to carry the things was not to be found, and they were obliged to tell Dr. Cullen that they could not get away. He declared they should go, and as there was nothing to prevent his putting their furniture in the street, Flora volunteered to go and try to get the Yankees to help her. So she sallied forth and found her way to the quarters of some general officer who listened kindly to her story, and ordered an officer to go out and stop the first wagon that passed, whether loaded or not.

Very soon a luckless countryman with a load of corn that he had perhaps hidden from the Confederates, and was now bringing to sell to the Yankees, passed by. He was stopped, and his load emptied in the street, two soldiers directing the operation. He was then ordered to proceed to the place designated by Flora, and move their furniture. The man rebelled, and swore lustily, but it did not benefit his cause, for he was made to drive on immediately, the armed soldiers on each side of him, Flora leading the way to show them which way to go. She walked beside the wagon after it was loaded, till it was driven to the place where the furniture was to be taken, and all day walked with it, back and forth as each load was carried, for fear the man and the soldiers would make away with the things.

We who were away from the scene knew nothing at the time of the horror of it, and I can only tell of the despair with which we heard the ill news, and of the fear and terror with which we looked for what must follow. Nothing was wanting to our misery; we heard tales of blood and horror, accounts of the numbers and power as well as the unresting activity of our pursuing foes, and nothing but destruction seemed to be in store for us.

The struggle had been desperate, all along that line of nearly forty miles, at Petersburg as well as at Richmond, and in those dark and desperate days the boys and old men were obliged to go out and join in the defense of the city.

I heard some one describing the pitiful sight of a school boy brought in mortally wounded, from the outworks of the city; and a grey haired man, his white hair dabbled in blood; but I had seen the fair dead faces of the boys, in the early days of the war, when all were eager for the fray, and our cause seemed so prosperous; so it was no new thing to me. I had seen so much of real suffering, of conflict, danger and death, that for years I could read neither romance or history, for nothing equalled what I had seen and known. All tales of war and carnage, every story of sorrow and suffering paled before the sad scenes of misery I knew of. As those early April days went by, more and more stragglers came from the army. They said it was melting away. Though I pitied the men who had done so much and suffered so long, I could not help despising them for giving up while Lee was still there.

The eventful 9th of April came, and the day after we heard of Lee's surrender. I can never forget the effect the intelligence had on me and on my family. I felt as if the end of all things had come, at least for the Southern people.

Grief and despair took possession of my heart, with a sense of humiliation that till then I did not know I could feel. The distress of the children was as great as mine; their poor little faces showed all the grief and shame that was in their hearts, and each went about sad and dejected as if it was a personal matter. I remember once glancing out at the window and seeing Donald who was too proud to show his concern to the family, walking up and down under the window with his fat little face streaming with tears, and wringing his hands in utter despair. By and by the dismal train of returning refugees began to pass by. Mr. Sherrard and Mr. James Marshall came, and called to see me as they passed by.[63] Their white hair was whiter than ever and their faces hopeless and sad. They were on their way to their ruined homes, which they had not seen for three years, to try and gather up the remains of their scattered fortunes, or to find some place of rest where they could be with their families. Every day came by returning soldiers and refugees and some among them were glad to have the privilege of going back to reunite their broken households. Though it came in so dreadful a shape, it is certainly true that the return of peace brought joy to many; to them at least, it was a "white winged angel," and they were glad to bury pride, patriotism, all, if they could see an end to destruction and bloodshed. And so, of the crowds that lined the roads, though some were gloomily going up, not knowing if they should find any house remaining, others were happy at the thought of being released from danger, hunger and weariness, and of seeing their homes again, even if they were robbed of so much that had made them happy, and though death had left its shadow there.

By far the greatest number, however, seemed to regard peace as a dire misfortune, and many had resolved, and were on their way to leave the country. Among those who were returning came old Dr. Foote of Romney,[64] one who in earlier and happier days I had cordially disliked, and who, though he was a Presbyterian minister, was very bitter and inimical to my husband on account of some difference about the management of a public institution. This difference and bitterness extended itself to the two families, and had arrived at such a pitch that the different members of each ceased all intercourse. My surprise was great then, when the door opened and Dr. Foote entered. A feeling of sympathy prompted me to offer my hand; he did not speak, but burst into a flood of tears.

For some time nothing was said. At last he sobbed out, "I could not believe it, I would not believe it, when they came to tell me Lee had surrendered. I told them I could not hear it, that it was false. I laid on my bed and covered my face and would not see or speak to any one for fear they would tell me that false and harrowing story. I prayed that God would take me then." "Yes," he said, "I laid for days. I would not look out to see the sun shine if it looked on our wretched country and ruined people." I wept, too, with the old man, and loved him then as much as I had once hated him. What was remarkable was that he was a Connecticut man. He had come to Virginia in his youth to teach, and had been living there for fifty years. He told me the coat he had on was made by his daughter of the skirt of her riding habit. He told me of privations that were great for any one, but for an old man dreadful. "And all for nothing," he said. "I would have borne ten times more if I could only have seen our country free from her enemies."

My house was full day after day, of passers by; friends, on their way, some to go home, others to leave the country. Not all of them were dejected, some seemed relieved to be rid of the awful strain, and to be content with defeat if it brought rest and peace.

Many young men came, members of the different regiments that had been disbanded. The Maryland Line, my old friends and neighbors, was represented by Mr. Thomas, young Sully, the son of the great painter, and a few others. I inquired about the rest of them. Only a few were left of the groups that used to gather about my fire on the cold winter evenings at Winchester. Mr. Iglehart who, on marching away had given me his Bible to keep, was killed in the trenches.

Those of them who lived could be counted on the fingers. One day a commotion among the children announced Harry's arrival. He looked worn and weary, and before he spoke, on coming in, he covered his face with his hands and wept. "To think it is all over and I did not strike a blow," were his first words.

He had reached Lee's army as they were on their retreat, and was set to guarding wagons. He worked on with the dispirited and starving throng till the end came. An officer offered him his horse as he did not care to surrender it, and taking it gladly he made his way home.

When the news of Gen. Lee's surrender was made known at Lexington, the quartermaster there divided among those persons who had been connected with the army the stores and provisions that were left there. Some fell to my share, some bacon and beans, and so I had something to give to the hungry men who daily came to ask a meal. Mr. Sherrard told me that his whole fortune being in bank stock, was gone when the currency became so depreciated, and that only a few months before he had received from California $7,000, left him by his son, Robert, who had died there; that to show his confidence in the cause, and inspire others with the same, he had invested it all in Confederate bonds. "Now," said he, "I have not a dollar." I could fully realize what that meant when I looked at his aged, withered face and snow white hair, and thought of the old wife, and the daughters who had for months been wanderers, driven from home by the enemy. After some days I learned that Edward had been dreadfully wounded on the last day of the struggle. Retreating with his command, he fought as he went, turning to fire on his pursuers.

Once as he turned, he received a ball in his face which passed through his jaw, splintering and tearing it fearfully. Finding himself severely wounded he made his way off from the scene of the fight, and determined to get to a place where he could receive attention, he rode on, weak and bleeding as he was, for sixty miles, in all that time not able to take a mouthful to nourish or revive him.

He reached Charlottesville, and there lay for many weeks with scarcely a hope of recovery.

I sent Harry as soon as I heard he was there to take care of him, but finding his brother Angus already there, he returned home.

All the Northern papers I saw were full of joy and exultation over the great victory; and there was much less bitterness expressed than I supposed would be; indeed, they seemed ready to welcome the poor Southern rebels as friends, now that they could fight no

234

longer, and compel them to waste their money on the sinews of war. Now they could return to their money-getting, thanks to the poor rebels who had been whipped.

Some papers even ventured to suggest that Gen. Lee should go to the North and show himself, saying that if he would do so, he would receive an ovation such as no Hero ever had, not even Grant.

They admired his high character, and appreciated his soldierly qualities, as well as his military greatness, and I believe that if his proud humility would have suffered him to make himself a spectacle to be gazed at, they would have showered honours on him. They were accustomed to such coarse-minded heroes as Grant, and such vain-glorious boasters as McClellan, and Pope,[65] and they could not understand such a man as our Hero was.

In a very short time the kind and forbearing feelings our late enemies seemed to entertain for us were displaced by bitter hatred and furious rage, for when the bullet of Booth took away the life of Lincoln they took for granted that it was the act of the Southern leaders and people who had, as they were persuaded, prompted the deed. I cannot deny that when I first heard of the taking off of Lincoln, I thought it was just what he deserved; he that had urged on and promoted a savage war that had cost so many lives; but a little reflection made me see that it was worse for us than if he had been suffered to live, for his satisfaction had been great when we were disarmed, and he was disposed to be merciful. Now no mercy was to be expected from a nation of infuriated fanatics whose idol of clay had been cast down.

We expected nothing but that the Southern people would be accused of planning the murder and procuring its execution; we knew that vengeance would be taken and that the crime would be visited upon our leaders, and prominent men who would be the most assailable objects for their vengeance; but were not prepared for the extent of diabolical rage which they manifested in their treatment of President Davis when he fell into their hands, or that their pitiless fury should demand that a helpless and innocent woman, innocent, as their own failure to prosecute her son proved, should perish at the hands of the hang man.

We had heard nothing from Marshall since the surrender of Gen. Johnston's army. He had been with Johnston, and had gone, no one knew whither. We afterwards found that he had traveled partly on horseback and partly on foot from Greensboro, N.C., where Johnston's surrender took place, to the Mississippi, where he remained on a plantation, employed by a Dr. Taylor to teach his children with others of the neighborhood.

I had intended to return to Winchester as soon as the way was opened, where I had a house at least, but without money for the journey it was impossible; so I had to remain, and wait for whatever time might bring of better or worse fortunes. No one of the family had means or leisure to come and see about our welfare. As soon as Edward began to recover from his frightful and dangerous wound, William set out to go to the lower valley to find out if anything remained to us of property in Winchester, and to try to do something for a maintenance. On his way, being without money, and his horse requiring a shoe, he had to defray the expense by giving to the blacksmith one of two pairs of socks which, with a very few other articles of apparel he had saved from the general confusion of retreat and surrender.

From that, some idea may be formed of the moneyless condition of the whole family, and of the gloom of its present prospects.

He found the house at Winchester so ruined as to be uninhabitable and even if I had had the means to get there, there was nothing to live on, nothing could be cultivated as there was not a fence on the place, and we could by no possibility replace them. So therefore I remained in Lexington, seeing no prospect of relief, and having no hope of assistance from any source.

May 1865

Our condition had been desolate before, but now was forlorn to the last degree. Not even the poor sum of Confederate money we sometimes had was to be hoped for now. I did not give up, but kept my drawing class and devoted its poor proceeds to supplying our most urgent needs. A man offered to take my garden and cultivate it, half for me and the other half for himself, allowing me to select my half. On one side grew two apple trees, which had served a good purpose in supplying apples to roast, so I selected the side on which they grew. It was cultivated carefully but produced nothing but the apples, while I was all the summer daily tantalized by seeing the men come and gather and carry away nice baskets of fresh vegetables, peas, beans and new potatoes, while I and my children sat down to our dinner of dried beans and roasted apples. Our afflictions at that time, however, were not want of food alone: in every way possible the town people were annoyed and persecuted, I among the rest. Some new and oppressive prohibition or arbitrary command would be inflicted on us every day, so that at last we began to lose patience. Small tyrants in the shape of Freedman's bureau men were our principal persecutors. The negroes were at all times encouraged to be impudent and aggressive, and there was danger of their coming in contact with the whites in a hostile manner at every place where they happened to meet; for passions were excited that only a small cause would kindle to a flame of resentment and retaliation. At the slightest offense given to a black, or a bureau man, the wrath of the officials would be brought down on the head of the luckless offender. One afternoon a clerky looking man in a round hat and jaunty coat stepped up on my porch as I stood there and requested in an impudent manner to know which of my sons had torn down a handbill which had been pasted on our garden fence by his order; saying if he could find the offender he would have him severely punished.

I had seen yellow bills posted over the town with some warning or admonition respecting the negroes, and had also seen Roy busying himself tearing down those on our place. I, thinking that when he saw the small size of the offender, it would make the great man regard it rather a subject for laughter than otherwise, went into the backyard and called Roy and presented him as the culprit. He turned on him a threatening brow, and began to scold him severely, saying that if the offense was repeated he should suffer for it. Turning to me, he said, "You should know better how to bring up your children than to encourage them to break the laws." This outburst was, I think, occasioned by his seeing in the little mocking face and fiery black eyes as they looked up from under the yellow curls, something that did not express contrition for his offense, or promise that it should not be repeated; so his reception of his admonitions had a most provoking effect. Turning to me, he said, "You must learn how to control your children, and I can tell you that if the offense is repeated you may find yourself in the Old Capitol prison." Before I had time to reply Harry came riding by, and looking in and seeing the Freedman's bureau man there, concluded that something was wrong.

He dismounted at the back gate, and coming through the house appeared at the door with his whip in his hand. I heard him come behind me and was not surprised when he advanced towards the man with the whip upraised in his hand, saying "Get out of this house, you rascal." I was afraid he would apply the whip or kick him out, so held him by the arm and exhorted the man to go while he was unharmed; he said he would if I would "keep that man off of him." He hastened away while I held Harry, effecting a rather disorderly retreat.

June 1865

In our great straits some weeks before, my two dear boys, Harry and Allan, knowing that every penny that could be made was of consequence, had volunteered to go and try to get work of some kind to do. Harry found employment at Col. Reid's farm, and ploughed from six in the morning till seven at night.[66] Whatever he did he did well, and faithfully, and though his earning were trifling, he determined to do what he could. The thought was terrible to me, of his working for the same wages, and by the side of negroes, but he insisted, and I suffered him to do it; but how my heart would ache when he came home at night with soiled and hardened hands, and rough working clothes, and would fall down asleep anywhere from utter weariness. Not a word to say, and never, as he was accustomed to do, taking a book to read as soon as he came into the house. Allan was more fortunate, being smaller and not so strong, he found some light work to do for Mrs. Cameron, making hay, I think, but his sprightliness and fondness for talking won him such favor in the sight of the young ladies, Mrs. Cameron's daughters, that he was adopted by them as a companion and protector in their drives through the country, as well as entertainer in the parlour. How often I wished then that of all the land their father had owned, I had only a few acres on which I could live with my children and try to make a living. That would have been independence, and none of us would have shrunk from labour. But to have my boys work as hired labourers for other people! It almost broke my heart. Others worked, the first young men in Virginia went cheerfully to the plough; but the land was their own; the farms they had been born and bred on, and that was so different. It seemed as if there was nothing left for us in the world but to starve or descend to the lowest level by working as labourers; and even then we could expect nothing but squalid poverty. To see my noble sons, little daughter, and pretty little boys dragged down so low, how could I bear it.

With all these tormenting anticipations and fears, there was the ever-present wolf to keep from the door; but he was always there, for at times I was so weak from hunger that I could scarcely go up and down stairs. Others had enough, but no one had time then to think of us, for all were trying to care for their own; and they were at home, and had all their possessions around them, and I was a stranger, in a strange land, and there was no ear into which I could pour my tale of suffering and poverty, but that of God, and He heard, and in His own good time sent relief. Gen. Pendleton had come home and when all was over, and had set himself to provide food and a support for his family. With his own hands he ploughed his fields, and his daughters, accomplished ladies as they were, went into the fields and planted the corn and potatoes.

Poor old gentleman, I often wondered if he did not almost break his heart for his only son whom the grave had hidden from his sight; and who would have been his natural helper and staff to lean on in his old age.

July 1865

In those dreary days I used to go and see Mrs. Dailey, the one person left to whom I could speak of my situation. Her's was little better, for her husband had gone back to his old home to see if a living could be made, and to try to establish his family. While he was gone they were in a great state of distress, being even for a time without bread. One morning when I went there I found her eyes red with weeping, and she told me she had just sent her mother's silver bowl to the mill to exchange for a barrel of flour; it was a great trial to her to part with it and she was of course very sad. I had been obliged to do the very same thing, only it was a ladle that we bought bread with. Her messenger soon returned with the bowl and the flour also; he brought also a message from Dr. Leyburn, owner of the mill, that she must keep the bowl and send for flour whenever she wanted it.[67]

It seemed to me at this time that matters were so bad that they could by no possibility be worse, but I found that they could be much worse; and I found also that God was so good, that with the trial he provided the needful help. One morning when the servant was engaged in another part of the house, I had taken her place in the kitchen.

There was a large fireplace but no stove, and it was very difficult for my inexperienced hands to take the kettle from it without setting fire to my clothes. With great effort I succeeded in taking it off full of boiling water, and having poured it into the tea pan took the pan by the handles and attempted to carry it upstairs to the dining room for the purpose of washing the breakfast things. It fell from my hands, I know not how or why, but all the boiling water poured over my right foot.

Of course I shrieked out with pain and fright, and in a moment many persons had gathered around the house to see what the trouble was. I ran by them all up stairs, and on taking off the stocking all the skin came with it.

For many weeks I was confined to the bed and suffered greatly. My boys had to remain at home to take care of the younger children and attend to me. I could not turn in the bed, and could not endure a footstep that would occasion the slightest jar. A door shut too suddenly, would occasion a nervous shock and intense pain. All this time my good boys, Harry and Allan, lifted me, and did all they could to keep the house quiet and me undisturbed.

How they fared, poor things, I did not know. I could not even think of them. I was remembered by my friends in the village, who sent every day nice breakfasts and dinners, so that I suffered for nothing in the way of food.

All my friends came to see me and were very kind. The Pendletons especially were more like relatives than strangers. Little Madge Paxton came every morning, and with her neat ways and pretty gentle face made me feel happy and cheerful as she moved about the room setting things in order and arranging all as nicely as possible.

She also superintended the washing and dressing of Nelly and Hunter, and when Nell had diphtheria during my sickness, Madge attended to her and washed her throat out every morning with the utmost care. Whenever she came in the morning she brought a bunch of grapes or an orange or something else nice for Nell and me. Dear little Madge, good and sweet she is, and I hope she may be as happy in this world as she deserves to be, and meet with her reward in the next one. Dr. Graham attended my injuries with constant care and skill,[68] and in two months I was able to move about the room on crutches.

In the mean time, Dr. Dailey returned and prepared to take his family away to Romney. Mrs. Dailey spent the day before she left with me in my room, and I felt that I was losing my only real intimate friend; one who knew all my circumstances, and to whom I was not ashamed to confess my destitution. I wished to go when they went, to go anywhere that some change might be effected in our sad, hard lot. When they were gone I felt doubly forlorn and undone, and when I could go about the house, the sight of the destitution, the want of every thing was more than I could bear. Then came the darkest and saddest of all those sad times. I had no one now to whom I could confide any part of my misery.

Mrs. Powell had been long gone, and now Mrs. Dailey and the Doctor, who had been my friends for long years, ever since I was married, and to whom I had no hesitation in speaking of my trouble, were also gone, and I felt forsaken. It is true I had many friends, but though they were kind, and would have helped if they had known the condition of things, yet they were friends of a very recent date, and how could I, when they came to pay a visit, make them uncomfortable by telling them we had nothing to eat! No, I would sit and talk to them, and be as cheerful as I could, but not the less did I when they were gone, go up stairs and throw myself on my knees and cry to God for food.

Aug. 1865

One day, I can never forget it. I had been sitting at the table eating nothing. How could I eat bean soup and bread? I loathed it and could not taste it. The children did not ever, though it was easy to see they disliked it. But I was starving; I felt so weak and helpless and every thing seemed so dark, that for a time I was seized with utter despair. I felt that God had forsaken us, and I wished, oh! I wished that He would at one blow sweep me and mine from the earth. There seemed no place on it for us, no room for us to live.

I laid on a sofa through all those dreadful hours of unbelief and hopelessness; I had lost the feeling that God cared for us, that He even knew of our want. The whole dreadful situation was shown to my doubting heart; the empty pantry, for even the beans and bread were exhausted, and I should have to send the servant away. The house rent to be paid, and no money for it, although it had been due and demanded some time before. The coming cold weather and the want of everything that could make life bearable, made me wish it would end. I did not think; nor did I dare to pray the impious prayer that God would destroy us, but I wished it; I desired at that moment to be done with life, for no one seemed to care for us, whether we lived or died. How long I lay there I do not know, but after a while came the remembrance of the goodness my God had shown me in the former dark hours I had passed through; how He had been near, my Heavenly Father, and how I had leaned on and trusted Him; with that remembrance came the resolve, "Though He slay me, yet will I trust in Him." I got up, saying, or trying to say:

"Although the vine its fruit deny,
The budding fig tree droop and die,
No oil the olive yield
Yet will I trust me in my God,
Yea bend rejoicing to his rod,
And by His stripes be healed."[69]

For days the remembrance of that dreadful hour clung to me, and made me afraid to dwell in thought for a moment on my own miseries. I feared the attacks of the Tempter, and so tried to busy myself about something. But what was there to do, what had I to do anything with? My drawing class had melted away as the summer advanced, and when my foot was scalded, of course it had all to be given up.

One day a package was sent me from Winchester by some friends who had not forgotten me. Some frocks and shoes for Nelly, and underclothing for myself. I was thankful for it, but how many more wants were there for which there was no supply. I determined at last to try to get the class together again, and with the assistance of Miss Baxter succeeded in getting back two or three of my scholars. But how small a sum it brought, not enough to do more than buy bread. The struggle went on seeming more and more hopeless every day as the cold days and nights drew near and no provision for them. When October came and brought its mellow sunshine, and the soft veil lay over the mountains and river, I used to walk, to take long walks, and try to enjoy the delight of breathing the pure air, and to get back a little of the pleasure I used to have in the woods and fields at that sweetest of all seasons. But I could scarcely lift my heavy eyes to the blue hills, or endure the light of the lovely sunsets.

The sight of the smooth, peaceful river gave me no joy of heart, or the songs of the birds, the incense-laden air, nothing, for always the thought of the desolation of our penniless home was before me, and my heart ached continually.

Sept. 1865

Gen. Lee having been invited to take the presidency of Washington College, and having accepted it, was daily expected to come to Lexington. One afternoon Allan came into my room in an excited manner and announced his arrival. I went to the window and saw riding by on his old war-horse, Traveler, the great old soldier, the beloved of the whole country, and the admiration of the world. Slowly he passed, raising his brown slouch hat to those on the pavements who recognized him, and not appearing conscious that he more than any body else was the object of attention.

He wore his military coat divested of all marks of rank; even the military buttons had been removed. He doubtless would have laid it aside altogether, but it was the only one he had, and he was too poor to buy another.

The people loved and admired him more than ever when they heard that he had refused the gift of a fortune from some of the southern people who were still wealthy, and requested the generous persons who offered it, to give what they could spare the families of the dead soldiers. How different from the great man on the other side who accepted a brown stone house and a hundred thousand dollars, though widows and orphans were plenty who needed help.

Allan flew up stairs and made himself presentable, and betook himself up to the hotel to be present when Gen. Lee dismounted. When he returned he had a lock of horsehair in his hand which he said he had pulled out of Traveler's tail, and announced his intention of preserving it for his wife to wear in her breastpin. It became quite common afterwards for the students to rob Traveler's tail, and Gen. Lee said one day at my house that he would allow no one to go behind him without becoming restive.

243

While every one else that I knew was interested in, and assisting with the preparations for Mrs. Lee's reception, I was wholly occupied with my own trouble and distresses. I could have helped when the other ladies went to the house to put down the carpets, make up the linen, and arrange the house, all of which was a labour of love, done by willing hands; but how could I go among them with my sad face and sorrowful heart. So I kept away, feeling that I had no part in working for their comfort, or of welcoming them when they came.

Oct.

The misery of those weeks in October, I must remember always, for with the pressure of present want and the knowledge that though I was there close to a college where the sons of my neighbors would go and be educated, that mine could not have the benefit of an education, as they could not pay the fees, or procure clothes to wear. I had written to Missouri to a lawyer to employ him in collecting my dower in land my husband owned there, but as yet had received nothing.

One evening I went out to walk, as much to get away from the gloomy house as for any thing else, and as I passed up the street, saw into the pleasant houses the bright fires, looking so cheerful, and the people that sat by them looking so contented, that it made me feel all the more desolate.

I felt too wretched and forlorn to go where people were, but turned and went into the cemetery. I sat there by Sandy Pendleton's grave for some time, trying to regain courage and hope. The evening was cold and clear, and the shadows were darkening over the lovely mountains opposite where I sat. The deep purple became deeper, till at last their huge outlines began to grow dim, and I could not stay longer, but turned and came out.

Near the gate I met Mrs. Pendleton going to visit her only son's grave. She met me and as she looked in my face she exclaimed: "What can be the matter, you look so dreadfully? Come home with me now, I will go back."

I only burst out crying, for her words of kindness upset all my composure. She held my hands and begged me to tell her. I smothered pride and said, "We are starving, I and my children." "Comfort yourself," she said. "I meant to have come and told you that help is coming for you. You are to receive a sum of money in a few days. William has given in your name to those who have charge of it, and you and Kate will each receive one hundred dollars. You must not ask where it comes from."

I went to bed that night with a happy heart and a thankful one.

I learned long after that the money was a part of a sum that had been sent to Canada for secret service; that after the surrender those in whose hands it was, determined to devote it to the relief of the destitute widows and orphans of Confederate soldiers. Gen. Edmund Lee was there,[70] and gave my name and Kate Pendleton's, Sandy's widow, to them. General Pendleton having suggested it in writing to him.

The next morning I felt cheerful enough to go and see Mrs. McElwee, intending to spend the day, not to get something to eat, but to enjoy her kind and friendly talk. After staying a while she told me she had just had a quarter of beef sent, and insisted on giving me a roast. I accepted it gladly, and immediately decided on returning home to have it cooked for the children's dinner. This I did, wrapping it in paper I put it under my shawl and carried it home.

Mrs. McElwee had received a sum of money from the estate of her brother who had been killed at Chickamauga, and a few days after she came and offered to lend me three hundred dollars. I accepted it, and with a light and happy heart set about making provision for the winter. Some time after Edward came and brought me money to pay my rent. He had found and collected a bond of his fathers, and brought me part of the money. He and William had rented a farm in Clarke County, and he farmed while William taught school. Susan and Flora kept house for them. Edward wanted one of the boys sent to them, so I decided on sending Allan, as Harry was old enough to go to college, and I had determined to send him.

And here ends my account of my trials; and though they were not at an end entirely, I was able in various ways to take care of my family till they were fitted to be of use themselves; and when they were able to bear the burden they took it up manfully, and acquitted themselves well.

Recollections of the year 1861

In November 1860 my husband returned from his mission in Europe. He came full of joy at again seeing his own country, and of exultation that he was an American and a Virginian. More especially the latter, for on Mr. Mason's coming to see him, which he did in half an hour after his arrival, he related to him with pride, that at the New York Custom House when he was questioned about the contents of his baggage, he had pointed to his trunks saying that they contained his clothes, a few articles of jewelry, and a silk dress for his wife and daughters. "That," he said, pointing to a huge seaman's chest packed with books and papers concerning the adjustment of the boundary between the states of Virginia and Maryland, "contains only matters concerning the business on which I went," mentioning its character. The officer after a pause asked what state he was from. On receiving his answer "from Virginia" he turned to his assistant and said: "Let this gentleman's packages pass without examination." He afterwards said to him: "I seldom find anything wrong in the boxes of persons from Virginia." The eyes of both Mr. Mason and himself were filled with tears of happy pride at the high compliment to their beloved state.

In his joy at being at home, and pride in his own country, so much happier he thought than any of those he had visited, he forgot for the time his lifelong hatred for everything Northern and puritanic as he expressed it, for in those days he rarely gave any one credit for a commendable quality if he was born north of Mason and Dixon's line, that circumstance served always to detract from any recommendation the person might have. In his softened mood he seemed to have buried the ill will he had always borne them as well as his remembrance of their approval of, and sympathy with, the atrocious attempt of the murderous John Brown.

The stormy scenes of '59 and '60 also seemed to have faded from his memory, when the mere attempt to elect a Speaker to the House excited the rage of both parties, and the "Black Republicans" as they were called made such furious attacks on the South and her people,

246

made more furious by the recollection of the swift punishment meted out to Brown and his gang in Virginia. None but gentle feelings filled his heart then, and that night he asked Mary to sing "New England, New England, my home o'er the sea." That was a wondrous change, for nothing of New England had before found favor in his eyes.

When Congress again assembled after the election of Lincoln the strife re-commenced with greater fury than before. Nothing was talked of but secession, in every company, at every street corner, whenever two people met that was the subject discussed. The gentlemen, most of them, were of the opinion that that was the only remedy for our troubles: the only way to settle the differences between North and South. They declared that once separated from the North we should have peace and prosperity to a degree before unknown; that we could never have peace with them while we had our slaves, and that we could not, and would not give them up. Some insisted that it was jealousy of our comfort and leisure that made them so oppose slavery, and it seemed strange now, to recall some of the conversations I heard and took part in, on that hateful subject.

I never in my heart thought slavery was right, and having in my childhood seen some of the worst instances of its abuse, and in my youth, when surrounded by them and daily witnessing what I considered great injustice to them, I could not think how the men I most honored and admired, my husband among the rest, could constantly justify it, and not only that, but say that it was a blessing to the slave, his master, and the country; and, (even now I say it with a feeling of shame), that the renewal of the slave trade would be a blessing and benefit to all, if only the consent of the world could be obtained to its being made lawful.

They argued that it was owing to the restrictions put upon the trade that the slaves suffered in the passage; and but for the laws against the traffic, and if it was legitimate they would be far happier if brought away from their own country even as slaves, than they could be if they remained in freedom and barbarism. They insisted also that it was to the interest of the Cotton States and the dignity of the South to revive it. Such men as Mr. James M. Mason, Mr. Ran. Tucker[2] and many others did not hesitate to avow their intention in case the South did secede and achieve her independence to use their best endeavors to establish the iniquitous practice again. Many there were, however, who did not go so far and though they were no advocates of slavery or the slave trade, were unwilling to be dictated to by a hostile section, and were in favor of secession for the sake of independence. For some time the people of Virginia had been trying to carry out an oft expressed intention of buying nothing at the North, not even importations from other countries; so the ladies, some of them wore linsey, and the men homespun. All the woolen factories in the lower valley were hard at work to supply the demand for woolen fabrics of every kind. But I confess that few besides the elderly and very patriotic were heroic enough to adorn their charms with linsey woolsey. I was at a large dinner party at Mrs. Conrad's given to the bride of a young relative who had married in Memphis.[3] The bride was very richly dressed, and the company moderately so, while Mrs. Conrad presided at her table in a linsey gown. Few people could have appeared, however, as she did in such a dress. Her dignity and grace were unequaled, her manners perfect in their composure, and her face the most beautiful I ever saw a person of her age have, with its sparkling black eyes, regular and beautiful features, with the snow white hair parted on her forehead, and the dainty white cap half covering it.

In Congress the scenes daily became more alarming to the lovers of peace, and more gratifyingly spirited to the wishers for separation. The opinion was almost unanimous that separation was inevitable, but that it would be peaceful; that the importance of the supply of cotton was such that the North dared not go to extremities. And if it did, that Europe and the rest of the world would interfere. "Cotton is King" was the cry, and it was sufficient for people to believe it to make them willing to abide the issue whatever that might be. The secession of South Carolina on the 20th of December was hailed with delight by our extremists, and when it was followed by that of the other cotton states there was great rejoicing.

At the same time there were many men and women of my acquaintance who did not regard it as a cause of joy. As for me, I mourned over it, I had a constant sense of coming evil, and felt almost certain that such a matter could only be settled by war and all its train of woes. The excitement of the time was such that no one could judge calmly, every day some additional news, or some fresh occurrences would serve to keep alive the interest and ardour of the people. The Senators from the seceding states were leaving Washington for their homes; and when Senator Brown of Mississippi came to Winchester after vacating his seat he was greatly toasted and admired. Dinner parties were given and feasting went on as if we were not all standing on the brink of an abyss. It has since often been a matter of wonder to me, that so many men of sense could have agreed in being so shortsighted. No one then took much time to think. Everybody seemed to be frantic, bereft of their sober senses. The gods must have meant to destroy us as the old heathen said; for they made us mad.

The morning we heard of the attack on Fort Sumpter, the 11th of May, '61, I came into the room where my husband was, and found him in a state of great excitement not unmingled with pleasure. "Gallant little state," said he, "she deserves to lead all the rest, for she has always been true to her principles." "What," said I, "if there is war, and war means misery, deserted and desolate homes, and the loss of all we hold dear." "There will be no war," he said; "those Northern rascals will be afraid to fight us, and we will have the world on our side, for the world will have cotton." Ah, how the scales fell from his eyes! There was no dearth of excitement at any time in Winchester, for some of the recusant statesmen in passing through, on their return to their homes at the summons of their seceded states, made inspiring addresses and appeals to the people, assuring them of triumph over the North, in the event of war, but scarcely admitting the idea that war would come. The Virginia Convention had been sitting for weeks in sad deliberation; for there were many of the best and truest men in it who thought secession fatal to the Southern interests, and had seen with sorrow the hasty action of South Carolina and the gulf states. A peace commission recommended by Virginia had been sent to Washington, but its overtures were rejected.[4] Still, the moderate men in the Convention and in the whole country hoped for peace, and opposed extreme measures; but when Lincoln's proclamation came, calling on Virginia to contribute her quota of 75,000 men, necessary to "put down the rebellion of the other states," what a change! Those who had been calm and moderate were now furiously indignant at the insult to Virginia. Not a dissenting voice was raised when the ordinance was passed that took her out of the company of the states which were ruled by the vulgar rail-splitter, who had sneaked into Washington disguised, for fear of assassination; and who had had the insolence to call on her for aid in crushing the sovereign states which had only acted as she believed she as well as they had a right to do. Some days before the proclamation was known, some friends requested me to go to Mr. Sherrard's to assist in making a Confederate flag, as it was afterwards called.[5] "The stars and bars" had been adopted by the seceded states, and as we were cutting out the white and red stripes Judge Parker came,[6] and sent for me and another lady, and begged us to relinquish the idea of making it, as there was danger of an attack on the bank building, in which Mr. Sherrard lived, if we persisted in making a secession flag, as the mechanics and trades-people were so opposed to secession that it would enrage them if they knew a flag was being made. We put it away, but at the end of a week, when the odious proclamation had decided Virginia's course, a change had come over the feelings of all classes; and the flag was brought out, and triumphantly unfurled to the sound of ringing of bells that announced the secession of Virginia.

Apr. 1861

On the morning of the seventeenth of April I was at breakfast, when my ears were greeted by the ringing of all the bells in town. Many bells were ringing, and as the tones softened by the distance, came on the sweet morning air, they seemed to have a sound of joy and exultation. Edward had half done his breakfast,[7] and at the sound of the bells he jumped up from the table, and running down the avenue was soon on his way into the town at a swift run.

The bells rang on, and shouts of people mingled with the sound. I did not for a moment think what it meant, but went about my household affairs, and about ten o'clock set out to go to town, taking with me the beautiful dress pattern my husband had brought me from Paris, to have it made. At the gate I stopped to ask a man who was passing what the bell ringing meant; he said, "Virginia has passed the ordinance of secession." I turned and went back to the house, folded up the dress and put it away; for I felt that in the days that were coming I should have no use for finery.

When I got in town every person I met was full of joy; those who a week ago were so violently opposed to secession had completely turned round, and were as ardent and exultant as any one. A few flags showing the stars and bars were on some of the houses, but when we had made and unfurled the large one which had been so obnoxious over the Farmers Bank, it excited great enthusiasm. I did not see Edward for three weeks; he had reached the Taylor Hotel and found that men were volunteering to go to Harper's Ferry to take possession of the armory and to hold the place; he immediately started off with them, and was in the war, from which he never returned except on a hurried visit, till that dreadful day at Appomattox, when, wounded and suffering, he made his way off the stricken field to find a place, as he thought, to die in. In a few days we learned that the Federal troops stationed at Harper's Ferry had evacuated the place after destroying a large part of the public property; and in a few days more, men began to gather towards that point from all parts of the state, men of all grades and pursuits; farmers from their ploughs, boys from their schools came in companies which in sport they had formed for drilling, students from the colleges, all were making to the point of expected conflict. I saw the students of the University of Virginia, gaily marching through the town, in their red shirts and black trousers, utterly unprovided with such sordid things as overcoats and blankets, but full of ardour at the prospect of encountering the Yankees. Col. Jackson of the Virginia Military Institute was summoned there and assumed command. My husband was in Richmond when the ordinance was passed, and immediately proceeded home, or rather to Harper's Ferry, and offered himself as volunteer aid to Col. Jackson. He came up to Winchester one night while the assembling of forces was going on; he was anxious and uneasy; for even his ardour could not blind him to the dangers of an attack on the undisciplined forces there. He spoke of the arrangements to guard against surprise; of the students who had been placed to guard the bridge. When he spoke of them he almost wept: "To think of those noble fellows being slaughtered like sheep, as they will be if an attack is made on them in their unprepared condition."

May 1861

Soon the news reached us of the approach to Baltimore, of troops from Massachusetts and Pennsylvania; and of the resolve of the citizens to dispute the passage. At midnight a messenger reached Harper's Ferry from Gen. Stuart, of Baltimore, for arms for the citizens.[8] Prompt action was necessary, and when an appeal was made for someone to go in charge of the arms, no one responded to it, till Edward came forward and offered to go. His offer was accepted, and procuring an engine and tender he had it loaded with arms from the stores of the Ferry, and started off in the night to Baltimore with only an engine driver and fireman. When he reached the station an excited multitude was there to receive him; and old Gen. Stuart clasped him in a close embrace in his joy of seeing him with the wished for arms. The bloody scenes that were enacted in those streets there can never be forgotten; bravery and patriotism were of no avail. Under the pretense of protecting the National Capital more troops were hurried from the North. Passing around Baltimore, they reached Washington, where they remained to keep the rebellious city of Baltimore in subjection by cutting her off from her friends, and to threaten Virginia. Maryland now was powerless. The people no more sang their beautiful patriotic songs in the streets, for they were captive; and the best and truest men were seized and sent away to Northern prisons. Her whole legislature was imprisoned in Fort Warren. Then the young and the ardent came pouring over the river into Virginia, to fight Maryland's battles on her soil; and on many a hard fought field did the Maryland Line maintain the honour of their old state. Those days of preparation for battle were holiday days compared with what came after. We, the ladies, worked unceasingly making lint, rolling bandages, (alas! for limbs that then were sound and active) making jackets and trousers, haversacks and havelocks, and even tents were made by fingers that had scarcely ever used a needle before. Up to the 29th of May, no hostile foot had ventured on Virginia soil, though Alexandria was closely watched and threatened, for the war vessel Pawnee was anchored in the Potomac opposite the city, with guns bristling, ready to open fire if any movement of troops was made to invade Washington. So we at least thought and we imagined that that was all they dared do, that they would not venture to cross to Virginia to offer battle, fearing to meet her armed hosts. They were not only watching, but were holding Alexandria in their grasp. Like the cat that knows the mouse is in its power, lets the poor thing imagine it is at liberty, when the claw has only to close down and crush it. So the Pawnee held the old city. Full of confidence and determined, the people made their preparations for fight if it should come. The troops stationed in the town were daily paraded, guards were stationed, and every means adopted to repel an attack. Still they felt secure that no attack would be made, that the enemy would be content with protecting his own side of the river, and would not venture to cross; but they were fearfully awakened from their delusion, when on that calm night, as the moon shone quietly down on the sleeping town, a band of men stole into it without the note of drum or martial trumpet, and took possession. Then the blood of the "Martyr Jackson" was shed, and all Virginia was aroused to avenge him.[9] Troops were now pouring into Winchester on their way to the gathering of the clans at Harper's Ferry. Among the rest came a body of men from the upper valley, from Rockingham county; I heard that when asked if they had arms, having nearly all arrived without them, they acknowledged that they had none, but expressed their willingness to try the issue with stones!

I, who had always loved the Union, and gloried in the stars and stripes, was surprised at myself when I felt my pulses bound at the sight of the first Confederate flag I saw borne at the head of a marching column. It was carried by the Culpeper minute men, who in passing through had halted in the street. I had gone to see them come in, as Wood was among them.[10] It was night, and the line of shadowy forms occupied the middle of the street, while admiring crowds thronged the pavements. Above them the flag chosen by the Confederacy slowly furled and unfurled its stars and bars, as the wind rose and fell, and as I beheld it my heart beat high, for it seemed a promise of glory and greatness, and of triumph over those who would deprive us of our right to do as we pleased with our own. Ah! I did not know then what a portentous sight it was, I only thought of the attempted coercion of our free state and country, and felt that no sacrifice was too great to ensure their defeat. I knew that blood must be shed, but the trial would be soon over, and we would be forever free. We were conscious of strength and courage, and were fully possessed of the idea of the importance of our part of the country as the producer of cotton for the world. The seat of the Confederate Government having been, on the secession of Virginia, transferred to Richmond, the Carolinas and Gulf States began to send their troops to defend the noble old state that had so manfully placed herself between them and her enemies, making their cause her own, and provoking them to fight the battles of the South on her soil, and make her a desolation. The first regiment that came from the South was from Alabama; a splendid body of men, and a grand welcome did they receive as they came marching through the streets of Winchester, all along the length of which the windows streamed with banners, and expectant crowds awaited them. Loudon Street from end to end was draped with Confederate flags, the same flag that a few weeks before we dared not show for fear of the people. Now it was the people who flung it to the breeze, and who crowded to fight under its folds.

Soon a Georgia Regiment came, commanded by Col. Bartow, and the same greeting was extended to them.[11] Every house was opened to them, and instead of their being obliged to seek soldiers quarters they were received and entertained as honoured guests.

I drove out one afternoon to the Georgia camp, and we were invited to Col. Bartow's tent. Over it floated a splendid banner of silk, displaying the red, white and red, and richly embroidered with the arms of Georgia, and fringed with gold; a gift from the ladies of Georgia. We saw the parade, a beautiful sight; the uniforms were dark green and gold, and the men went through all their maneuvers with perfect order, so well were they drilled. After it was over, the boys, for boys most of them were, began to play games, leap frog and others; so joyous they looked, so full of life and gaiety, that I could not help contrasting their happy looks with the melancholy face of their commander. As he stood looking at them a deep sadness was on his countenance, and I heard him say to Mrs. Ambler,[12] "I cannot drive from my mind the thought of the terrible struggles in which they will have to bear their part." I thought afterwards that his sadness was prophetic, for when the sun had set over the dreadful field of Manassas two months afterwards, Col. Bartow lay dead with the best part of his splendid regiment around him.

My husband, as I have said, had gone immediately from Richmond, where he was when the ordinance passed, to Harper's Ferry, and offered himself as volunteer aid to Gen. Jackson.[13] He was employed in assisting to organize the forces assembled there, and aiding by his military knowledge in all the measures taken by Col. Jackson for the protection of the border. Ashby's troop of Black Horse cavalry,[14] organized in Prince William County, had been placed on a sort of picket duty near the Point of Rocks, and along the river, by Gen. Harper,[15] the commander of the state militia, and was thus engaged when Col. Jackson arrived at the place from Lexington with the cadets.[16]

June

My husband had applied to the War Department for permission to raise a regiment of cavalry, and Ashby's troop was the first to join him. His object was to employ his command in guarding the boarder of the Upper Potomac. His rendezvous was at Winchester, and so many applications to join him by gentlemen who had raised troops of horse, were made, that the regiment was rapidly filled, and by the 17th of June was ready for service.

Ashby had been appointed Lieut. Col., and his troop was assigned to his brother Richard. Headquarters were at our house, and it was thronged day and night by armed men passing to and fro, while preparations were going on for the removal of the regiment. The hall was the place where military affairs were attended to, and in passing back and forth the ladies of the family not infrequently had their flounces caught by a spur, or would run against a carbine. The clashing of sabres and jingling of spurs became a familiar sound, and in the activity and excitement we nearly lost sight of the object of the preparations.

The men slept under the trees in the yard, and though the two Ashbys were pressingly invited to sleep in the house they declined, preferring to share the discomforts of their men. On the morning of the 17th of June the regiment marched away, with orders to move along the North Western turnpike and destroy the bridges of the Baltimore & Ohio Railroad over the Cheat river,[17] in order to break the communication between Washington and the West, so as to prevent the advance of troops in that direction till forces could be sent from Staunton to Western Virginia to relieve the remnant of the Confederate forces lately commanded by the ill-fated Garnett.[18] My husband had only one of his older sons with him, Angus, who was Adjutant of the regiment. He seemed anxious to have one of the younger boys, and poor Harry had fixed his hopes on being the one selected; but he talked with him, and told him that though he, being older and stronger would be better able to assist him, he could not think of taking him from home where his presence was necessary, as no man was on the place but negroes. He told him he had such a high opinion of his sense of duty and willingness to do it, that he knew he would not repine. So he took Allan with him, and though Harry was flattered at being placed in the position of guardian of the household, he could not command stoicism sufficient to see without tears the regiment march away to its glorious destiny, while he was left behind; so he retired to hide his grief, while Allan gleefully went off with his father. The second day after leaving Winchester they reached Romney, where they remained to perfect their arrangements, and to await the arrival of some of their equipments which were to come from Richmond. In the meantime scouts were sent out to ascertain the whereabouts of McClellan's force which was still threatening an advance from Western Virginia.[19] In order to secure forage for their horses and provisions for their men, it was deemed advisable for the regiment to separate and go to different points on the railroad. Six miles from Romney Col. Ashby established his camp, calling it Camp Washington, in compliment to Mr. George Washington, on whose estate the camp was.

On the morning of June 26th Col. Ashby selected his brother Richard to command a party of eleven men who were commissioned to arrest some mischievous individuals of suspected Union proclivities. Finding on arriving at the place that the men he sought had put themselves out of the way, he determined to push his scout nearer to the Federal lines. Proceeding along the railroad, and turning off to avoid a cattle guard, he was startled by a volley of musketry which was poured into his ranks. Rapidly forming his little band of men to receive the coming charge, he perceived that he was outnumbered. Determining to withdraw to a more favourable position, he endeavored to effect a retreat, himself bringing up the rear, when the Federal column of a hundred charged on them. Firing as they rapidly retreated down the railroad, they were suddenly brought to a stop by the cattle guard they had turned off to avoid in the morning. Most of the men made the leap, but Ashby's horse, as he turned to fire at his pursuers, lost his footing, and fell into the cattle guard with his rider. Ashby sprang to his feet and seeing the danger called to his men to shelter themselves. He was then alone, attacked by a large body of men who fired on him as they advanced. He fought bravely, but was soon cut down in a hand to hand encounter with the bravest of his foes. He fell, pierced by more than a dozen wounds; and gasping as he was, when they asked if he was a secessionist, and he said "Yes," they gave him a thrust in the abdomen which was his death. Col. Ashby had gone with a party on a scouting expedition in another direction, and being informed of the firing heard in that taken by his brother, he went at full speed and overtook the enemy at Kelly's Island. Plunging into the Potomac, he charged them with his men and soon routed them. Three of his men fell, and he received a slight wound. Gathering up his wounded he returned to the Virginia shore in search of his wounded brother. He was still alive, but survived only a week, for on the 3rd of July he died, mourned by all who knew him. His death was a terrible blow to his brother who I heard many say, was never the same man. Always brave and daring, he was now fierce in his recklessness, and in the one short year that he lived after his brother's death, he won such a name by his dashing bravery and by his splendid soldierly qualities, that he was placed in command of a brigade. His connection with my husband's command ceased in a month or two after he went to Romney with the regiment, as he and several companies were assigned to duty on the lower Potomac. In one year, from the time of which I have written, his eventful career was closed. On the 6th of June, 1862, he fell near Port Republic while leading his squadrons in a charge on a body of cavalry commanded by Sir Percy Wyndham, an Englishman, Col. of the 1st New Jersey Cavalry. He was supported by the celebrated Pennsylvania Bucktails, and other troops; they were defeated, and both commanders taken prisoner, Wyndham, and Col. Kane, of the Pennsylvania Bucktails.[20] Wyndham being left alone by his retreating regiment, surrendered to Edward, then in command of the 11th Virginia cavalry, and Holmes Conrad.[21] The flag of the Pennsylvania regiment was captured by Edward's men; it was made of the wedding dress of Mrs. Kate Chase Sprague.[22] The victory was dearly bought by the valuable life of one of the most brilliant cavalry officers in the Confederate service. The story of the death of the two Ashbys has been told often; but I repeat it here, on account of the connection of them both with my husband's command. I so well remember the two brothers as they sat together on my right at the breakfast table; Richard, with his handsome brown eyes and hair, his bright smile and pleasant manners, while Turner, with jet black piercing eyes, black hair and beautiful coal black beard, sat grave and quiet, but enjoying the chat. It seemed that morning as if some gay pleasure excursion was on foot, so bright and spirited they all were as they marched away, but for the cannon it might have been taken for a holiday expedition. Edward, who had joined the 10th Virginia regiment as a private, went with it and the 1st Tennessee to Romney under command of Col. A. P. Hill.[23] He had been since the John Brown raid in command of a militia regiment[24] and was still occupying that position when on visiting Hampshire County while the troops were collecting and organizing, he saw a man about to march off with a volunteer regiment, leaving his wife in great distress. The tears of the woman were more than he could bear, so he volunteered to take the place of the man, thus losing his chance of a command which he could readily have had, as he was well esteemed for his courage and energy, and thoroughly acquainted with the country. His first experience as a foot soldier was not an agreeable one, but he was rewarded after his wearying march by the warm welcome of the people of Hampshire who had known him from a boy and knew his worth. He regarded the place and people with great affection, as Romney was his birthplace, and of the county of Hampshire and some adjoining scarcely a corner was unknown to him, as when a boy he had in his hunting expeditions roamed over them at will.

A few days after his regiment arrived at Romney, he was sent with a detachment of it to destroy the Baltimore & Ohio Railroad bridge at New Creek. They marched all night and at daylight arrived at the bridge. They found there a few home guards who had been left to defend the place. Col. Vaughan, who commanded the expedition, led his Tennessee regiment by columns of two instead of line of battle, while Captain Robert White was sent with his own company and a detachment of that to which Edward belonged to cross the river below the bridge and attack the defending party in the rear.[25]

When the detachment commanded by Capt. White reached the river, the head of the column stopped and fell into confusion, as no one seemed disposed to lead them on to the attack. Edward at his place in the ranks, was appealed to by one of the Lieutenants, and asked what had better be done. He told him if he would take ten men and protect their crossing that he would lead them on over the river. He plunged in, followed by the whole command, and when he reached the opposite shore, the surgeon, who was the only officer who had crossed with the command, dismounted and offered him his horse and sword, saying that he was better fitted to command than those whose duty it was. He took the horse and assumed command, thereby violating all military rules, being only a private.

As soon as the home guards (Union men) perceived them crossing the river, they beat a disorderly retreat, and the fleetest of foot could not overtake them. The Confederates captured two pieces of old artillery, burnt the bridge, and returned that evening to Romney, having marched about forty miles in twenty-four hours. Finding that McClellan's object was not to march any further in that direction, he having apparently relinquished the design of uniting with Patterson in an advance up the valley,[26] as was supposed he intended doing, Gen. Johnston ordered the two infantry regiments to repair to Winchester, my husband's cavalry to take their place in Romney.[27] There they remained till the 17th of July, when orders were received to march to Winchester. On the 19th they began the march.

Gen. Johnston had on the 10th of June evacuated Harper's Ferry, marching all of his army to Winchester. He had found Harper's Ferry an untenable position, as it could be easily flanked by any one of the three bodies of troops which then threatened the valley. He removed all the munitions of war that he could get away, and destroyed the bridge. I think that I, with my own hands, made the cotton bag to hold the powder for the train. A bag was brought to me to be made, many yards long, and about three inches wide, and I was requested to sew it up. I inquired what it was for, and was told it was to blow up the bridge at Harper's Ferry. It was not interesting work, but I was zealous, and sat up till far into the night to finish the never-ending seam. Gen. Johnston having arrived with his army, the old town was made lively again, it having worn rather a gloomy aspect after the departure of the cavalry two days before. The army was encamped near our house in the fields on the edge of town. We had plenty of company, for people were constantly coming and going, young men, friends of the girls and boys, and men of distinction both of the army and in civil life were our daily visitors and every meal was a festive occasion; for gay officers and pleasant young privates were always there, besides ladies from all parts of the state who had come to see their friends. The parades, the galloping back and forth, the music and the stir, made it seem a great gala time, for as yet there were no features visible of grim visaged war. Already though, the hospitals were filling up with sick men from the Southern regiments; they seemed less able to bear the hardships of camp life than the Virginians. The ladies organized parties for attending to the sick, making clothes for the soldiers, preparing bandages, lint, etc., but these doleful employments did not destroy their pleasure in the brightness and gaiety around them, or damp their enjoyment of the society of the pleasant people.

On Gen. Johnston's staff was Kirby Smith, Major Whiting, Captain Fauntleroy, late of the U. S. Navy, Col. Preston, Maj. McLean, Col. Thomas, besides the prominent men in command of brigades and regiments.[28] Scarcely a young man we knew in Virginia but was present in that camp, and the throngs of comers and goers was almost too much for my comfort, I often had to have three or four supper tables set at night, and the parlour floors were often covered with mattresses. Gen. Patterson, the Federal commander, and Gen. Patterson[29] had for some time hovered near Bunker Hill, a point between Winchester and Martinsburg, and we were daily in receipt of news concerning them. Now they were advancing, now returning to Martinsburg; but one day intelligence was received that Patterson was moving on Winchester. By noon Gen. Johnston's army was in motion, marching to meet him, but in two days they all came back, rather crestfallen at being compelled to retrace their steps without an encounter with the foe they had so long wished to meet. A few shots had been fired on either side, and only one casualty occurred on our side. One man had his head taken off by a cannon ball. Holmes Conrad was telling me of it, and said it was a man named Parks. During my refugee life[30] I lived opposite an old man of that name who was demented, and I learned that it was his son who was killed on that day, and that the first intimation he had of it was the arrival of the corpse at his door in the night. He lost his reason then. Thursday, the 18th day of July, Gen. Johnston received a despatch from Gen. Beauregard informing him that McDowell was about to attack him. The whole army was soon in motion, in gallant array, and a proud sight it was, with the Confederate banners waving, the bands playing and the bayonets gleaming in the noonday sun. They passed by our gate and we were all there to bid them good bye and to fill their haversacks with the food we had prepared for them in haste. Many of the companies were made up of mere boys, but their earnest and joyous faces were fully as reassuring as the martial music was inspiriting. Then we watched them out of sight, and saw the last of them; of some the last we should ever see; for on reaching that fatal field they rushed into the battle without rest or refreshment, and turned the tide and brought victory to us. Wood, who had been a private in one of the Virginia regiments for some time, had been appointed aid to Gen. Elzey.[31] He came in haste to get a horse, and the servant who had charge of the horses thought the best not too good for him, and so brought Sam Patch, a fiery young blooded horse, who before he had gone a hundred yards, took occasion to show his distaste to the service, by throwing him over his head. He hurried back and mounting the girl's pretty riding horse, the spirited and beautiful Kate, he dashed off after Elzey. A sad and deserted place was Winchester all those days after they were gone. Friday, Saturday and Sunday passed without news. When Sunday came, bright and peaceful as it was, it seemed as if an unnatural hush was over everything. Gloom and anxiety was on every face; but how would our hearts have fainted if we had known that all through those bright peaceful hours a deadly struggle was going on, that amid the rattle of musketry and the roar of artillery our ranks were being rapidly thinned, that the good and the brave were falling like leaves in Autumn. When night closed the dreadful battle of Manassas had been fought and won. We only heard rumours of a great and overwhelming victory, the enemy had been driven like sheep, so said the accounts, driven so far, and so well beaten that they would scarcely attempt to attack us again; it would end the war, many thought and said. How we watched and waited for news, and how we exulted over that we heard. I remember standing at the gate all day to hear what any passerby might have to tell. We did not begin to realize the horrors of our victory till Tuesday evening when the wagons began to come in with their loads of wounded men; some came, too, with the dead. One stopped at Mr. Charles Powell's, and left his son, Lloyd, killed in the early part of the battle. He had come from the West to join the army just one week before it marched. Another stopped at the house of a plasterer named Glaize.[32] His boy was one of a company of schoolboys who went with Harry to Mr. Clarke's school,[33] and had drilled with the school company till the troops were called to the defense of Virginia. These made a deep impression, because they were the first of the victims. The list is long, and I have no room to tell of more, but will only relate how the two young sons of Mr. Holmes Conrad fell,[34] together with their cousin, Mr. Peyton Harrison, killed by the same shell. They were found lying side by side. When the wagon was seen approaching his house Mr. Conrad went to meet it. Finding what its burden was, he turned and went into the house and into the room where his wife and daughter were sitting. "Let us pray," he said, and they all knelt, asking no question, but knowing full well that an awful calamity had happened. They had joined the army only two weeks before. I saw them when they rode into the camp that day, as they came galloping up, their black groom riding behind them, their rosy young faces bright with excitement and pleasure at the martial aspect of the surroundings.

These were the first fruits of the bitter tree our people had helped to plant and nourish for so many years. We soon learned all the particulars of that memorable battle; how the festive Congressmen had come with their wives, daughters and sweethearts, on the outskirts of the army, seated in luxurious carriages, with hampers packed with champagne and all good things, to regale themselves withal, as from a safe place they would view the triumphant career of their Invincibles as they made the rebels bite the dust, and then to march over their traitorous corpses to Richmond. There, there was to be a grand ball; ladies had provided themselves with magnificent dresses, certainly expecting, after the battle was over, and the rebels were wiped out, to proceed serenely on their way to the Confederate Capital without meeting an obstacle. When the "rebels" had been reinforced by the arch-rebels, Johnston and Jackson, with their worn out but gallant men, and when the Federals with their splendid army had turned and were frantically flying before those same "rebels," they cared for nothing but to get away. The flight of that panic-stricken mob has often been described, and by many pens, none however so graphic as that which after treating of their disgraceful race, styled them the "Bull Runners," the London Punch was, I believe, the author of that appropriate name. The battle was called the battle of Bull Run, because it took place near that stream, a poor little mountain brook, that I remember playing in when a child, as my sister's home was near it.[35] Near there was the great battle fought that might have decided the issue if God had not willed that it should be decided not then or there. And now the homely name has become classic, as much as any in ancient story, for as goodly men, and as glorious heroes dyed its waters that day with their blood, as any that ever fell on the hard fought battle fields of the world. All along the line of pursuit of the fleeing army, our men beheld the shattered trunks of the ladies with their ball dresses;

gossamer robes trampled under feet of men and horses, and which our men picked up and laughingly carried on the points of their bayonets. Huge baskets of wine and all kinds of delicacies strewed the way. We heard many laughable accounts of how the luxurious non-combatants made good their escape; of the prayers for a mule or a wagon horse, anything to bear them out of the reach of danger. The daughter of Thurlow Weed was seen on a mule that had been cut from a wagon making her way through the crowd and din, without saddle or bridle other than a robe around the neck of her steed.[36]

Henry Wilson, a senator, and afterwards Vice President of the United States, begged in vain of a teamster the privilege of a seat on his wagon. After repeated and emphatic refusals, he revealed his name and position. "I am Henry Wilson," said he, "United States Senator"; but the teamster, perfectly unmoved by the announcement of the dignity and importance of his petitioner, cried out, "I don't care a _____ who you are," and lashing his mules, sped on his way. Many noble and brave men laid down their lives on that day; Generals Bee and Bartow headed the list.[37] But of the rank and file whose names perished with them, there were hundreds who we had known of.

I heard the scenes and incidents described by many different actors in it; a shoe maker named Faulkner who had left the army the day after the battle on account of a slight wound, said, as I stood in his shop: "First came Sherman's artillery thundering down a slope, then an avalanche of red, I could not tell what, for I shut my eyes; but I afterwards found it was a regiment of Zuaves;[38] it seemed to me that all creation had turned red." Wood had been ordered to carry a message, and in galloping across the open space in front of the enemy's line, a shell fell and burst just before him. His gallant little horse showed no terror, but tossed her pretty head after a slight pause, and galloped on her way quite composed. William was then a private in the ranks,[39] and his regiment was on that fearful left, while the enemy was making such desperate efforts to flank them. He said they were in a sort of thicket surrounded by a close undergrowth; they could see no enemy to fire at, but without ceasing the bullets whizzed through the bushes, and generally found a mark in some poor fellow, for they fell thickly around. He said that as they were falling behind him and at his side, he feared to look at them lest his own heart should fail and his hand become unnerved. Holmes and Tucker Conrad he saw fall wounded by the same piece of shell. He and others declared that the enemy carried the Confederate banner to deceive our troops.[40] On the 18th my husband reached Winchester with his cavalry, in obedience to an order from Gen. Johnston to join him at Manassas. He arrived at Winchester the day after Gen. Johnston had left. He did not reach Manassas till the day after the battle, greatly to the regret of his regiment. Col. Hill, commanding the 10th Virginia and the 1st Tennessee,[41] had been as related, called to Winchester on the 17th of June, and were encamped near there, forming part of Gen. Johnston's army. When Johnston marched to Darkesville to meet Patterson, Edward was with his regiment. In his diary he says, "We were drawn up in line of battle for three days expecting an attack, but Patterson gave us the slip, and marched off towards Charlestown." When he made his appearance there, to the great disgust of the inhabitants, my boy Harry, who had been sent to act as protector to his sister Mary when Mr. Green left for the army,[42] thought it incompatible with the dignity of a man of thirteen to remain and be captured by the Yankees, so as they entered the town on one side, he left it at the other and walked all the way to Winchester that day, a distance of twenty miles.

While the army of Gen. Johnston was encamped at Winchester, Edward was sent by him to call out the 77th regiment of Virginia Militia of which he was Colonel. Before he had done so, however, Gen. Johnston had left Winchester, and was moving by forced marches to join Beauregard in repelling the attack of the Federals at Manassas, and as Edward was without a commander, his father having left to join Johnston, he thought it best not to call out the militia for the defense of the border, as many of them whose homes were near it were not entirely free from Union proclivities, and he had serious doubts of their reliability if called into action. Under these circumstances he thought it best to follow his father's command and reached Manassas with him the day after the battle. After consultation, his father advised him to return to Hampshire and resume command of his militia, which he decided to do; but on reaching Winchester he found that all the militia of that district had orders to rendezvous there.

He reported to Gen. Carson, in command, who ordered him to order his regiment out and bring it there.[43] His orders were accordingly issued, but only about forty men responded, the rest, or many of them, having gone into the volunteer service. Soon after he was authorized to mount and equip his forty men to do scouting and picket duty. This was the beginning of his cavalry company, with which he afterwards did good service. My husband being ordered to join Gen. Lee in Western Virginia, who was opposing Rosencrantz,[44] marched his regiment towards Staunton. On reaching that place the order was countermanded, and the whole force returned to the valley. Part of the regiment was sent to do picket duty on the border, and formed the guard of all the country from Martinsburg to Harper's Ferry. This part of it was under command of Lieut. Col. Ashby, which six companies under my husband went into camp near Winchester, he having his headquarters at home. I was greatly pleased to have the regiment back again, and especially that my little boy Allan was at home once more. He has a great deal to tell of what he had seen, but unfortunately for his martial and ambitious spirit, he had no adventure of his own by flood and field to relate; but he made up for it by telling of those of others, of which he had heard. While they were encamped near Winchester, sometime in August, I was returning from church one day, and as I reached the gate I observed a carriage standing near, guarded by six cavalrymen. An old gentleman sat inside. When I got to the house I saw my husband sitting in the hall leaning on a table with his face buried in his hands, in an attitude of deep dejection. I asked what the matter was, and he told me that a part of the cavalry commanded by Ashby had, in scouting near Martinsburg, taken and brought in as a prisoner Col. Strother, his father's old companion-in-arms, and his own good friend.[45] He was much distressed but could do nothing till he could communicate with Richmond. The consequences to him of this unfortunate arrest are well known, and I will not dwell on the subject here, except to say that Col. Strother was accused of communicating with the enemy, and nothing could be done to effect his release till his case was examined by the proper authority. My husband did all in his power to prevent any anxiety or suffering from any inconvenience on his part. He desired to entertain him at his house, but Col. Strother preferred going to camp. In the latter part of August my husband went to Romney with six companies of his regiment, about 400 men. The rest of the regiment was still with Ashby near Martinsburg, engaged in protecting the border, and preventing the enemy from rebuilding the railroad and canal which our forces had destroyed. The command was sent to Romney to protect the border there, and also to prevent the rebuilding of that part of the railroad, Baltimore & Ohio, it being the great line of communication by which they received their supplies for the army. Edward now joined his father in Romney, and this time succeeded in organizing about a hundred and fifty of his regiment of militia. These with his company of mounted men formed part of the force for the protection of the border. A great effort was now being made by the Federals to draw the forces away from Romney, as they could do nothing to repair the bridges, culverts and canals while they were here. Upon the 29th of September they began the advance upon my husband's position. I had constant letters from him at this time, expressing regret at the smallness of his force, and fear of his inability to hold the position. In one of his letters he told me of Edward's routing a force of 200 with about seventy of his command. They stationed themselves, part on a precipice overlooking a narrow road formed on the mountain side, where it seemed to have parted for the passage of the river, a place called Blue's Gap.[46] Part were placed a short distance from the narrow pass. Orders were given not to fire till the word of command, but as the dark column moved along on the shelving road, and approached the point overlooked by the precipice, one gun went off by accident, when the enemy opened on the position of the men stationed near. At this moment those on the top of the precipice began to roll down on their advance huge rocks which fell crushing among them, making them all turn and flee for life, overriding in their mad course the infantry that followed. It being too dark to see their enemies, or guess their numbers, they did not pause till safely out of their way. This delayed the advance on Romney for some time. At one time he wrote that anticipating an attack on Romney for some time, he had withdrawn his force six miles out of the town, in order not to have his retreat cut off; that they had occupied the town on his withdrawal, and he had determined to attack them there. That as his troops advanced they retreated rapidly from the town, and that as they were making good their escape Edward was sent in pursuit, and overtaking them while crossing the South Branch of the Potomac, charged them with his mounted men, and they all fled precipitately, never pausing till they were within their fortifications.

Oct. 1861

On Sunday morning, the 7th of October, I was awakened at daylight by the tramp of horses under my window, and the voices of men calling me. I got up and raising the window asked who they were. One answered, "We are men of Col. McDonald's command; the regiment has been cut to pieces, and he is either killed or captured. The last seen of him was standing in the street of Romney with his bridle in his hand, and only one officer with him. We saw him mount his horse, but do not know whether he escaped or not, as the town was then full of the enemy advancing along all the streets." All that day the fugitives were passing, the broken remnants of the once gallant regiment. Not until Tuesday night did I learn of my husband's safety by his arrival at home. He said the enemy were moving to attack him in two columns, one under Col. Kelly from New Creek, the other under Col. Bruce from Green Spring Run, both places on the Baltimore & Ohio Railroad. He had withdrawn his baggage to a point east of the town, and disposed his troops to meet the attack. He had under his command six companies of his cavalry, a small company of artillery, which had been organized by Edward from his militia, and which was provided with one howitzer, one rifled six-pound gun and one old iron four-pounder which had been captured by Col. Hill's command. The 77th Virginia Militia under Edward, numbering 100 men, the 114th under Col. Monroe, numbering 400, in all about 700 men, to oppose a force of 4,000; Col. Monroe was sent to defend the wire suspension bridge, Edward to Blues, while four companies of the cavalry were sent to defend the turnpike road along which one column was to advance.[47]

They skirmished all along the route back to the bridge, and when the enemy attempted to cross, charged and repulsed them, throwing them into great confusion, they retreating on their infantry.

One officer, bolder than the rest, made a desperate charge under the bridge, protected by the piers, and succeeded in gaining the opposite bank. This unexpected maneuver threw the Confederates into a panic, and they retreated back to Romney, passing through the town without pausing.

My husband with two companies of the cavalry and the rifled gun had placed himself at Cemetery Hill as a reserve; but as the panic-stricken men rushed by, they communicated their fears to the reserve, who without ceremony broke ranks and fled after the rest. My husband only escaped capture by mounting his horse and riding quietly out of the town by a road that led over a high hill covered with laurel bushes. One officer accompanied him, whose name I cannot now recall. Knowing the country well, he made his way to a place of safety, where he procured rest and refreshment, and from there slowly made his way home.

On the 29th of October, a few days after the occurrences narrated, my little Bessie was born. My husband had suffered from rheumatism, exposed as he necessarily was in command of the regiment, and being unable to take the active post that a cavalry officer should do, he was convinced that it was his duty to resign it to one younger and more active than himself. He resigned accordingly, and was placed in command of the post at Winchester. Ashby was now promoted and assumed command of the regiment.[48]

General Jackson had returned to the valley after the battle of Manassas, and the neighborhood of Winchester was again the camping ground of the Stonewall Brigade, as it was then called. Ashby scoured the country along the border, keeping Geary at bay, and driving him back when he attempted to emerge from his place of safety.[49] We often drove out to the camp to see our friends, and they were near enough often to slip into town to see the girls or get a good supper. We saw Will often, as his camp was near.

One evening in November Jackson marched his troops out to meet Geary, who had advanced from Charlestown, and the brigade was kept in line of battle for several hours. Those who saw Jackson as he rode down in front of his line that evening said that his face beamed at the prospect of an encounter, but he had no battle that day, for Geary retired to fight another day. Those were dreary months, November and December, nothing but mud or rain and snow. All the glory seemed to have departed from the eager and enthusiastic army of the summer before. Christmas night we gave a party to the Stonewall Brigade, and our sweet and comfortable home was for the last time the scene of a gay assemblage. New Year's day General Jackson marched his army off to Bath. The weather was very inclement, and in little more than a week the wagons began to pour in with sick men; the hospitals were filled, and the ladies had to organize a system of cooking for the sick, which we did, taking turns in the kitchen each day. Gen. Jackson, after many battles and skirmishes, finally went to Romney, from whence he sent for my husband to assist him with his knowledge of the country in planning movements. In February Jackson returned to Winchester, and news came that preparations were making by the Federals for another advance up the valley. It then began to be whispered that our army must evacuate, as that at Manassas had long since fallen back and a retreat seemed general. The consternation of the people was great when they learned of their probable fate, but the evil hour was, as we thought, far off. My husband had returned from Romney with Jackson, and shortly after told me that he was compelled to go to Richmond. He told me that Winchester would have to be given up, that he would probably see me no more till better times. That was when we should have driven off the Yankees which we were sure to do. He begged me to keep up a good heart, and not give way to sorrow at parting with him, or to apprehension at being left with the enemy. He then made the request that I should keep a diary, and record every day's event so that nothing should be forgotten when we met again. He left, and from that time preparations for evacuating went on rapidly. The sick went first, and the stores and supplies followed, heavily laden wagons and rumbling artillery filled the streets. Friends began to call to take leave. Edward came to tell us good bye, and that night, the 11th of March, at twelve o'clock, the long roll was heard in the streets, the trampling of men and horses, and in an hour they were all gone.

Appendix
Notes
Index

Appendix

Children of Cornelia Peake McDonald and Angus W. McDonald III

Harry Peake	Born April 14, 1848
Allan Lane	Born October 30, 1849
Humphrey Peake	Born December 31, 1850
Kenneth	Born July 18, 1852
Ellen ("Nelly")	Born September 30, 1854
Roy ("Rob")	Born August 25, 1856
Donald	Born September 5, 1858
Hunter	Born June 12, 1860
Elizabeth ("Bessie")	Born October 29, 1861 (died in infancy

Children of Leacy Anne Naylor and Angus W. McDonald III (Cornelia Peake McDonald's Stepchildren)

Mary Naylor	Born December 27, 1827
Angus W. IV	Born May 16, 1829
Anne Sanford	Born October 30, 1830
Edward Hitchcock	Born October 26, 1832
William Naylor	Born February 4, 1834
Marshall	Born October 18, 1835
Craig Woodrow ("Wood")	Born May 28, 1837
Susan Leacy	Born December 10, 1839
Flora	Born June 7, 1842

Notes

Introduction

1. Page numbers in parentheses refer to this edition of Cornelia Peake McDonald's diary.

2. The text of this edition was taken from a scrapbook made available to me by Hunter McDonald of Nashville, Tennessee, now deceased, the grandson of Cornelia McDonald. The scrapbook remains in the McDonald family. Bound in leather, the handwritten book remains in excellent condition. There are 491 pages in the book; the pages measure 11 by 9 inches with 25 lines of writing per page. McDonald's handwriting is flawless and always legible. On the second page is a hand-painted picture of a U.S. flag and a Confederate flag crossed with the sun setting in war clouds behind them. Crossed rifles and a drum are under the flags. There is other art work in the scrapbook.

3. Janet Varner Gunn, "*Walden* and the Temporal Mode of Autobiographical Narrative," in *The American Autobiography*, ed. Albert E. Stone (Englewood Cliffs, N.J.: Prentice Hall, 1981), 82.

4. Domna Stanton, "Autobiography," in *The Female Autograph*, ed. Stanton (Chicago: Univ. of Chicago Press, 1984), 13.

5. Gunn, "*Walden* and the Temporal Mode," 83.

6. Josephine Donovan, "Toward a Women's Poetics," in *Feminist Issues in Literary Scholarship*, ed. Shari Benstock (Bloomington: Indiana Univ. Press, 1987), 103.

7. Anne Firor Scott, *Making the Invisible Woman Visible* (Urbana: Univ. of Illinois Press, 1984), 149.

8. Joan Scott, *Gender and the Politics of History* (New York: Columbia Univ. Press, 1988), 9.

9. C. Vann Woodward, *The Burden of Southern History*, rev. ed. (Baton Rouge: Louisiana State Univ. Press, 1970), xi.

10. Sidonie Smith, *A Poetics of Women's Autobiography: Marginality and the Fictions of Self-Representation* (Bloomington: Indiana Univ. Press, 1987), 7.

11. Suzanne L. Bunkers, "Diaries: Public and Private Records of Women's Lives," *Legacy: A Journal of Nineteenth-Century American Women Writers* 7, no. 1 (Fall 1990): 17.

12. Anne Goodwyn Jones, "Southern Literary Women as Chroniclers of Southern Life," in *Sex, Race, and the Role of Women in the South*, ed. Joanne V. Hawks and Sheila L. Skemp (Jackson: Univ. Press of Mississippi, 1983), 79, 85.

13. Jean E. Friedman, "Women's History and the Revision of Southern History," in *Sex, Race, and the Role of Women in the South* (see note 11), 9.

14. Bunkers more generally argues that women's diaries and journals are "*both* 'public' and 'private' writings" ("Diaries," 17; (see note 10).

15. Judith Newton, *Women, Power, and Subversion: Social Strategies in British Fiction, 1778–1860* (Athens: Univ. of Georgia Press, 1981), xx.

16. Hélène Cixous, "The Laugh of the Medusa," in *New French Feminisms*, ed. Elaine Marks and Isabelle de Courtivron (New York: Schocken Books, 1981), 252.

17. Gerda Lerner, ed., *The Female Experience: An American Documentary* (Indianapolis: Bobbs-Merrill, 1977), xxi.

18. Karl J. Weintraub, "Autobiography and Historical Consciousness," *Critical Inquiry* 1, no. 4 (June 1975): 837–38.

19. Anne Firor Scott, *The Southern Lady: From Pedestal to Politics, 1830–1930* (Chicago: Univ. of Chicago Press, 1970), x.

20. Anne Goodwyn Jones, *Tomorrow Is Another Day: The Woman Writer in the South, 1859–1936* (Baton Rouge: Louisiana State Univ. Press, 1981), 14.

21. Wilbur J. Cash, *The Mind of the South* (New York: Knopf, 1941), 86.

22. Stanton, "Autobiography," xi. For examples of such critical practice, see the broad variety of essays collected in Brodzki and Schenck (see note 24) and Stanton (see note 3), as well as Smith's *A Poetics of Women's Autobiography* (see note 9) and Bunkers' two essays (see notes 10 and 25). See also Stanton's and Bunkers' bibliographies.

23. Minrose C. Gwin, *Black and White Women of the Old South: The Peculiar Sisterhood in American Literature* (Knoxville: Univ. of Tennessee Press, 1985), 81–84, 99–102.

24. Bella Brodzki and Celeste Schenck, eds., "Introduction," in *Life/Lines: Theorizing Women's Autobiography* (Ithaca: Cornell Univ. Press, 1988), 1–2.

25. Suzanne L. Bunkers, "Subjectivity and Self-Reflexivity in the Study of Women's Diaries as Autobiography," *a/b: Auto/Biography Studies* 5, no. 2 (Fall 1990): 115.

26. I am using James Olney's term, which is also the title of his book *Metaphors of Self: The Meaning of Autobiography* (Princeton: Princeton Univ. Press, 1972).

A diary with reminiscences of the war

1. Harry Peake McDonald, born April 14, 1848, and Allan Lane McDonald, born October 30, 1849. The names and birth dates of Cornelia McDonald's children and stepchildren are listed in the appendix.

2. Ann Powell.

3. Maj. Gen. Nathaniel P. Banks, U.S. Army.

4. Zuaves: regiments of either side whose uniforms included bright red baggy trousers.

5. Wife of George W. Seevers of Fairfax County, proprietor of the Taylor Hotel. No first name is recorded.

6. Col. Othneil de Forest, 5th New York Cavalry.

7. Brig. Gen. Alpheus S. Williams, U.S. Army, Commander of the 1st Division, 2nd Corps.

8. Capt. William D. Wilkins, Assistant Adjutant-General.

9. James Murray Mason's home, Selma.

10. Col. George D. Chapman, 5th Connecticut Regiment, 5th Army Corps.

11. Gen. Thomas "Stonewall" Jackson.

12. Col. Charles Candy, in command of the 1st Brigade (5th, 7th, 29th, 66th Ohio regiments, and the 28th and 147th Pennsylvania regiments).

13. Maj. Gen. James Shields.

14. Although Dr. Robert Baldwin was too old to enter the Confederate Army, Union Gen. Robert H. Milroy, whose headquarters were in Winchester, nonetheless "exiled" Baldwin from the town for condemning Federal authorities.

15. Col. John S. Clark, Aide-de-Camp to Gen. Banks.

16. Lethea was the McDonalds' slave, whose services were rented from a neighbor to help care for the younger children.

17. Lincoln R. Stone, Assistant Surgeon 2nd Massachusetts Regiment.

18. Maj. Gen. Franz Sigel, organized and commanded 3rd Missouri Regiment, U.S. Volunteers.

19. The Taylor Hotel, in which Stonewall Jackson made his private quarters when he came to Winchester from his camp at Centreville, Virginia, in November 1861. The hotel was later used as a hospital by Federal Gen. Nathaniel P. Banks, and as headquarters by officers of both armies. Sigel occupied the building in June 1862.

20. Tuss was one of the McDonalds' slaves; he and his mother, "Aunt Winnie," were bought with Hawthorne by Angus McDonald III.

21. Jacob Baker and his brother George opened in 1837 a wholesale business in Winchester.

22. According to Hunter McDonald, Cornelia McDonald's son and editor of the 1935 version of her journal, a row of cedar trees flanked the driveway on each side from the gate at the foot of the hill to and around the turnway at the house.

23. First Battle of Manassas, or First Bull Run, fought July 21, 1861.

24. Battle of Kernstown, about three miles south of Winchester, March 23, 1862.

25. "Aunt Winnie," Tuss's mother, cooked for the family; she and Tuss were bought in 1856.

26. The Tennessee Brigade at Kernstown consisted of the 1st, 7th, and 14th regiments. Hunter McDonald noted that Jones belonged to the 1st. Since the commander of the 1st, Col. Peter Turney, later lived in Winchester, McDonald could have bypassed the sketchy regimental officer lists and gotten a first-hand identification of the man. If Cornelia McDonald's assertion that the man was from a Tennessee regiment is incorrect, then he could have been Capt. James Y. Jones of the 1st Virginia Battalion, who was injured at the Battle of Kernstown and died five days thereafter on March 28, 1862.

27. Ann Hunter Tucker Magill, widow of Alfred T. Magill.

28. Possibly Capt. William Townes of the 38th Virginia Infantry. This man knew Capt. John Ambler, also well known to the McDonald family, but survived the Battle of Kernstown to be sent, a month later, to the General Hospital in Williamsburg for diphtheria. Townes's service records fail to mention a neck or spinal injury.

29. A Lieut. Gwynn is not listed in the rosters of regiments that fought in the Battle of Kernstown.

30. Judge John McLean, born in 1785, was the first Ohioan to sit on the U.S. Supreme Court. Prior to his tenure on the high court, which lasted from 1830 to 1861, and which was distinguished by his dissent in the Dred Scott decision, McLean was a U.S. Representative, state supreme court judge, and Postmaster General.

31. Hunter Holmes McGuire, born in Winchester in 1835, graduated from Winchester Medical College in 1855 and shortly afterward became a professor of anatomy at the school. During the Civil War he was Chief Medical Officer under Generals Jackson, Ewell, Early, and Gordon. McGuire established reserve hospitals, organized the Confederate Army's Ambulance Corps, and rigorously promoted the release of the captured medical officers of both armies.

32. Conrad, who practiced law in Winchester, was one of two delegates representing Frederick County at the Secession Convention of 1861. In 1864 he was elected mayor of Winchester, but, according to Winchester historian Garland Quarles, was most likely not allowed to serve because of his animosity toward the Federal government.

33. Sherrard, of Frederick County, was a lawyer, a cashier for the Farmer's Bank of Virginia, and after the war a Frederick County judge.

34. William H. Seward, Secretary of State under President Lincoln.

35. This is a misquoted verse from Byron's poem "The Devil's Drive." Seward's "great prototype" is the devil.

36. Mary Naylor McDonald Green, Cornelia McDonald's stepdaughter. See appendix.

37. Capt. W. P. Pratt, 5th New York Cavalry.

38. In reports of Maj. Edgar A. Hamilton of the 7th New York Cavalry, also known as the 1st New York Mounted Rifles, no mention is made of a Lieut. Col. Johnson. In Col. Othneil de Forest's report of the valley operations on May 24 and 25, a Lieut. Col. Robert Johnstone, of the 5th New York Cavalry, is mentioned. McDonald possibly refers to Johnstone.

39. Maj. Gen. George B. McClellan.

40. Maj. Gen. Irvin McDowell.

41. Maj. Gen. Charles H. Frémont.

42. Smith, formerly of the Walnut Grove plantation, lived across from the Cumberland Valley Railroad Station.

43. The 1st and 10th Maine regiments were in Winchester at the time.

44. Fannie L. Jones Barton, wife of David Barton, an attorney in Winchester.

45. Granddaughter of Chief Justice John Marshall. Her home was at Prospect Hill, Fauquier County.

46. Richard Parker, circuit court judge in Frederick County until 1869, who tried and sentenced John Brown in 1859, in what is now Charlestown, West Virginia.

47. Craig Woodrow McDonald, Cornelia McDonald's stepson. See appendix.

48. Col. Arnold Elzey, 1st Maryland Infantry.

49. Col. Carr B. White, in command of the 12th, 34th, and 91st Ohio regiments, and the 2nd West Virginia Cavalry.

50. Brig. Gen. Louis Blenker, whose division consisted of three brigades, eighteen pieces of artillery, one New York cavalry regiment, and a total of 8,627 men. In a report dated July 5, 1862, Maj. Gen. Franz Sigel informed Col. Daniel Ruggles that Blenker's division had been abolished because of the differences between the commanding officers of the three brigades.

51. Confederate Ministers James Murray Mason, bound for England on the British steamer *Trent*, and John Slidell, on his way to France, were captured on Nov. 8, 1861, by the U.S. warship *San Jacinto*. They were incarcerated in Boston until pressure from the British forced their release. The incident, known as the Trent Affair, almost caused a war between the United States and Great Britain.

52. There is no reference to a Col. Sweeny in the official records covering northern Virginia from March 17 to September 1862. Possibly the man is Thomas W. Sweeny, commanding the 3rd Brigade, 2nd Division, Army of the Tennessee. Winchester historian Garland Quarles refers to a Sweeny as the Provost Marshal under Gen. Julius White.

53. Col. Frederick G. D'Utassy, 39th New York Volunteer Infantry, "Garibaldi Guard."

54. Hunter McDonald believed that Capt. Canfield commanded the Home Guards in Winchester and was a member of the Virginia Militia. Confederate service records for Virginia soldiers do not record a Capt. Canfield of the militia.

55. Maj. Gen. Robert Patterson commanded the Department of the Shenandoah until July 21, 1861. Brig. Gen. George Cadwallader commanded the Department of Annapolis.

56. Col. Edward Charles McDonald, C.S.A., of Hannibal, Mo., who died January 15, 1862.

57. Lethea's daughter.

58. Major Joseph Page Whittlesey.

59. Hunter McDonald indicated that the man may have been Joseph E. Snyder, a captured scout sent to Maj. Gen. Franz Sigel from Richmond.

60. Brig. Gen. Turner Ashby, killed on June 6, 1862.

61. Manuel's wife, a slave whose services were also rented by the year to do the McDonalds' laundry.

62. Maj. William N. Bronaugh, commander of the 2nd Arkansas Battery, was killed at the Battle of the Chicahominy on June 25, 1862.

63. 1st Lieut. Frank Sherrard.

64. Daughter of Sen. James M. Mason.

65. Glen Burnie, the estate of James Wood, the founder of Winchester.

66. R.B. Hampton, Battery F, Pennsylvania Light Artillery.

67. Brig. Gen. Julius White, U.S. Volunteers, assumed command in Winchester in late July 1862.

68. Wife of Robert Dailey. Her first name is not recorded.

69. Capt. Hampton (see note 66).

70. It is uncertain as to whether McDonald wrote these lines herself or is quoting from a poem or song from the period. They are not listed in current indexes.

71. Formerly Elizabeth Whiting Powell.

72. Phillip Williams, an attorney in Winchester, later arrested in 1864 as a hostage for Federal soldiers who had been captured by Confederates and confined in Atheneum prison at Wheeling, West Virginia.

73. The Burwell sisters were nieces-in-law of Annette Lee, wife of Hugh Holmes Lee.

74. The evacuation took place one week later than McDonald dates it, on Sept. 2, 1862, under orders from Maj. Gen. Halleck. Fort Garabaldi on the hill in the rear of Hawthorn was evacuated on Sept. 2.

75. 2nd Battle of Manassas, ending Aug. 30, 1862.

76. The battle of Antietam, or Sharpsburg, fought Sept. 17, 1862. Federal troops numbered about 75,000 and Confederate casualties were estimated at 13,724 out of 40,000 total Confederates engaged in the battle.

77. Possibly Capt. William B. Clarke of the Washington Artillery of New Orleans.

78. 1st Lieut. J. B. Richardson, Washington Artillery.

79. Martinsburg, West Virginia, is approximately twenty-two miles northeast of Winchester.

80. Maj. Gen. Sterling Price, C.S.A.

81. Edward McDonald's name does not appear on a list of the captured members of George W. Kendall's party. He may have escaped capture. Most of the prisoners were Texans.

82. Susan Peake McDonald.

83. Thomas Fayette Buck, Cornelia McDonald's brother-in-law.

84. Gustavus Tyler of the "Warren Rifles," which afterwards became Company B of the 17th Virginia Infantry.

85. The Rapidan River joins the Rappahannock near Fredericksburg and is south of Winchester. The Potomac travels around Winchester, along the Maryland line, and into Washington, D.C.

86. 1st. Lieut. George Thomas, 1st Maryland Battalion, C.S.A.

87. Abbey Hopkins.

88. Thomas Claiborne Green, Mary's husband.

89. Federal Brig. Gen. John Pope.

90. Wife of Judge Parker (see note 46). Her first name is not recorded.

91. See notes 77 and 78.

92. Lynchburg area records do not mention a Rev. Kimble.

93. Rev. A. F. Scott.

94. Hunter McDonald identifies the woman as Mary Jackson Tooley, a widow of a Winchester tanner. An occupational survey of the town in 1850 does not list a tanner by that name, nor do local marriage records include anyone named Tooley.

95. Rev. W. C. Meredith took the ministry of Christ Church in Winchester in 1860 and, except for four years as chaplain in the Confederate Army, he was rector there until 1876.

96. These lines are quoted from "We Parted in Silence" by Julia Crawford.

97. Anne Sanford McDonald, Cornelia McDonald's stepdaughter (see appendix).

98. Possibly Capt. Alexander Murray, 8th Maryland Volunteers.

99. Hugh Holmes McGuire of Winchester enlisted as a private in Rockbridge Artillery and became private secretary to Gen. Stonewall Jackson. Later a Capt. in Company E, 11th Virginia Cavalry, he was mortally wounded at the Battle of Amelia Springs and died May 8, 1865.

100. Hunter McDonald identifies the man as Rev. Robert M. Baker, an Episcopal minister.

101. An Assistant Surgeon Iglehart is mentioned in the official records, in regard to a battle fought from the C.S. steamer *Gaines.* Thomas is probably the "Lieut. Thomas of the Maryland line" previously mentioned in the diary.

102. Maj. Gen. Earl Van Dorn.

103. Confederate Maj. Gen. Braxton Bragg defeated Maj. Gen. Don Carlos Buell at the Battle of Perryville, or Chaplin Hills, on June 8, 1862. Union losses numbered 4,211 out of the estimated 37,000 soldiers engaged. Bragg's troops numbered 16,000.

104. Brother of Dr. Robert Dailey.

105. Warren County, Virginia, formed from Shenandoah and Frederick Counties in 1836.

106. Canandaigua, county seat of Ontario County, New York, thirty miles southeast of Rochester.

107. Maj. Gen. James Longstreet.

108. Brig. Gen. Charles H. Tyler of Rockingham County, Virginia, Cornelia McDonald's brother-in-law.

109. Those members of the legislature who had met in the summer of 1861 to consider an ordinance of secession were arrested by Gen. B. F. Butler and imprisoned in Fort Warren, along with other citizens of Maryland who were arrested as political prisoners. All were released by Gen. John A. Dix on orders of the Secretary of War in Nov. 1862.

110. Maj. Gen. Ambrose E. Burnside. A day earlier, Lincoln had ordered Burnside to replace Maj. Gen. George McClellan as Commander of the Army of the Potomac.

111. Rev. James B. Graham, Presbyterian minister.

112. Richard Bickerton Pemell Lyons, 1817–1887, British Ambassador to the United States.

113. Mary Charlton Greenhow Lee, Winchester diarist. Her detailed and lengthy journals cover the period from March 11, 1862 to October 19, 1865. A small portion of Lee's diary was published in 1958 in the *Maryland Historical Magazine.*

114. Wife of the principal of the Winchester Academy. Her first name is not recorded.

115. Maj. Gen. A. P. Hill.

116. Son of Mary Elizabeth Dandridge. Her father was President Zachary Taylor, and her second husband, Philip Pendleton Dandridge.

117. There are two Leacys listed in the Confederate service records for Virginia: Private John Leacy, 7th Virginia Calvary, and Private William Leacy, 33rd Virginia Infantry. Leacy is probably a colleague of 1st Lieut. George Thomas, of the Maryland Line, although information on a Maryland Leacy is not included in the official records.

118. Marshall McDonald, stepson of Cornelia McDonald, and a 2nd Lieut., Corps of Artillery, C.S.A. (see appendix).

119. Lieut. Gen. John C. Pemberton.

120. Cornelia McDonald's stepdaughters, Sue and Flora. Flora wrote for newspapers and magazines, and published both a novel and a McDonald family history. Angus McDonald III bought Hawthorn from the Tidballs.

121. Dr. A. H. H. Boyd, pastor of the Loudon Street Presbyterian Church.

122. Formerly Virginia Lee Cabell, wife of James Smith Gilkeson. McDonald misspelled her name.

123. Lieut. Col. James R. Herbert, 1st Maryland Infantry Battalion.

124. See note 101.

125. Brig. Gen. John W. Geary of the 12th Army Corps.

126. Rev. John Bell Tilden Reed.

127. The home of Cornelia McDonald and Angus W. McDonald III from 1853 to 1857 at New Creek, Virginia, a station on the Baltimore & Ohio Railroad, now Keyser, West Virginia. Edward was sent to Camp Chase and confined for several months. As he was being moved with a boatload of prisoners to Vicksburg to be exchanged, he escaped and rejoined his command.

128. Lieut. McHenry Howard of the Maryland Line; W. G. Williamson, 2nd Lieut. Engineers, Provisional Army Confederate States; Brig. Gen. William E. Jones, C.S.A. In 1914 Howard published his recollections of the war.

129. Cummings may be Abraham Cummings, some of whose sermons were published, or Jeremiah Williams Cummings, who published a collection of scriptural texts and epitaphs for a child's headstone.

130. Hunter McDonald indicates that Buchanan was from Martinsburg, West Virginia.

131. Pontoon bridges were used for crossing; there is no indication that the bridges collapsed and that many people consequently drowned.

132. Maj. Gen. A. P. Hill and Maj. Gen. J. E. B. Stuart.

133. Buck was a member of Company E, 7th Virginia Calvary.

134. Confederate casualities were 595 killed, 4,061 wounded, and 653 missing, totaling 5,309. The Federal Army suffered 12,653 casualities.

135. Brig. Gen. Thomas R. R. Cobb, C.S.A. and Brig. Gen. Maxey Gregg, C.S.A.

136. Brig. Gen. Gustav P. Cluseret, commanding the First Brigade of Milroy's Division.

137. Maj. Gen. R. H. Milroy of Indiana was court-martialed for surrendering Winchester, but exonerated by Lincoln. He had other commands and was in charge of the Nashville and Chattanooga Railroad between Nashville and Chattanooga in 1862. In 1865, his conduct again being questioned, he resigned his command.

138. In the original version, which McDonald inverts, Oliver Hazard Perry thus announced to Gen. William Henry Harrison his victory at the Battle of Lake Erie on Sept. 10, 1813.

139. On Dec. 19, 1862, a caucus of Republican Senators sent a committee to Lincoln demanding that Secretary of State William H. Seward be dismissed. The Senators alleged that Seward held too much influence over Lincoln. Seward and Secretary of the Treasury Salmon P. Chase offered their resignations a few days later. Lincoln refused to accept them, and both men resumed their duties.

140. Charles Wilkes, U.S. Navy. He was made a Commodore in 1862.

141. The capture of Mason and Slidell angered the British government, which demanded an apology from the United States and the release of the Confederate Commissioners. Realizing the political and military ramifications of detaining Mason and Slidell—during the crisis England seemed on the cusp of full Confederate sympathy—Seward, in his letter of Dec. 26, 1861, assured the British that Mason and Slidell would be promptly freed and that Commander Wilkes had violated the American freedom-of-the-seas policy.

142. Brig. Gen. John Hunt Morgan; Maj. Gen. J. E. B. Stuart; Gen. Joseph Wheeler.

143. Isaiah B. McDonald of Virginia, 2nd Lieut., 17th Indiana Infantry.

144. Angus McDonald II.

145. At the close of the battle of Murfreesboro on Jan. 1, 1863, Maj. Gen. Braxton Bragg retired southward and made his headquarters for the winter at Tullahoma, Tennessee. He withdrew because of reports that Federal commander William S. Rosecrans was to receive reinforcements.

146. Dr. Fred Holliday, husband of Hannah McCormick. (Dailey, Boyd, and Parker are noted earlier in this chapter.)

147. Horatio Seymour, Governor of New York. He opposed the Emancipation Proclamation, the draft, and arbitrary military arrests.

148. Confederate Maj. Gen. Earl Van Dorn. The capture of Holly Springs, Miss., temporarily suspended Gen. Ulysses S. Grant's planned operations against Vicksburg. The Federal commander of the town, Col. R. C. Murphy, 8th Regiment, Wisconsin Volunteers, was subsequently court-martialed and discharged for his failure to anticipate Van Dorn's approach.

149. Commander Matthew Fontaine Maury, C.S.N.

150. Maj. Gen. Joseph Hooker.

151. "Mick" Tidball was Millicent McGuire, cousin of Angus W. McDonald. She married Alexander Tidball. Portia Baldwin was the wife of Robert Baldwin.

152. The Libby Prison, on the James River in Richmond. Only officers were held there.

153. Brig. Gen. Fitzhugh Lee, 1st Virginia Cavalry, nephew of Robert E. Lee and James Murray Mason.

154. The "Battle of the Handkerchiefs" occurred on Feb. 20, 1863, as Southern officers who had been imprisoned left the city to be exchanged. The spectators, who were mostly women, waved handkerchiefs, cheered for the Confederacy, and shouted angrily at Federal soldiers. Disturbed by the women's hostility, Union officers called for reinforcements and dispersed the crowd. The incident convinced many of the Federals that New Orleans was irrecoverably Confederate.

155. On Dec. 12, 1864, when Commanding Gen. William Tecumseh Sherman captured Savannah, Maj. Gen. W. B. Hazen took Fort McAllister. Confederate Maj. G. W. Anderson and 250 of his men occupied the fort at the time.

156. John Van Buren, lawyer and politician, was Martin Van Buren's son. He lobbied in 1860 for a states' convention to guarantee slavery interests and to prevent war. He opposed the draft, the suspension of the writ of habeus corpus, and the use of African-American troops in the Union Army. Phineas C. Wright, of New Orleans: After Lincoln indicated his intent to free his slaves, Wright began criticizing the administration. In his pamphlets he supported states' rights. In the spring of 1863 he established the Order of American Knights, naming himself Supreme Grand Commander. His organization was closely allied with the Cooperhead movement, although more pro-Confederate. Union supporters applied the term *Cooperhead* to Northerners who favored peace and opposed the president's war policy. The crux of the Cooperhead oath was the promise to "take up arms, [if needs be], in the cause of the oppressed—*in my country first of all*—against any . . . Power or Government usurped, which may be found in arms, and waging war against a people or peoples, who are endeavoring to establish, or have inaugurated, a Government for themselves of their own free choice, in accordance with, and founded upon, *the eternal principles of Truth!*"

157. Edward Everett, Unitarian clergyman, politican, orator, of Massachusetts. During the war, he traveled throughout the North, urging his audiences to support the restoration of the Union through peaceful means.

158. Federal Lieut. Gen. Winfield Scott, a native Virginian, relinquished his General-in-Chief position to Maj. Gen. George B. McClellan on Nov. 1, 1861. Scott resigned voluntarily, but had been pressured by the thirty-four-year-old McClellan, who believed Scott was too old to lead the Federal forces. Scott's military career dated from the War of 1812. McClellan was finally relieved of his command in November of 1862 because of his failure to secure a Federal victory at Antietam.

159. Gen. Joseph Wheeler.

160. Maj. Timothy Quinn, 1st New York Cavalry, 3rd Brigade, 2nd Division.

161. British-born John Ericsson, spelled Ericcson by McDonald, of New York, mechanical engineer who designed the Union vessel *Monitor*, among others.

162. A political organization which originated in Ohio in 1862; sent troops and supplies to the Federals and distributed political literature; supported the radical reconstruction of the post-war South, punishment of Southern leaders, and African-American voting rights; disbanded in 1870. See also note 156 on the Cooperhead Movement.

163. Col. James Montgomery.

164. Maj. Gen. Robert Schenck in command of Middle Department, 8th Army Corps, with headquarters at Baltimore.

165. From chapter 1 of *Lamentations*, and *Revelation* 18:23.

166. *Micah* 2:10.

167. Wife of Lloyd Logan, a retired tobacco merchant. Her first name is not recorded.

168. Jessee (spelled Jesse by McDonald) Scouts: Union scouts often disguised as Confederate soldiers or sympathizers.

169. William Dooly, a Union sympathizer.

170. Penelope Eichelberger, second wife and widow of Rev. Lewis F. Eichelberger, who came to Winchester in 1828 as pastor of the German Lutheran Church.

171. On March 6, 1863, Maj. Gen. David Hunter applied to Admiral S. F. DuPont for naval cooperation in his expedition to capture Jacksonville, Florida. The plan was for Cols. James Montgomery and T. W. Higginson, each with two African-American regiments, and Col. John D. Rust, commanding a white regiment from Maine, to take the town and there establish a haven for fugitive African-Americans. The men, fugitives from any Southern state, were to be trained as soldiers and used in the capture of Florida. Offering little resistance, the town was taken on March 10, and evacuated on the 29th. Brig. Gen. George Finegan, C.S.A., later reported to the Confederate Chief of Staff at Charleston, S.C., that he had seen much of Jacksonville in flames on the day of the capture.

172. In 1857 the British East India Company, which practically governed India, introduced to Indian soldiers, called *Sepoys,* an ammunition cartridge greased in beef and pork fat. The end of the cartridge had to be bitten off in order to use it, and because the Hindu and Muslim Sepoys could not put the meat products in their mouths, they launched a two-year revolt during which several major Indian cities were taken back from the British. The British government ended the rebellion through force, although a promise was made to the Sepoys, and India, that British interference with religious practices would end.

173. The Kingdom of Poland unsuccessfully revolted against Russia in 1863, resulting in wholesale executions, confiscations, and deportations ordered against the Poles by Russia. Shortly after the rebellion, Tsar Alexander II tried to eliminate Polish culture by making Russian the official language of the overcome Polish region.

174. Maj. Gen. John G. Foster, 18th Army Corps.

175. Nine Federal ironclads attacked Fort Sumter, in Charleston harbor, on April 7, 1863. The *Weehawken* was hit fifty-three times in forty minutes, and the *U.S.S. Keokuk* sank the next morning after being hit ninety times. Four Union ships managed to retreat intact.

176. Robert Steele, Winchester florist.

177. See note 175.

178. Brig. Gen. Nathan B. Forrest captured thirteen hundred Federal cavalry under Col. Abel D. Streight in April 1863. The previous month, Forrest and Maj. Gen. Earl Van Dorn captured parts of regiments from Indiana, Michigan, and Wisconsin under Union Col. John Colburn.

179. Brig. Gen. Henry A. Wise, C.S.A., governor of Virginia, 1856–60.

180. Charles Rumley.

181. Annette Tyler, wife of Dr. James H. Turner of Front Royal, Va.

182. These lines are not included in current poetry indexes.

183. James Monroe Tyler, Cornelia McDonald's grandnephew, was seriously wounded at the Battle of Shiloh, also known as the Battle of Pittsburgh Landing, Tennessee, April 7, 1862. Tyler did not die as a result of his wounds. Hunter McDonald speculates that Tyler's Union brother-in-law, engaged in the same battle, removed him to safety and medical care. Tyler died in 1868.

184. On April 20, Brig. Gen. John D. Imboden began a raid which lasted until May 14, severing the Baltimore and Ohio Railroad in Northwestern Virginia. He captured many horses and cattle. Brig. Gen. William E. Jones began his month-long raid on the B & O in (West) Virginia on April 21.

185. Brig. Gen. A. G. Jenkins.

186. See note 35 on Byron's "The Devil's Drive." This line may be a paraphrase of the line, "For the field ran so red with the blood of the

dead," which follows the partial verse McDonald quotes earlier in this chapter.

187. Brig. Gen. George Stoneman.

188. Maj. Gen. John Sedgewick.

189. Possibilities for this man's identity include: Capt. George H. Purdy, 4th Indiana Cavalry; Orderly James Purdy, 15th Ohio; 1st Sgt. Gilbert H. Purdy, 4th U.S. Artillery.

190. Benjamin F. White of Fauquier County, Virginia, 17th Infantry. His records are incomplete, and do not mention his death at Fredericksburg, but indicate that six medical cards were included. White possibly was wounded in the battle and died several months later. The Lyle family was a prominent Valley family, of which at least five members were Confederate soldiers. Only two Lighters are mentioned in the *Confederate Service Records*, neither of whom were killed at Fredericksburg. The men could have been from what is now West Virginia.

191. See note 168.

192. George and Julian Ward, sons of Julia Funston of White Post, Virginia, and George W. Ward of Culpeper, Virginia.

193. Three Butterworths are mentioned in the official records: one, a civilian; another a Lieut. Butterworth, no other information provided; and the third, Capt. Ebenezer Butterworth, supposed to have been mortally wounded at the Battle of Bull Run, or Manassas, 1861.

194. Maj. Gen. Isaac R. Trimble.

195. Col. James A. Mulligan, 23rd Illinois Volunteers.

196. Maj. Gen. Jubal A. Early.

197. See note 78.

198. Brig. Gen. John B. Gordon.

199. Possibly Dr. Robert Patton, surgeon.

200. Lieut. Gen. Richard S. Ewell.

201. Maj. C. E. Snodgrass, Quartermaster for Gen. Ewell; Maj. Gen. Washington L. Elliott, U.S.A., spelled Elliot by McDonald.

Narrative of our refugee life

1. Rev. Joseph P. B. Wilmer.

2. A Julia Clarke is not mentioned in local records. In *The Glengarry McDonalds of Virginia*, Flora McDonald Williams indicates that she was the daughter of William Clark (*sic*) and sister of Peyton Clark, principal of the Winchester Academy. Evelina Devoe, Frances E. Yain, and Lydia E. Hyatt each married a William Clark in Frederick County, Virginia; one of these women may have been Julia Clark's mother.

3. Maj. Gen. Robert C. Schenk, Federal commander whose headquarters were in Baltimore, had sent women and children away from the city, which was under martial law. In *The Glengarry McDonalds of Virginia*, Flora McDonald Williams notes that Julia Waring and her daughters were among those forced to leave.

4. James W. Green.

5. Charles H. Tyler.

6. Elizabeth Tyler. Cornelia McDonald's sister Julia married Elizabeth Tyler's brother.

7. James River and Kanawaha Canal via branch line at Balcony Falls.

8. The Lexington Hotel.

9. Robert Dailey, or his son Griffin, also a doctor.

10. Rev. William Meeks McElwee.

11. McDonald refers to one of Fontaine's older sons, John Herndon Fontaine. In January of 1863, Fontaine left Vicksburg to reconnoiter the Federal forces and was not seen again.

12. Joshua L. Deaver.

13. E. S. Tutwiler.

14. Hunter McDonald identifies her as Ellen Lee Powell, wife of Confederate Capt. John Simms Powell. Various Virginia genealogies do not include information on Ellen Lee Powell, her husband, or her brother Charles, in connection with his sister. A Shenandoah Valley history lists a Mary Lee as Charles's sister, but does not mention her husband's name. In 1820, a Lucy Peachy Lee married William A. Powell, in Frederick County, Virginia.

15. McDonald obviously meant Feb. 1864.

16. Maj. Brig. Gen. Thomas L. Rosser.

17. Battles of the Wilderness, May 5 and 6, and Spottsylvania, May 8–19, 1864. Federal losses numbered close to 33,000 men of about 110,000 engaged. Confederate casualties have been estimated at about 10,000 of at least 60,000 engaged Confederates.

18. Maj. Gen. David Hunter.

19. Francis H. Smith.

20. John McCausland.

21. Brig. Gen. William W. Averell, spelled Averill by McDonald, Commander 1st Cavalry Division, Department of West Virginia.

22. Hunter McDonald was born June 12, 1860.

23. Col. Robert L. Madison, M.D.

24. Matthew X. White, 1st Virginia Cavalry.

25. Maj. Thomas H. Williamson.

26. Richard G. Prendergast, 1st New York (Lincoln) Cavalry.

27. Wife of Col. William Gilham. No first name is recorded.

28. Jacob Fuller.

29. Matt Berry, attached to General Hunter's staff.

30. Elizabeth Letcher, the oldest daughter in the family.

31. Rockbridge Co. records show a Col. A. W. Cameron. His wife's name is not mentioned.

32. Although there were several Wilsons in the area, the identity of this man is not recorded.

33. Possibly John M. Greenlee, 1st Virginia Cavalry.

34. North branch of the James River, called the North River.

35. See McDonald's extremely negative opinion of the writer and journalist David Strother expressed later in this chapter. David Hunter Strother ("Porte Crayon"), born in Martinsburg, Virginia (now West Virginia) in 1816, was widely known for his journalistic travel and descriptive pieces on Virginia and North Carolina and the drawings which accompanied them. Most of these sketches first appeared in *Harper's Magazine* before being published in book form. Much to the dismay of his southern friends, Strother joined the Union Army when the Civil War broke out. His first-hand knowledge of Virginia terrain made him invaluable in campaigns in the Shenandoah Valley, and he rose to the rank of Brigadier General. After the war, as a high-ranking assistant to Virginia Governor Francis Pierpont and as Adjutant General of the Virginia State Militia, he attempted to carry out Pierpont's reconstructive policies, which were eventually overruled by more radical elements bent upon vengeance against the South. He then returned to his writing and drawing for *Harper's* and in 1878 was appointed Consul-General in Mexico City. He died in 1888.

36. Brig. Gen. George Crook and Brig. Gen. William W. Averell.

37. Now Bedford.

38. Twenty-eight miles west of Lewisburg, West Virginia.

39. George W. Effinger.

40. A Col. Beard is not mentioned in Valley records, but, on the basis of information from Beard's grandson, Hunter McDonald identifies the man as Josiah Beard, operator of a mill.

41. Alexander Beresford-Hope, conservative politician and writer. During the war he published lectures on the "American Disruption."

42. Margaret J. Preston, wife of Col. J. T. L. Preston, C.S.A.

43. James A. Seddon.

44. Hunter McDonald identifies his cousin as Private John Thompson Peerce, 7th Virginia Cavalry. A John Pierce is also listed in the Confederate service records for the 7th Virginia Cavalry.

45. Samuel D. Myers, Company C, 7th Virginia Cavalry, C.S.A.

46. Angus McDonald III once wrote that he "never felt a sentiment of the slightest unkindness or ill will against Strother," and that his most painful war duty was his incarceration of Strother.

47. In a letter dated September 6, 1864, Angus McDonald informed Maj. Gen. George Crook, David Hunter's successor, that he was aware of the retaliatory order against Col. Samuel J. Crooks, New York Cavalry, and that he opposed it.

48. Eliza Welch Goodwin.

49. Berkley Springs in Morgan County, Virginia.

50. Gen. William N. Pendleton of Richmond, Virginia.

51. Maj. Gen. Ethan Allen Hitchcock, Commissioner for Exchange of Prisoners of War, and military adviser to President Lincoln.

52. Millicent McDonald Holliday, sister of Angus McDonald.

53. *Psalms* 7:3–5.

54. Gen. S. Cooper, Adjutant and Inspector General, C.S.A.

55. Sarah A. Warwick Daniel.

56. Their remains were later removed to the Confederate cemetery at Richmond.

57. Sallie Alexander Moore, author of *Memories of a Long Life in Virginia*, published in 1920.

58. *Psalms* 146:9.

59. Margaret J. Preston's poem, "Beechenbrook, A Rhyme of the War," was printed and bound in Richmond. Fifty copies were sent to Preston's friends before the capture of Richmond. During the evacuation, the publishing house was burned and the approximately fifteen hundred remaining copies of the poem destroyed.

60. Louisa P. Baxter and her sisters operated a school in their home at Lexington.

61. George Shearley owned the Lexington Tannery.

62. Papers found on twenty-two-year-old Ulric Dahlgren, son of John A. B. Dahlgren, indicated that Jefferson Davis and other southern leaders were to be murdered during Dahlgren's raid on Richmond. The U.S. government charged that the papers were forgeries and that Dahlgren had acted independently in the latter stages of the raid. The authenticity of the papers has never been determined.

63. John Broome Sherrard and James Markham Marshall.

64. Rev. William Henry Foote, historian and Presbyterian minister, of Romney, (West) Virginia, was the author of several histories of Virginia and North Carolina.

65. Union Generals Ulysses S. Grant, George B. McClellan, and John Pope.

66. Samuel McDowell Reid.

67. Alfred Leyburn, M.D.

68. Edward L. Graham.

69. "Although the Vine Its Fruit Deny" is a hymn written by Henry Ustic Onderdonk, 1789–1858, a Bishop of the Philadelphia Diocese. The verses are a paraphrase of *Habakkuk* 3:17–19.

70. Brig. Gen. Edwin Gray Lee, son-in-law of Brig. Gen. William N. Pendleton.

Recollections of the year 1861

1. U.S. Senator James M. Mason, who resigned a year later to become a Commissioner for the Confederate government; he and John Slidell, also a Confederate Commissioner, were captured on the British mail steamer *Trent*; Mason was bound for England, and Slidell for France.

2. John Randolph Tucker of Winchester.

3. Formerly Elizabeth Whiting Powell, wife of Robert Y. Conrad, a state senator and member of the Virginia Convention of 1861.

4. The Peace Conference, initiated by Virginia in a resolution of its General Assembly adopted on January 7, 1861, met in Washington on February 4, 1861. In the preamble to its resolutions, the Assembly indicated its desire to employ "every reasonable means to avert so dire a calamity as a [permanent dissolution of the Union]." The resolutions themselves, however, defended Virginia's right both to maintain its statehood independent of federal coercion, and to withdraw from the Union, if the Commonwealth so desired. Twenty states were represented, including Maine, Massachusetts, New York, New Jersey, Pennsylvania, Maryland, North Carolina, Kentucky, Ohio, Indiana, and Iowa. None of the seven cotton states sent delegates to the convention. Prior to the conference, a joint resolution was also adopted by the Assembly, which called for delegates from the Commonwealth to consider Virginia's position in the midst of the "problems and dangers of the hour." The result of this resolution was the Secession Convention.

5. Joseph H. Sherrard.

6. Circuit Court Judge Richard Parker.

7. Edward Allen Hitchcock McDonald, Cornelia McDonald's stepson.

8. The name is misspelled. McDonald is referring to George Hume Steuart, Major General in the Maryland Militia.

9. The first casualty in the war was Union Col. Elmer E. Ellsworth, who was shot and killed by James W. Jackson on May 24, 1861, as Ellsworth hoisted a Federal flag over Alexandria's principal hotel, the Marshall House. Jackson, the proprietor of the hotel, was subsequently killed by Ellsworth's regiment, and Alexandria surrendered immediately to the Union forces.

10. Craig Woodrow McDonald, Cornelia McDonald's stepson, enlisted as a private in the Brandy Rifles at Culpeper in April 1861.

11. In the space of fewer than three months in 1861, Francis Scott Bartow was elected Captain of Company B, Oglethorpe Light Infantry, 8th Regiment; commissioned Brigadier General of the Provisional Army, C.S.A.; and killed at the First Battle of Manassas, also known as First Bull Run.

12. Anna Mason Ambler, James M. Mason's daughter.

13. Official records show that McDonald was ordered in June 1861 to report to Gen. Joseph E. Johnston. The reference to "Col. Jackson" in the next sentence is to T. J. "Stonewall" Jackson, who was then a Colonel.

14. Brig. Gen. Turner Ashby of Rose Hill, Fauquier County.

15. Maj. Gen. Kenton Harper of Pennsylvania, Virginia Militia, later Col., 5th Virginia Regiment.

16. Actually, Col. Jackson came from Richmond. The cadets went to Richmond to train troops rather than to Harper's Ferry.

17. The Cheat River Viaduct was located near Rowlesburg in Preston County, Virginia.

18. Brig. Gen. Robert Selden Garnett, C.S.A., was killed July 13, 1861, on the Cheat River.

19. Maj. Gen. George B. McClellan.

20. Col. Thomas L. Kane.

21. Conrad, of Winchester, Private in the 11th Virginia Cavalry.

22. In a report to her father, Salmon P. Chase, Lincoln's Secretary of the Treasury, Maj. Gen. Joseph Hooker (U.S.A.) remarked on Kate Chase Sprague's wedding and her "exquisitely tasteful" gown. The report was dated Dec. 28, 1863.

23. Actually, he went with the 3rd Tennessee under Col. John C. Vaughn.

24. The 77th Virginia Militia.

25. Capt. Robert White's company was assigned to the 13th Virginia Infantry under Col. A. P. Hill.

26. Maj. Gen. Robert Patterson was then Maj. Gen. of U.S. Volunteers, Military Department, Pennsylvania, Delaware, Maryland, and District of Columbia. For failure to cooperate with Gen. Winfield Scott at the First Battle of Manassas, he was mustered out of service.

27. Maj. Gen. Joseph E. Johnston, C.S.A.

28. Gen. Edmund Kirby Smith, of St. Augustine, Florida; Maj. W. H. C. Whiting, C.S.A., of Biloxi, Mississippi; Archibald McGill Fauntleroy of Winchester, Surgeon, C.S.A., 1861–65; J. T. L. Preston of Lexington, Virginia, professor of languages at Virginia Military Academy, commissioned in 1861 Lieut. Col. and aide to Col. Francis H. Smith, who commanded the fort at Craney Island; Eugene McLean, Major Quartermaster, C.S.A.; Col. F. J. Thomas, Johnston's chief ordinance officer, killed at Manassas.

29. Probably refers to Joseph E. Johnston.

30. In Lexington, Virginia.

31. Brig. Gen. Arnold Elzey, C.S.A.

32. Isaac N. Glaize, 2nd Virginia Infantry. The Glaizes were a prominent family in Winchester, chiefly involved in the lumber business and farming.

33. Peyton Clarke was principal of Winchester Academy.

34. David Holmes Conrad.

35. Julia Peake, who married George G. Tyler, was Cornelia McDonald's older sister.

36. Shenandoah Valley histories show two Weeds in the area, one a minister, the other a liquor merchant.

37. Brig. Gen. Bernard E. Bee of South Carolina.

38. Regiments on either side whose uniforms included bright red baggy trousers.

39. Cornelia McDonald's stepson William Naylor McDonald, 11th Virginia Calvary.

40. In *An Autobiographical Sketch and Narrative of the War Between the States,* Lieut. Gen. Jubal Early, C.S.A., describes an advance on the Union army which Lieut. Craig Woodrow McDonald halted. McDonald claimed the regiment directly in front of Early's, which had been firing on Early's troops and had disappeared over a ridge, was actually a Confederate regiment. "The very confident manner of Lieutenant McDonald" persuaded Early to survey the regiment. He found men dressed similarly to his own Confederate volunteers and a rolled-up flag, the army of which he could not identify. Early assumed the regiment was a Confederate one, until a Confederate force flanking him fired on the regiment and it retreated. As it did so, the flag was unfurled, and Early saw that McDonald had mistakenly identified a Federal regiment.

41. This was actually the Third Tennessee.

42. Mary Naylor McDonald of Romney, Virginia. Her husband was Thomas Claiborne Green of Charlestown, Virginia, now West Virginia.

43. Brig. Gen. J. H. Carson, Virginia Militia.

44. Brig. Gen. W. S. Rosecrans.

45. According to McDonald family biographer Julia Davis, Strother had brought home from the War of 1812 Angus McDonald II's last messages and sword, subsequent to McDonald's death in 1814. Strother was accused of communicating with the Federals, and after refusing Angus McDonald III's invitation to stay at Hawthorne, was placed under house arrest in Winchester. Strother was acquitted but died shortly after returning home. He was the father of the writer and artist David Strother. See also note 35 of the previous chapter.

46. This engagement occurred at Hanging Rock Pass near Romney, Virginia, on September 24, 1861.

47. Federal forces under Gen. Benjamin F. Kelley were stationed at and around New Creek. William Naylor McDonald, in his history of the Laurel Brigade, lists the three pieces of artillery as "a rifle gun called the 'Blakely,' one howitzer, and one six-inch rifle gun." Official records recounting Kelley's position do not mention Col. Bruce. Col. A. Monroe's forces actually numbered abut two hundred.

48. Col. Turner Ashby.
49. Col. John W. Geary, 28th Regiment, Pennsylvania Volunteers.

Index

Perry, Oliver Hazard, 284*n138*
Perryville, battle of, 282*n103*
Philips, Mr., 196
Pierce, John. *See* Peerce, John Thompson
Pleasants, Sally McCarty, 76
Polish Revolt, 138, 287*n173*
Pope, John, 76, 235
Powell, Ann, 25
Powell, Charles, 261
Powell, Eleanor, 205
Powell, Elizabeth Whiting. *See* Conrad, Elizabeth Whiting Powell
Powell, Ellen Lee, 181, 190, 205, 210–11, 219, 226, 241, 289*n14*
Powell, John Simms, 289*n14*
Powell, Laura, 205
Powell, Lloyd, 261
Powell, Lucy Peachy Lee, 289*n14*
Powell, Simms, 219
Powell, William A., 289*n14*
Powhattan Hotel, 168
Pratt, W. P., 45–47, 56–57
Prendergast, Richard G., 188
Preston, J. T. L., 202, 260
Preston, Margaret J., 201, 222, 291*n59*
Preston, Phoebe, 202
Price, Sterling, 75
Purdy, George H. (?), 149, 288*n189*
Purdy, Gilbert H. (?), 149, 288*n189*
Purdy, James (?), 149, 288*n189*

Quarles, Garland, 278*n32*, 280*n52*
Quinn, Timothy, 132, 134, 144, 187, 194

Reed, John Bell Tilden, 96
Reid, Samuel McDowell, 238
Richardson, J. B., 74, 77, 160, 161
Richmond, Va.: battle at, 65–66; Cornelia McDonald at, 169
Rosencrans (Rozencrantz), William S., 115, 136, 140, 142, 147, 265, 284*n145*
Rosser, Thomas L., 183, 184
Ruggles, Daniel, 279*n50*
Rumley, Charles, 141
Rust, John D., 286*n171*

Savannah, Ga., 122
Schenck, Celeste, 17
Schenck, Robert C., 133, 289n3
Scott, A. F., 78

Scott, Anne Firor, 9
Scott, Dred, 278*n30*
Scott, Joan, 9–10
Scott, Winfield, 131, 286*n158*, 294*n26*
Secession: as issue in Virginia, 247–48, 250
Seddon, James A., 203
Seevers, George W., 277*n5*
Seevers, Mrs. George W., 25
Self-conceptions: of women, 11–12
Sepoy Revolt, 138, 287*n172*
Seward, William H., 41, 108–9, 284*nn139, 141*
Seymour, Horatio, 117, 284*n147*
Sharpsburg. *See* Antietam, battle of
Shearley (Shirley), George, 226
Sherman, William Tecumseh, 114, 285*n155*
Sherrard, Frank, 66, 219, 250
Sherrard, John Broome, 232, 234
Sherrard, Joseph H., 40, 66, 279*n33*
Sherrard, Robert, 234
Sherrard, Virginia, 63, 66, 137
Shields, James, 29, 32, 33, 48
Shirley, George. *See* Shearley, George
Sigel, Franz, 31–32, 277*n18*, 279*n50*, 280*n59*
Slavery: Cornelia McDonald's attitude toward, 12–14, 247–48
Slidell, John, 57, 89, 108–9, 279*n51*, 284*n141*, 293*n1*
Smith, Francis H., 185–86, 294*n28*
Smith, Kirby, 179, 260
Smith, Patrick, 48
Smith, Sidonie, 10
Snodgrass, C. E., 162
Synder, Joseph E., 280*n59*
Spottsylvania, battle of, 185, 289*n17*
Sprague, Kate Chase, 257, 294*n22*
Stanton, Domna, 12
Staunton Female Institute, 196
Steele, Robert, 140, 159
Steuart (Stuart), George Hume, 251–52
Stone, Albert E., 11
Stone, Lincoln R., 30–31
Stoneman, George, 144
Streight, Abel D., 287*n178*
Strother, David, 194, 206–7, 208–9, 217, 265, 290*n35*, 291*n46*, 295*n45*
Stuart, George Hume. *See* Steuart, George Hume

302